THE GUIDE TO BUYING PLANTS

THE GARDENER'S CATALOGUE series was conceived and is independently produced by Harvey Rottenberg and Tom Riker

THE GUIDE TO BUYING PLANTS was edited and designed by Tom Riker, whose years of experience as a horticulturist and botanical art specialist made the book possible

John Krausz was production man, and did the photography and photoconversions. Special thanks to Lars Skattebol for his editorial and technical knowhow, Lenore Stein, actor, who did the horticultural research, and Michael Edstrom, board person.

Other books in the "THE GARDENER'S CATALOGUE" series: "THE GARDENER'S CATALOGUE" the nationally best selling how-to-do-it, where-to-find-it guidebook for gardeners, "FOOD GARDENS Indoors, Outdoors, Under Glass", the critically acclaimed most definitive guide to home grown food available, "SEX IN THE GARDEN" exposes the real secret life of plants in intimate detail.

William Morrow & Company, Inc.
105 Madison Avenue
New York, N. Y. 10016

ISBN -0-688-03123-1

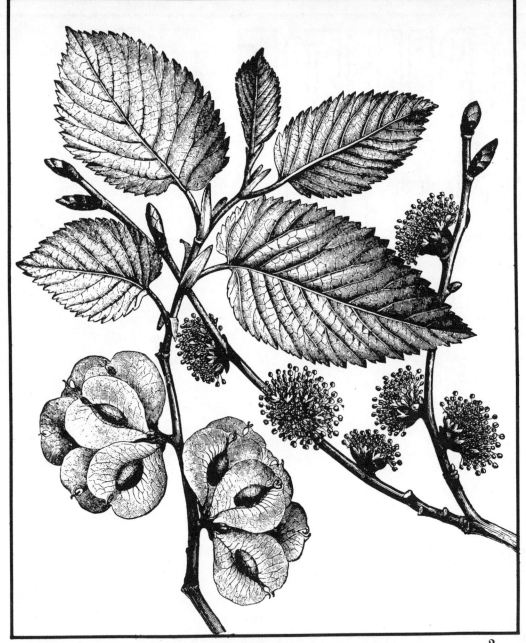

Special thanks to:

The American Association of Nurserymen for Green
        Survival & The Environmental Crisis, pg. 158
LaMotte Chemical Products Co., Chestertown, Md.,
        Soil & Nutrient Guide, pg. 184
United States Dept. of Agriculture Yearbook Staff,
pg. 216

Printed in the United States of America

1 2 3 4 5 6 7 8 9 10

Library of Congress Catalog Card Number 76-22864   ISBN 0-688-03123-4

TABLE OF CONTENTS

4

AMERICAN BEECH. *Fagus Americana.*

INTRODUCTION

To successfully operate a garden center, a small plant store or landscape service, the operator should be prepared to answer hundreds of questions about his special services. The home gardener or amateur plant collector seems to be getting more and more sophisticated as the "green plant boom" continues in the cities and suburban areas. There is a demand for more precise answers concerning plants and their cultivation. Granted many of the questions are the same year-in and year-out, nevertheless the garden center operator should not try to give pat answers and dismiss questions in the old traditional ways. We have a new generation of plant lovers and new gardeners that read and are sincerely interested in proper cultivation of plants. During the sixties with the ecology movements, the national interest in Earth Day, and more recently the "grow your own vegetables" craze, the young people of this country and all countries are concerned and want real answers for thought-out questions. These are the new customers, spending money and demanding service.

I must defend the store owners for a moment. Some of the customers do ask questions that tend to irritate and some questions are funny enough to make your day. I have operated a suburban garden center and managed the biggest garden center in New York City. So I have heard most of the questions and have had my share of laughs and incomprehensible conversations with "up tight" gardeners holding a dead vine or rose that was alive and well only days before. "A rose is a rose is a rose" might be a profound line but to the customer standing with a brown thorny branch complaining that I sold a "bad plant" to him, a rose is a dead rose is a rose. I have tried to consider all possibilities when a plant dies or does not develop properly. For a rose is many types, grown in many conditions and cultivated by various levels of competence. The obvious answer would be "you must be putting me on," after I found out the customer sprayed the rose with a weed killer strong enough to kill a well-established shade tree. Many times the customer is not right but if you answer the questions properly more plants will live and more plant lovers will grow roses that turn green rather than brown.

The point I am trying to make is that a lot of interested new gardeners and garden center operators do not have a background in wide areas of horticulture and related fields, and are in essence only plant collectors. The plant store operator collects from the grower or wholesaler, keeps the plants alive long enough to sell to the smaller collector, the customer. Most plant stores have a wide cross section of botanical life, from the hardy native plants to the rain forest foliage plants. Most people who have studied horitculture do not have knowledge of many kinds of plants from thousands of different types of ecologies. A maple tree is not a palm tree and a rare orchid needs more care than a philodendron. Buy what you can handle, do not get in over your head. The store will sell plants in bloom, nice and green without any markings but they just came out of a greenhouse or were shipped up from the south. To expect to keep the plant looking like it did in the greenhouse or tropical field you must have a greenhouse or live in a tropical field.

Many plant store operators or local landscape people are experts in native hardy plants indigenous to their part of the world but their expertise is lacking when indoor plants or imported southern plants are required because of the design or specifications of the landscape architect. These plants, indoors and outdoors, need special care and I suggest you seek help from an expert in your locality. Try the Department of Horticulture or Botany if a university is nearby. At least consult someone who has had experience growing such plants.

Many of the "plant society people" are indeed experts, for many have spent years cultivating and propagating certain species or types of plants.

The garden product customer should realize that operating a garden center is a business, and that most of the overhead is paid for with the sales of commercial fertilizers and bottled chemicals. Only a very few garden centers deal only in plant material. The customer should also realize the many problems the nursery has in maintaining the healthy plant under summer conditions. It costs a great deal of money in both material and labor to keep plants looking as healthy and fresh as the day they came off the truck or were shipped from the greenhouse to the retail store. Plants by and large should be sold in the same season, the sooner the better. Any plants left around for a long time, even if balled or in containers, tend to become neglected if the retailer does not keep up with the proper maintenance and care. Many of you have probably noticed sale signs around the middle of summer for shrubs, trees, roses and evergreens. Be very careful, and pick and choose. These plants were probably dug almost six months before and some were dug in the fall months and kept in cold storage for early spring shipments. I have seen magnolia stella not bloom until fall due to cold storage holdovers. This plant blooms usually in the early spring but the buds were dormant and "held back" due to the handling procedure.

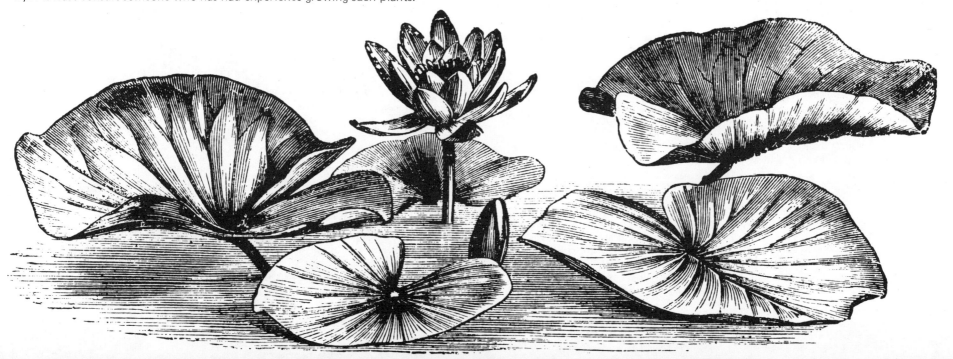

PLANT CHECK LIST

Over the years I have developed a basic check list for the shopper buying plants in various seasons and here it is:

1. The plant should be uniform in color. Yellow leaves or black spots on the foliage indicate lack of fertilizer, some sort of insect on the plant, or plant disease. Turn the leaf over and look underneath for insects. When buying roses beware of black spots on the foliage and aphids (small green sucking insects) on the tender stems or buds.

2. If the plant (tree or shrub) is dormant (without leaves) scratch the bark and see if the color is green and moist. Brittle stems indicate winter kill or that the plant has dried out. Buds should be very firm in the spring.

3. Plants should be balled or in containers after the dormant period. Never buy evergreens without a dirt ball. This includes broadleaf evergreens such as rhododendrons and azaleas. It is cheaper and all right to buy deciduous plants before the growing season (early spring) bareroot (without soil around the roots). You must plant them before they dry out, or heal them in and keep wet. Many roses are bought each year bareroot as are fruit trees. The soil around the plant if balled should be firm. A broken ball or loose container will cause severe damage to the root hairs.

ON BUYING TREES AND LARGE SHRUBS (DECIDUOUS)

1. If you are buying shade trees make sure the trunks are straight and without any crooks. A very young tree may not show a disfiguration but as the plant matures it will begin to lean. Make sure you have proper branching. (Example: A maple tree of twelve to fourteen feet should have branching six to nine feet from the base.) You can usually look at the tree and judge the proper distance. The plant must look in balance. Properly raised shade trees coming from good nurseries are pruned and thinned. Buy from someone you can call on the telephone or visit. There are good mail-order nurseries but check them out.

2. Tree should be without breaks on the bark and without sunscald. Sunscald is a split in the bark caused by the winter sun striking the tree on the south side. The difference of temperature causes the bark to split and the result is damage to the growing layer of the plant (cambium layer) directly under the bark. Insects may over-winter in such openings. Walk around the plant and see what it looks like from all sides.

3. All trees and shrubs should be properly pruned. The cuts should be even with the branch or trunk. If a plant is pruned to encourage growth the cut should be made back to the bud.

HOW TO DETERMINE PLANT PROBLEMS

The first step in determining the abnormalities that affect plant growth and cause damage is getting a check list of the various elements that cause problems. They are: plant diseases, fertilizer or nutrient deficiency, damage by local animals (roots as well as tender stems), insect damage including nematodes, and chemical damage such as weed killers or over-fertilizing.

Winter kill caused by cold weather or windy conditions usually damages the tender stems. Damage caused by transporting the plant is usually a break or scrape on the trunk, or broken limbs. The dirt ball can be water-logged causing the root sections to rot.

After you understand how the problems are caused, then you can examine the plants you want to buy. The most important advice is to look at the plant very closely. Some insects are very small and you must look at the foliage close up or with a magnifying glass. Make sure the whole plant is without broken limbs or scars. As the plant matures the crack or scar gets bigger and bigger and will become an eyesore if planted in your front yard.

While you are inspecting the plants keep the following in mind:

On leaves. Any discoloration or color patterns are usually caused by lack of fertilizer. Leaves may also drop if under fed. If leaves are curled the cause is usually insects or chemical spray. If the leaves are under-developed for the time of year the cause is probably some sort of root damage. If the leaves are wilting the cause could be many things but usually trunk damage or root damageage and too much water. Any white or black spots on the foliage usually mean disease. If the foliage has breaks that look like chewing, insects may still be on the plant. Holes in the middle of the leaf are caused by pollution. The only solution for pollution damage is to write your congressman demanding cleaner air and better controls over the environment.

On branches or trunk of plant. Brittle stems or branches usually are caused by winter kill, chemical injury and sometimes insects (borers). Split bark is caused either by cold weather or careless handling. Holes in the trunk are caused by borers or birds.

Not all plant store operators are experts. Do not take all they say as the truth. Follow other expert advice as can be found in books, and ask the advice of local horticulturists. Your state extension service people can help. Although they are over worked, they always try to help.

Read the fertilizer or chemical labels very carefully. Do not over spray or over fertilize. Be careful while spraying and never spray in the wind. Chemical drift may damage surrounding plants and harm other living things. I cannot say enough about careful use of these very dangerous chemicals. If you must use herbicides, fungicides, chemical fertilizers and insect killers, do so with all precautions.

LANDSCAPING

If you are going to have a landscape job done at your home, and usually this is a big investment, careful planning and consideration are in order. I would buy all of the plant material from a good local nursery or landscape center that will guarantee the plants for at least one growing season. If a professional does the planting he or she should guarantee the job. Under almost all normal conditions good healthy plants, properly planted, will survive. I would insist on a plan with a plant list that shows not only the design but also spacing requirements, size of plants, price of plants, amount of peatmoss and fertilizer to be used during the planting, and staking of shade trees with guide lines for the first season or two.

Sometimes it is impossible to determine the amount of labor, for problems do come up. The workers could hit rocks directly under twelve inches of topsoil and have to break the stone. Get the hourly rate per man. Many times the contractor will quote an hourly rate, say ten dollars per hour. This usually means per person, so if you have three men on the job the price is thirty dollars an hour. Get it in writing. Sign a contract. I can recall a man who had to dynamite holes in back of his house to plant trees. It was a good place for a house on that rock, but very expensive for landscaping.

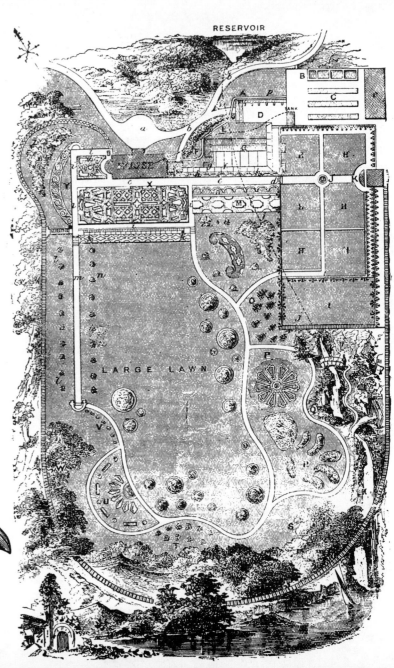

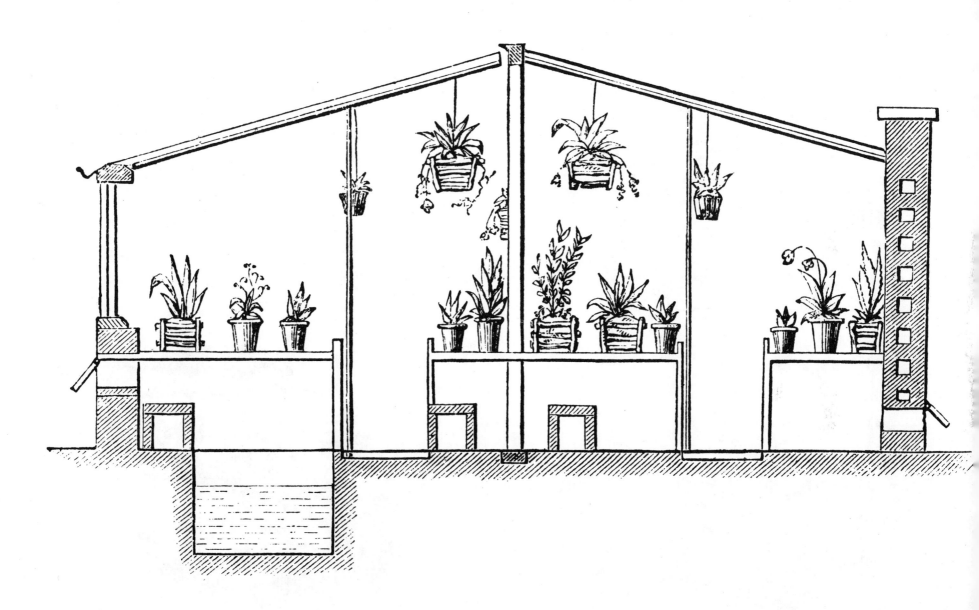

11

Go to the nursery and look at the plants. Make sure the plants are planted beyond the drip line on the house if you do not have gutters. Winter water dripping on the plants will kill them.

Have the nurseryman explain to you the mature sizes of plants and check the spacing so the plants will have room to grow. I have seen very expensive landscape jobs planted too close and within a few years it looks like a jungle.

Care of the plants is critical in the first few years. Different types of plants need different care. Get a check list for the whole job with specific instructions for the various kinds of plants. Evergreens including broadleaf evergreens need an acid soil, so if the PH is wrong you must feed them a special fertilizer. Some plants should be pruned heavily, and some not at all. Have the professional explain how to care for your plants. You are paying for it. After the landscape crew departs the yard should be neat and clean. The beds should be cut right and the plants properly planted. Take a very close look at the final job with the landscape foreman.

I would not try to help or bother the crew while they are working. Let the plantsmen do their job but make sure you are getting your money's worth. Demand total professionalism. If something does not look right or if you feel something is out of balance, you must speak up. You have to live with the plants. The nurserymen go on to the next job.

NEPENTHES RAFFLESIANA.

The experiences of gardners and plant collectors are varied and sometimes very strange. I have seen all ends of the spectrum from the coffee merchant in lower New York City who had a collection of miniature plants in a file cabinet, to the man in the suburbs who collected maple trees. Everyone has a certain way of looking at the world. Some want to look at it through a microscope, some want to grow everything under plant lights in the basement, and some plant corn in the front yard. All have their problems and successes. Some of the problems are simple to solve with the right information and some of the mistakes are very costly.

It seems the most costly and tragic mistakes occur when a gardener gets his hands on a sprayer and fills up the bottle hooked to the hose or puts the tank on the back. Chemicals have a way of being over used and misunderstood.

It's a nice late spring morning in the northeast. The rain has left the lawns just wet enough so the hose does not have to be used. This "gardener" wants to kill the weeds in his lawn. So he sprays the whole area with a common type weed killer and goes about the day's business. The next day I get a call and the herbicide sprayer explains on the phone that he thinks something may be wrong with the plants I sold him. I go have a look. The man had not only sprayed his lawn but decided to spray the weeds in the beds around his home.

In the spraying process he had sprayed everything—roses, shrubs, evergreens, flowers and his pride and joy, a group of rose trees. They were turning brown, the foliage was dropping off and turning up. I explained the weed killer not only kills weeds but also kills plants with a root section that directly draws fertilizer and water out of the soil. Within a few days he had the only brown planting in the area and it cost him thousands of dollars. A hard lesson that could have been avoided by a phone call or by reading the instructions on the bottle or can.

I have operated a garden center in the suburbs and managed the biggest garden center in New York City, in the shadow of the World Trade Center. This gives me a special view of gardening that most horticulturists never see or even consider. People in the city have special needs and little space. They tend to crowd a lot of plants in windows, boxes on fire escapes, roofs (some of the roof gardens that I have designed and seen are very beautiful and would put many suburban backyards with twice the amount of space to shame). The idea of moving ten weeping willows, eighteen feet high, to the top of a thirty story building is not the usual garden. I have designed formal rose gardens on the roofs as well as old style New England Perennial Gardens. The problems

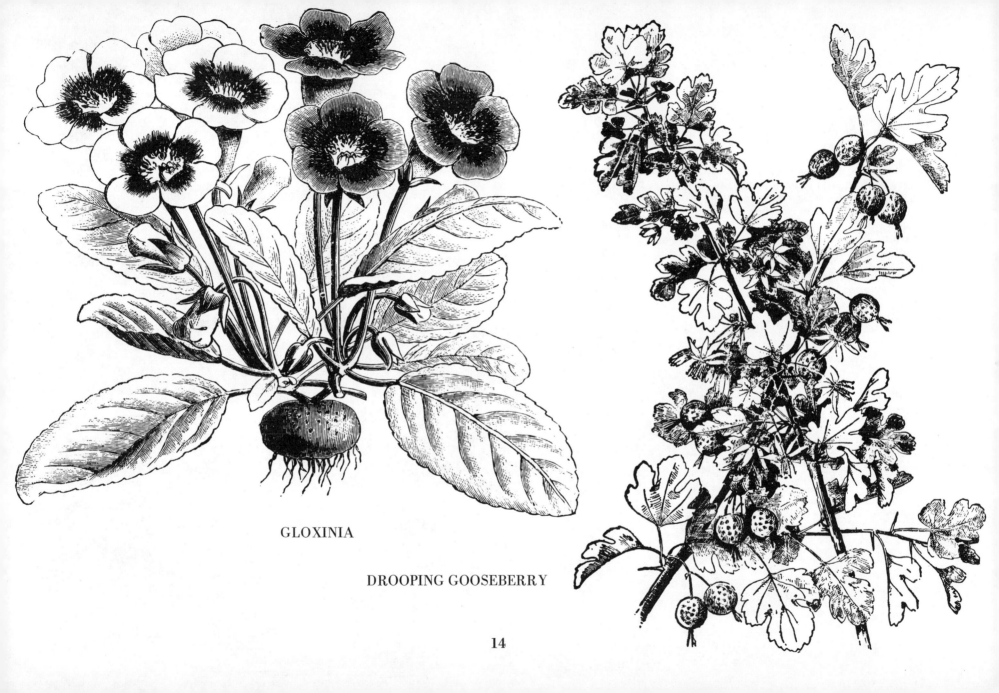

GLOXINIA

DROOPING GOOSEBERRY

14

and grief of city gardeners are costly when a mistake does occur. One must realize that the main cost of city gardening (terrace or roof) is not the cost of the plants but the cost of the containers and soil. Barrels and boxes, gravel and stone, soil and peatmoss all have to be put on elevators or walked up to the roof. A mistake could put the owner of the roof garden in bankrupt court.

One example that will forever remain in my mind concerns a very wealthy woman who called and wanted a garden consultant to help her plan her new garden. I arrive and am shown out onto the terrace roof garden. As I pass through the garden I notice that everything is in bloom, the dogwood and flowering crabs. The boxes have bulbs and the ivy growing on the brick walls is nice and green with new growth. She is sitting at a glass table dressed in pink with a pink poodle. I introduce myself and she shows me a picture that is about one inch by two inches. It is a picture of a formal Japanese garden— the racked sand in the right patterns, the stone and statues, and the contorted pine and dogwood. I mention to her that this particular garden would take a great deal of space and from what I could see her garden was completely filled with large trees, shrubs and evergreens. There was absolutely no space to put such an additional design.

She looked rather bewildered and said, "Oh, all of this will have to be taken out."

That example proves that if you have enough money you do not have any gardening problems. If you are not a gardener and have a lot of money you can have the professional come in and do it all. Most people have problems and do not have that kind of money. I have received phone calls from Paris from wealthy New York roof top dwellers concerned about their Ficus trees. I would rather deal with real gardeners with real problems.

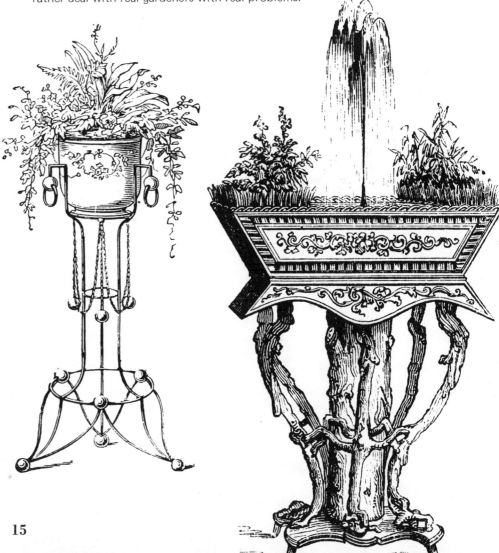

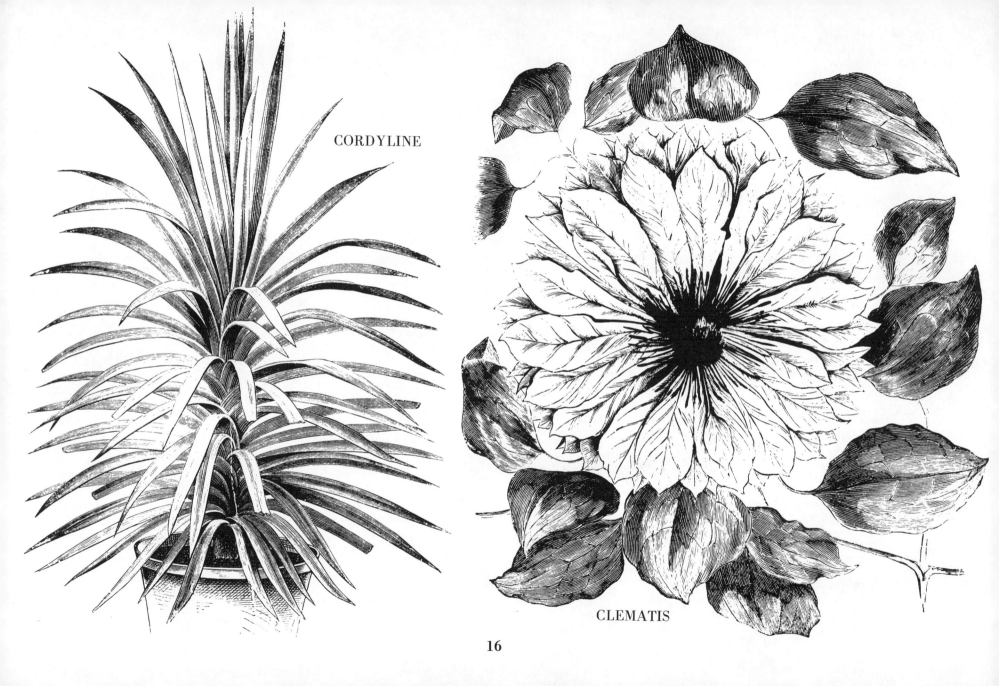

CORDYLINE

CLEMATIS

16

Another extreme example took place in the suburbs. A man calls early in the spring and tells me his tree died. This tree is a three inch crimson king maple that I sold. The tree is twenty feet tall, had a dirt ball that weighed over one thousand pounds. It took three men to plant and was brought directly from a local nursery that had been growing shade trees for over fifty years.

I look at the tree. It is very dead. I look more closely and notice holes in the trunk that have been drilled in by some mechanical means. I turn and ask the man did he notice the holes in the trunk. He said he had put them there to feed the tree exactly as the instructions indicated. I ask him to show me the print. The instructions read as follows: "Drill holes around the tree and put pellets into the ground." I look at the man in amazement. He actually drilled holes in the tree. I laughed and lost a customer, but as the saying goes, "Who needs such customers?" An extreme case? Yes, but very costly.

I have seen people plant cherry trees in their living rooms so the monkeys could have an exercise tree. I have sold a beautiful blue spruce to a photographer that was needed only for a day's work. After he bought the spruce, and at a cost of over one hundred dollars, he asked for a saw and cut the dirt ball off, called a cab and went on his way. I have helped plant willow trees in bathrooms with the crown of the tree sticking out the window. I have moved and removed, uprooted, transplanted, and cut plants from the most obvious places and from places that plants should not grow. During all this I have tried to keep a straight face and listen as the gardeners and collectors told me their tales of woe and joy.

Gardening is still the biggest hobby in the world. More people dig in the garden, grow tomatoes on the window sill, plant peas in the pod and grow ferns in bottles than ever before. Let's hope it continues. Try not to lose your sense of humor if the peas do not germinate, the tomatoes are smaller than the picture on the seed pack, and the ferns are not quite the same as you remember as you walked down the country road.

17

ANNUALS

BEDDING PLANTS

Flower gardening hints for new gardeners or for accomplished gardeners are offered by Bedding Plants, Incorporated, the international organization of plant growers. The sturdy, well-branched plants produced by Bedding Plant growers are found at your local garden supply store, all ready for planting in your garden. Often the plants are showing flower colors to aid in your variety choice.

For sunny gardens the most reliable and popular kinds of annuals are ageratum, marigolds, petunias. salvia, snapdragons and sweet alyssum. For the shady garden where there.is some good light, the most useful annuals are wax (or fibrous-rooted) begonias, coleus and impatiens.

Marigolds are produced in several varieties and sizes of flowers and on plants of different heights. Choices include the low bedding varieties, the remarkable "hedge-type" marigolds and the taller-growing specimens which flower later in the season.

Petunias are the mainstay of the sunny flower garden, and the new hybrids are better than ever. Choose the colors and forms you like; remember, in this bicentennial year red, white and blue varieties of petunias are available. Snapdragons are produced in clear vibrant colors on tall, medium or short-stemmed plants. They are good for display and for cutting. There are open-faced kinds, as well as the familiar hooded varieties.

Wax begonias can be used in sunny gardens, but they also do well in partial shade. Begonias are available in heights from 10 to 18 inches, characterized by green or bronze-colored foliage. Other valuable plants for the shady garden include impatiens, now appearing in wider color ranges and increased flower size, and colorfully-leaved coleus.

If you're gardening on level ground, try building a mound slightly higher in one area for another dimension in your garden. Ageratum, alyssum, asters, begonias, calendula, gazania, geraniums, marigolds, petunias, vinca and zinnias are some good kinds of bedding plants for a mound garden. A mulch spread between plants will prevent possible erosion before plants grow together.

For cutting flowers buy plants of asters, bells of Ireland, calendulas, carnations, larkspur, marigolds, stock and zinnias. Strawflower plants produce flowers for colorful dried arrangements. Heliotrope and flowering tobacco plants produce fragrant flowers. Ivy-leaved geraniums, lantana, dracaena, petunias and variegated vinca vines are excellent for container gardens.

BEDDING PLANT COMBINATIONS CREATE EXCITING GARDENS

The bedding plant displays at garden supply stores each spring fire the imagination with many "mix or match" possibilities! Once the gardener decides whether the garden will be a bed of one kind of annual (such as impatiens or petunia) in one color or in mixed colors, or whether the garden will be a glorious mixture of kinds and colors, then the choice of plants is simplified. Be sure to buy enough plants to create the desired effect.

Ideas for the use of annual bedding plants include: a bed or mound garden of yellow petunias with a border of white sweet alyssum and blue ageratum; a mixed verbena collection facing a lily border; a white sweet alyssum or parsley border for a rose bed; yellow or orange hedge-type marigolds used with red or white tall snapdragons with mixed colors of dwarf snapdragons in front and cleome or blue salvia in the background.

Other interesting combinations include tall red salvia, French marigolds, white vinca or sweet alyssum with bachelor's buttons, larkspur or flowering tobacco plants worked in. A border of petunias around a bed of hedge-type zinnias, the flower colors complementing one another makes a striking display.

Islands of color by the terrace, on a balcony or suspended bring much enjoyment to outdoor summer living. When using bedding plants in containers, consider provision for drainage, a good soil or peat-lite planting mixture and colors and numbers of plants the container will hold. For containers with sloping or curved sides, plant the bedding plants half-way between the rim and the center of the container for best root growth and health of the plants.

Suggested plant combinations suitable for containers include: red geraniums, white cascading petunias, lemon drop or petite marigolds and dracaena; white geraniums, red cascading petunias with blue ageratum or lobelia; pink geraniums, pink-flowered wax begonias, trailing variegated vinca and pink cascading petunias; coral cascading petunias, coral coleus, blue ageratum and dracaena.

Some good hanging basket annuals which can be used alone are cascading petunias lantana, ivy-leaved geraniums, sweet alyssum, lobelia and impatiens. Let the impatiens plants wilt somewhat so that the stems droop; after this period of wilting, the stems will continue to droop more gracefully and when flowering begins, the effect is splendid.

ALYSSUM

DAISY

AFRICAN DAISY arcotis White, and varieties in red, violet, blue, yellow 25"-48" Full sun, average soil Long blooming season, resists drought, good for dry, sunny areas, massed in border. Sow in place.

AGERATUM ageratum Blue 4"-10" Sun to light shade, any soil Likes poorer soils, long blooming season, often reseeds itself. Good for borders, beddings, window boxes, potted, edgings. Sow in place.

ALYSSUM, SWEET lobularia maritima White to violet 3"-12" Sun, average soil Fragrant and good cut flowers. Withstands heavy, poor soil. Useful in rock gardens, borders, autumn gardens, cold climates. Sow in place.

ANCHUSA (CAPE FORGET-ME-NOT) anchusa capensis Blue 12"-18" Full sun, average soil Sow inside or in place. Use potted, in rock gardens, or in borders.

BALLOON VINE cardiosperum, halicacabum White flowers grown for balloon-like fruit vine to 14 feet Sun, average soil Quick growing vine, have to tie, use on trellis. Sow in place.

BABY'S BREATH gypsophila elegans, grandiflora White and various others 10"-20" Full sun, any soil (tolerate poor soils) Grown in rock gardens and edgings. Good cut flower. Can sow more than once a season in place or inside. Short blooming season.

BABY BLUE EYES nemophila menziesii White to bluish purple 6"-20" Partial shade, average soil Use in rock gardens, shady gardens, edgings. Sow in place.

BASKET FLOWER centaurea americana several colors 24"-60" Sun, average soil, sow in place Likes to be crowded, use massed, in borders.

BALSAM impatiens balsamina Several colors 24"-36" Partial shade, average soil Can take ligher shade than other impatiens. Use in shady gardens, under trees, massed, potted.

BARTONIA menzelia lindleyi Yellow 12"-36" Sun, average well-drained soil Very fragrant, opening in the evening and closing in the morning. Use massed, in borders, sow in place.

BEGONIA begonia, fiborous rooted in variety Several colors 4"-48" Partial shade, good soil (Rich, well drained) Sown indoors and easily grown, a houseplant all year round and garden annual. Can be transplanted from garden to houseplant. Grow potted, massed in borders, beddings.

BLUE LACE FLOWER trachymene coerulea Blue 24" Sun, average soil Sow indoors in flats or outdoors in place, likes to be crowded. Use massed in borders, beddings. Popular greenhouse plant, sown throughout the year for successive blooms.

BLUE WOODRUFF asperula orientalis Blue 12" Sun, average soil Sown in place, borders and edgings. Perennial varieties better suited to partial shade.

BROWALLIA browallia Blue 8"-20" Partial shade, average soil Can withstand wet, heavy soil and often used near aquatic plantings, also massed and edgings. Sow indoors or in place.

BUTTERFLY FLOWER schizanthus Several colors 18"-48" Sun, rich, well-drained soil Also known as poor man's orchid and grown in greenhouses. Use massed or potted in garden. Sow in cold frame or cool room in Feb., move to large pots as needed. Move out after last frost.

CALIFORNIA BLUEBELL phacelia, several varieties Usually blue, but white, or lavender, types too 6"-24" Full sun, well-drained soil (sandy) Grow massed in beddings or borders in a sandy soil. Will attract bees.

CALIFORNIA POPPY eschscholzia californica Yellow, orange 12"-36" Full sun, sandy soil Sow in place after last frost, does best in cool weather, can sow more than once a season. Use massed, on slopes, borders, beddings.

CAMOMILE, FALSE matricaria Yellow, white 8"-25" Full sun, any well-drained soil Not the herb chamomile, which is the perennial anthemis nobilis. This is a lovely plant useful in rock gardens, borders. Sow in place or indoors.

CANDYTUFT iberis Several colors 6"-12" Sun to slight shade, average soil An early bloomer, can withstand rocky soil. Use massed, in borders. Sow in place.

CAPE MARIGOLD dimorphotheca aurantiaca Several Colors 20" Sun, average soil Use in beddings, massed. Likes heat, used as a greenhouse plant and a perennial in mild areas. Sow indoors or outdoors (if season is long).

BELLFLOWER campanula White, purple, blue, pink 6"-48" Sun, average soil Good in borders, rock gardens. Sow in place. Campanula/isophylla is trailing and good in hanging basket inside or out; others are erect.

BELLS OF IRELAND molucella iaevis White 24"-36" Full sun, tolerates heat, fairly easy to grow Also called shell-flower, a popular cut flower, commonly forced by florists. Use massed and in borders. Sow indoors in flats or outdoors in place.

CAPE STOCK Heliophila Blue, yellow 12" Sun, average, but well-drained soil Popular border plant, can also be used massed. Sow indoors.

CARDINAL CLIMBER quamoelit sloteri Red with white throat vine Sun, average, but well-drained soil Sow in cold frame or cool room. Use on trellis, tie on.

CARNATION dianthus Several colors 6"-24" Sun, any well-drained soil Fragrant and popular cut flowers. Easily grown. Use massed, in borders.

CASTOR BEAN ricinus commusis Foliage all green, red stems and grey leaves, red leaves 72" and more Sun, average soil Grown for foliage and to 40 feet in the tropics. Use as bedding plant or free form. Sow indoors or out. Seeds are poisonous!

CATCHFLY silene Light pink To 24" Sun, average soil Can resist drought and rocky soil. Use in rock gardens, borders. Sow in place or indoors.

CELOSIA, PLUMED celosia plumosa Several colors 10"-50" Full sun, well-drained soil Use in backgrounds or massed. They like warmth and resist drought. Sow indoors or outdoors.

CHINA ASTER Callistephus chinensis Several colors; most often a shade of blue 6"-20" Sun, rich, well-drained soil Tallest types make good cut flowers. Grow in bedding and borders, don't grow in the same place in successive years. Sow indoors or out.

CHINESE FORGET-ME-NOT cynoglossum amabile Blue 12"-24" Sun, average soil Sow indoors or in place. Use in beddings, massed.

CHRYSANTHEMUM chrysanthemum, several varieties White, yellow, red 12"-48" Full sun, any well-drained soil Can withstand heavy soil, but does better with good drainage. Use in beds, borders, potted. (Includes crown daisy, marguerite, corn marigold, etc.)

CLARKIA clarkia elegans Several colors 15"-38" Sun, any soil Withstands rocky or sandy soil. Likes to be crowded, sow in place or indoors. Use massed or in borders. Long blooming period.

CLEOME (SPIDER FLOWER) cleome spinosa White, shades of purple 48"-60" Full sun, any well-drained soil Sow in place, but thin out, need room; or sow indoors. Often self-sowing. Scented, use massed, in borders or backgrounds.

COCKSCOMB celosia argentea cristata Several colors 10"-50" Full sun, well-drained soil Resists drought, sow indoors or out, in borders or background planting. Likes warmth.

COLEUS coleus blumei Foliage—several colors 40" Partial shade, well-drained soil Popular potted plant indoors and out. Sow indoors, use in borders, shady gardens. Cuttings easily rooted.

CONEFLOWER rudbeckia bicolor superba Yellow and black 25"-40" Sun, average soil Sow in place or in cold frame. Use massed, in borders.

CORNFLOWER (BATCHELOR'S BUTTON) centaurea cyanus Blue (other colors available) 12"-36" Full sun, average soil Good cut flowers; withstands poor soil and heat. Likes to be crowded. Use massed, in borders, beddings. Can sow more than once a season.

COREOPSIS coreopsis Yellow, yellow and brown 10"-40" Full sun, average soil Easily grown; likes to be crowded and resists heat, drought, and poor soils. Sow more than once a season for more continuous bloom. Sow in place.

COSMOS cosmos Several colors 40"-90" Full sun, sandy soil, low in humus Rich soil will produce lush foliage and fewer flowers. Withstands heat. Sow indoors or out, may need staking. Good cut flower, use massed, in backgrounds.

COTTON, ORNAMENTAL gossypium, herbaceum Yellow and purple 18"-36" Sun, average soil Use massed, good bee attractor, so indoors, outside in mild areas.

CREEPING ZINNIA sanvialia, procumbens Yellow 6"-trailing Full sun, well-drained soil Withstands heat and drought. Sow in place or in cold frame. Used in rock gardens, edgings.

CUP AND SAUCER VINE Coboea scandens Purple, white Vine Sun, average soil Quick growing and withstands sandy soil. Use on trellis, fence. Sow indoors or out in mild areas.

CUPHEA (CIGAR-FLOWER) cuphea, in variety Several colors 12"-45" Sun, well-drained soil Sow indoors, use potted, massed. Also used as greenhouse plant.

CUPID'S DART catananche caerulea Blue, white 24" Sun, average soil Used in dry flower arrangements, plant in borders, massed. Sow indoors or in place.

Bed of "China Asters," showing effect of well-grown annual plants in garden.

CYPRESS VINE quamoclit pennata Red Vine to 20 ft. Sun, well-drained soil Sow in cold frame or cool room in March. Tie on trellis.

DAHLIA dahlia, several varieties Several colors 24''-36'' Full sun, rich, well-drained soil Best started indoors but can be sown in place; not the bulbous types. Use in border backgrounds, massed.

DATURA METAL datura metal Several colors 36''-60'' Sun, average soil Usually fragrant, use massed in backgrounds. Sow indoors or in place.

DIANTHUS dianthus (annual pinks) Several colors 8''-20'' Full sun, average soil Sown indoors or out, tolerates poor soil, best flowering in cooler weather. Use massed, borders, rock gardens.

EVERLASTING helipterum Pale yellow, white 8''-18'' Sun, average soil Sow in place or indoors. Used massed or in borders. Popular dried flower.

FLOWERING FLAX linum, grandiflorum Blue to red flowers 10''-24'' Sun, average soil Easily grown, sown in place, in borders or massed, a perennial in the south.

FLOWERING MAPLE abiluton Several colors 18''-60'' Sun, rich, well-drained soil A potted plant indoors in a cool, sunny room, outdoors either potted or background planting.

FORGET-ME-NOT myosotis Blue 8''-18'' Parial shade, any well-drained soil Likes to be crowded, sow in place, use massed in beddings, keep moist, can reseed itself.

FOUR-O'CLOCK mirabilis jalapa Several colors 12''-30'' Sun, average soil The flowers open late in the day or all day when it is cloudy. Resists heat, drought, and poor soil. Sow indoors or in place, may resow itself.

FOXGLOVE digatalis purpurea Flowers—shades of red to white 24''-36'' Sun, average soil Sow indoors or out, noting it takes up to five months to bloom. Useful as a cut flower. Prefers cool, humid climates. Also listed in perennials.

GAILLARDIA (Blanket flower) gaillardia pulchella Red, orange, yellow 10''-20'' Full sun, average to poor soil Resists heat, drought, poor soil. Long blooming period. Sow in place or indoors. Good cut flowers. Plant massed, in borders.

GENTIAN, ANNUAL gentiana Violet 10''-14'' Sun, rich to average soil

GENTIAN

Sow in place in rock garden, massed, borders. Most gentians are perennial or biennial.

GILIA gilia, several varieties Several colors 8''-24'' Full sun, average well-drained soil. Sow in place; used in borders, rock gardens, massed. Good cut flowers, especially gilia capitata.

GLOBE AMARANTH gomphrena globosa Several colors 10''-18'' Sun, average soil Long blooming season, sow indoors or in place, in masses, borders. Used in dry arrangements.

GODETIA godetia Several colors 10''-30'' Sun to partial shade, any soil Can withstand sandy or heavy soil; likes to be crowded, plant massed. Good cut flowers. Sow indoors.

GOURDS, ORNAMENTAL cucurbita Vine, foliage and multicolored fruit Full sun, rich soil Multi-colored fruit used dried and varnished. Sown in place after last frost. Grow on trellis.

GYPSOPHILA, PINK gypophila muralis Pink 4''-8'' Full sun, any soil Pink baby's breath, can be sown several times a season for continuous bloom. Sow in place or indoors in flats. Easily grown; in rock gardens, borders, massed. Profuse flowers good for cutting.

HELIOTROPE heliotropium Shades of purple 24''-48'' Sun, rich, well-drained soil Needs warmth, sow indoors, fragrant. Plant in beddings, potted. Also grown as greenhouse plant, where fragrance is stronger.

HIBISCUS hibiscus, palustris Shades of red, white To 60'' Sun, fertile, well-drained soil Must be sown indoors if treated as an annual. Do not crowd. Grow as background, near water. Blooms in late summer, may become perennial if protected in winter, except in very cold areas.

HOLLYHOCK althea rosea Several colors 60''-96'' Full sun, average soil. Best sown indoors when used as annual. Good background plant or massed. May require staking, tolerates moist soils.

HOP, JAPANESE humulus, japonicus, va. variegatus Foliage—flowers hang in clusters and are green Vine Sun, average soil Sow in place, quick growing, used for covering areas in a hurry. Trellis, wall. Can become a weed.

HYACINTH BEAN dolichos lablab Purple, white Vine Full sun, average soil Resists heat and drought. Sow in place or indoors, grow on trellis.

ICE PLANT mesembry anthemun crystallinum Foliage—covered with shiny dots. Flowers—white, light pink Low, to 6'' Full sun, sandy soil Resists heat, drought, also called sea fig. Use as ground cover in sandy areas.

IMMORTELLE xeranthemum annum Several colors 24''-36'' Sun, average soil Used as dried flower; sow in place or indoors, in masses or borders.

HOLLYHOCK

25

IMPATIENS impatiens, in variety, including holsti, roylei, and sultani Several colors 12"-60" Shade, average soil Excellent potted plant indoors or out. Sow indoors. Edgings, shady gardens. Long blooming season (see balsam).

JOSEPH'S COAT amaranthus tricolor Foliage (which is red) 10"-40" Full sun, average soil Rich soil tends to make leaves larger at the expense of color. Sow indoors or in place. Withstands heat, use massed, in backgrounds.

KENILWORTH-IVY cymbalaria muralis Pale violet flowers, green foliage Short vine to 40" Sun to light shade, average soil Perennial grown as annual but may naturalize. Good houseplant in cool sunny rooms. Outdoors in window boxes, hanging baskets. Sow indoors or outdoors.

KINGFISHER-DAISY felicia bergeriana Blue 6"-10" Sun, average, well drained soil Grown in greenhouse or outdoors in window boxes, potted, or in borders. Sow indoors.

KOCHIA (Summer cypress) kochia scoparia Foliage—yellow, red, orange, green 24"-48" Full sun, average well-drained soil A bushy plant for background and borders. Sow indoors or in place.

LANTANA lantana Several colors Low and vine-like or up to 50" shrub Partial shade, average but well-drained soil Popular in California and south where it is a perennial. In the north an annual greenhouse plant or house plant. Sow in place; used potted, in windowboxes, or borders.

LARKSPUR delphinium Several colors 12"-24" Sun or slight shade Cool weather important to germination and growth, sow in place in early spring. Good cut flowers, used in borders and backgrounds. Staking may be necessary.

LAVATERA lavatera trimestris splendens Pink 18"-36" Sun, average soil Easily grown, sow in place. Used in borders and beddings.

LINARIA linaria maroccana Shades of pruple 10"-18" Partial shade, average soil Also known as toad flax; withstands wet, heavy soil. Sow indoors or out. Used in rock gardens, potted, windowboxes.

LOBELIA (Edging lobelia) lobelia erinus Blue, although several different varieties in varying colors 4"-12" Sun or light shade, average soil Sown in place or indoors, sow more than once a season for more continuous bloom. Edgings, massed.

LOBELIA

LUPINE

LOVE-LIES-BLEEDING amaranthus caudatus Red 40''-60'' Full sun, average soil Sow in place or indoors. Rich soil tends to produce larger leaves at the expense of color. Use in backgrounds, borders.

LUPINE lupinus, several varieties Several colors 8''-30'' Sun, average, well-drained soil Sow indoors or in place, but seeds started in place may rot before they germinate; in either case make a small cut in seed before planting. Use in beddings, borders.

OLD WOODCUT OF A MARIGOLD

LYCHNIS lychnis, several varieties Several colors 18''-36'' Sun, average soil Use in rock gardens; massed, easily grown, sow in place.

MALOPE malope trifida, grandiflora Shades of rose-red 24''-36'' Sun, average soil Sow in place or indoors. Use in rock gardens, beddings, or borders.

MARIGOLD tagates, in variety Yellow to red 8''-24'' Sun, any soil Easily grown, long-lasting bloom, helpful in repelling certain insects and animals. Resists drought, poor soil, wind, cold. Sow in place or indoors. Use massed, potted, borders, in vegetable patches, etc.

MAURANDIA maurandia, in variety Purple, rose climbing vine-like Sun, average but well-drained soil A greenhouse plant or summer annual, sow indoors. Use potted, on trellis. Dramatic, showy flowers.

MEADOW-FOAM limnanthes Several colors 4''-8'' Sun, any soil Sow in place, preferably near a body of water. Likes wet soil.

MEXICAN TULIP POPPY hunnemannia fumariaefolia Yellow 18''-28'' Sun, well-drained soil Very pretty flowers, use massed or in borders. Sow in place or indoors.

MIGNONETTE reseda odorata Yellow, green 4''-12'' Sun, average soil Fragrant herb, sown in place, and used in borders, massed, herb gardens.

MOLUCELLA molucella spinosa White or pink 48''-72'' Sun, average soil Easily grown and good as background planting or massed. Sow indoors or in place.

MONEY PLANT lunaria, annua Flowers, shades of purple pods, shiny, translucent 18''-36'' Sun, average soil Used in dry arrangements. Easily grown, usually planted as border or massed. Also called silver-dollar plant. Sow in place or indoors.

MONKEY FLOWER mimulis Yellow, reddish 10''-24'' Partial shade, well-drained soil Sow in place or indoors, use in shady gardens, potted. Keep moist, also a greenhouse plant.

MOONFLOWER calonyetion aculeatum White to pale pink Vine Sun, well-drained soil Both moonflower and morning glory withstand heat, sown indoors or in place. Trellis; potted; roof-gardens; fences. Moonflower night blooming and has a long blooming period.

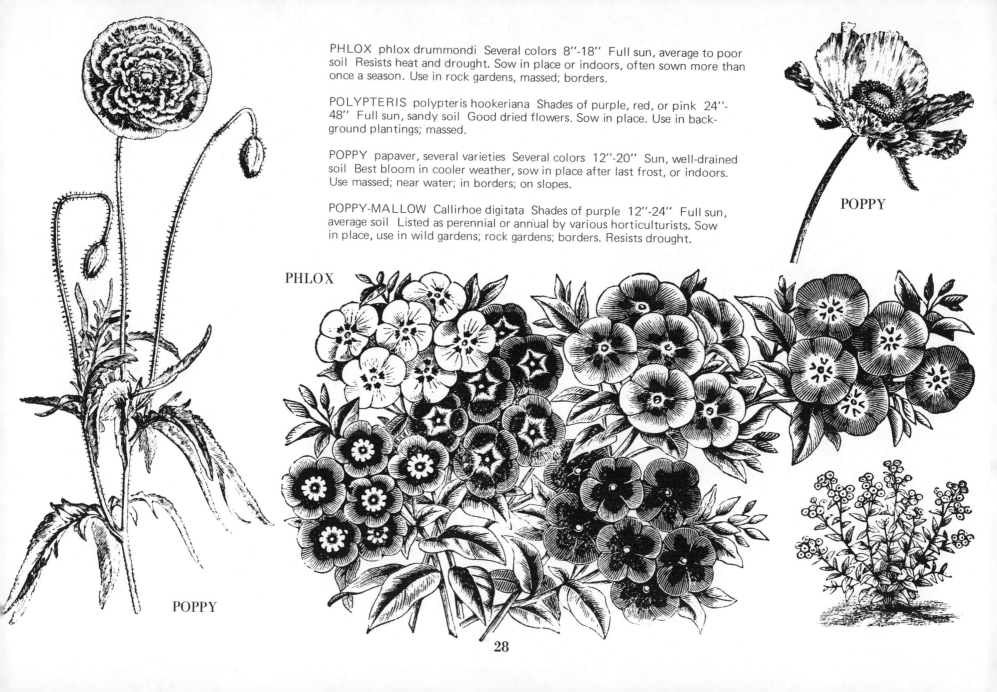

PHLOX phlox drummondi Several colors 8''-18'' Full sun, average to poor soil Resists heat and drought. Sow in place or indoors, often sown more than once a season. Use in rock gardens, massed; borders.

POLYPTERIS polypteris hookeriana Shades of purple, red, or pink 24''-48'' Full sun, sandy soil Good dried flowers. Sow in place. Use in background plantings; massed.

POPPY papaver, several varieties Several colors 12''-20'' Sun, well-drained soil Best bloom in cooler weather, sow in place after last frost, or indoors. Use massed; near water; in borders; on slopes.

POPPY-MALLOW Callirhoe digitata Shades of purple 12''-24'' Full sun, average soil Listed as perennial or annual by various horticulturists. Sow in place, use in wild gardens; rock gardens; borders. Resists drought.

POPPY

POPPY

PHLOX

POPPY

28

FANCY PANSY

MORNING GLORY ipomoea purpurea Several colors Vine Sun, well-drained soil Morning glory day blooming and also with long blooming period. Same culture and uses as moonflower. Especially nice when both are used on a fence.

MOUNTAIN FRINGE adlumia fungosa Pink Vine Shade, rich, well-drained soil Sow in place in rich but not acid soil. Grow in shade or wild gardens, or in protected places. Does not tolerate wind.

NASTURTIUM tropaeolum Several colors 7"-30" Full sun, average to poor soil Easily grown, long lasting, resists near drought. Sow in place or indoors. Rich soil will reap a lot of foliage but little bloom. Borders, banks, herb gardens, potted, trellis, windowboxes.

NICOTIANA nicotiana alata grandiflora White, pink, red 18"-36" Sun to partial shade, average to poor soil Also known as flowering tobacco, resists heat, drought, poor soil; sow in place or indoors. May re-sow itself. Use massed, borders. Most bloom in the evening and are fragrant.

NIEREMBERGIA (Blue cup-flower) niembergia caerulea Blue and a light purple 6"-12" Sun, average soil Use massed, in edgings. Sow indoors or in place.

NEMESIA nemesia strumosa suttoni Several colors 8"-24" Sun, well-drained soil Cool weather important to growth, sow in cold frame or cool room or greenhouse in March. Use potted, massed, in borders.

NIGELLA nigella damascena Blue, white 12"-24" Full sun, average soil Also known as Love-In-A-Mist. Sow in place, used massed; in borders.

NIGHT-SCENTED STOCK mathiola bicornia Dark purple Low growing, to 6" Sun, well-drained soil Fragrant flowers that open in the evening. Sow indoors. Use potted; in borders; edgings; beddings.

NIGHT PHLOX zaluzianskya White with shades of purple 8"-18" Sun, well-drained soil Sow indoors. Use in borders, beddings. Night blooming and fragrant.

PAINTED TONGUE salpiglossis sinuata Several colors 18"-24" Sun, well-drained soil Good cut flowers, sow in cold frame or cool room in early March. Use massed, in borders, potted.

PANSY viola tricolor hortensis Several colors 4"-10" Partial shade, rich well-drained soil Use in beddings, borders, potted. Keep cut back. Sow indoors in flats or in cold frame. Also good in shady gardens.

PERIWINKLE, MADAGASCAR vinca rosea Rose, white 10''-18'' Sun to partial shade, average soil Sow indoors. Use in windowboxes, borders, ground cover. Best in sun.

PETUNIA petunia in variety Several colors 12''-24'' Sun to light shade, average soil Many types both hanging and erect; cascade, double, grandiflora, multiflora, single. Popular in windowboxes, borders, beddings, potted. Long blooming period. Keep well watered but will resist some drought and heavy soil. Sow indoors in flats.

PORTULACA (MOSS ROSE) portulaca grandiflora Several colors Trailing, to 6'' Full sun, average to poor soil Easily grown, sow in place or indoors. Resists heat and drought; best bloom in heat of summer. Use in rock borders, edgings, walkways.

POT MARIGOLD calendula officinalis Yellow, orange 10''-24'' Sun, average soil Good cut flower, blooms best in cooler weather. Sow in place. It may reseed itself in following years. Use in borders; beddings; potted.

PRICKLY POPPY argemone grandiflora Yellow, white 24''-36'' Sun, average soil Sow in place or indoors. Use in beddings or borders.

PRINCE'S FATHER amaranthus lypochondriacus Flowers—red, auburn, foliage—reddish 24''-48'' Full sun, average to poor soil Rich soil tends to produce larger leaves at the expense of color. Withstands heat. Use massed; in borders; in backgrounds.

PRINCE'S FEATHER polygonum orientale pink, rose 72'' Sun, average soil Will attract bees. Sow in place. Use in background.

SAND VERBENA abronia Dark pink low, vinelike to 4'' Resists drought, sow indoors or in place. Fragrant; used in hanging baskets, rock gardens.

SCABIOSA scabiosa atropur purea Several colors 18''-36'' Sun, average soil. Fragrant and long lasting flowers. Use massed; in background border. Sow indoors or in cold frame after last frost. Good cut flowers.

SCARLET RUNNER BEAN phaseolus coccineus Red, white Vine Sun, average, well-drained soil Grow like pole bean; so in place or indoors.

SCARLET SAGE salvia spelndens Red—but pink & blue varieties as well 24''-72'' Full sun, average soil Sow indoors. Resists heat and poor soil; but keep well-watered in dry weather. Beddings, background.

SLIPPERY WORT calceolaria in variety Yellow, or yellow with orange brown spots 12"-36" Sun, rich, well-drained soil Houseplant; greenhouse plant and summer annual. Use potted; in beddings sow indoors in cool room; handle carefully when growing from seed.

SNAPDRAGON antirrhinum Several colors 6"-30" Sun, average well-drained soil Good cut flower; blooms best in cool weather; sown indoors or in place. Background, beddings. If cut back after first flowering may bloom again in the autumn, depending on weather.

SNEEZEWEED helenium tenuifolium Yellow 18"-28" Sun, any soil Easily grown, sow in place. Use in borders; massed; wild gardens.

SNOW-ON-THE-MOUNTAIN euphorbia marginata White and green 10"-24" Full sun, sandy soil Resists drought and heat. Do not over-water. Sow in place or indoors. Use in rock gardens; potted; sandy gardens.

SOAPWORT saponaria White to red 18"-40" Sun, well-drained soil Sow indoors or in cold frame. Use in rock gardens, borders. Can become an annoying weed.

STAR-OF-TEXAS xanthisma texanum Yellow 8"-30" Full sun, poor soil May behave like a biennial. Good for dry, sunny places, borders, etc. Resists heat and drought. Sow in place.

STAR-OF-THE-DESERT amberboa Purple to white 24"-36" Full sun, sandy soil Use in sandy gardens; in borders; massed. Sow indoors.

STATICE limphium Yellow, light purple 18"-24" Full sun, well-drained soil Use in borders; sand gardens; massed. Sow in place; good dried.

STINKING CLOVER cleome serrulata White, pink, red 18"-40" Sun, well-drained soil Used mostly to attract bees, especially in the west. Strong scent. Sow in place, but thin out. Use in borders.

STOCK, TEN WEEK mathiola, incana annual Several colors 12"-24" Sun, well-drained soil Fragrant flower that does not like heat and may flower after a frost. Can sow more than once a season. Use massed; in borders; potted. Sow indoors or in place. Good cut flowers and greenhouse plant.

STRAWFLOWER helichrysum bracteatum Several colors 24"-36" Sun, average soil Popular dried flower and cut flower. Sow in place or indoors. Use massed; in borders.

31

SUMMER FIR artemisia sacrorumviride Foliage—whitish To 60" Full sun, average to poor well-drained soil Does not do as well in rich soil. Sow in place as background.

SUNFLOWER helianthus annuus Yellow, orange red 24"-84" Sun, best in rich soil but tolerates poor soil Resists heat, drought, most soil conditions. Sow in place. Use as background planting, near fences.

SWAN RIVER DAISY bracycome iberidifolia Several colors 10"-30" Sun, well-drained soil Sow indoors. Use in borders; massed. Good cut flowers.

SWEET PEA lathyrus odoratus Several colors Vine 10"-60" Sun, rich, well-drained soil Likes cool weather, sow in place after last frost. Can be sown in fall and well mulched for spring bloom. Fragrant; may need vine supports. Good cut flower. Can tolerate heavy soil.

SWEET SULTAN centaurea moschata Several colors 12"-24" Sun, average soil Sow in place; likes to be crowded. No need to thin out. Fragrant, use in borders, massed.

SWEET WILLIAM dianthus barbatus Shades of red, white, pink 12"-30" Sun, well-drained soil Grow as annual or perennial in milder climates. Sow in place or indoors. Use massed; in borders.

TARWEED madia elegans Yellow 8"-24" Partial shade, average soil Heavily scented, use in beddings; shade gardens. Sow in place or indoors.

TAHOKA-DAISY machaeranthera tanacetifolia Bluish lavender 12"-24" Full sun, average soil Best in well-drained soil. Sow indoors and use massed or in borders.

TASSEL FLOWER emilia sagittata Yellow, orange, red To 24" Sun, average soil Sow in place; use massed; in borders. Also called Flora's Paintbrush.

TIDY TIPS layia elegans Yellow with white 12"-24" Sun, average soil Sow in place; use in wild gardens, massed.

TITHONIA tithonia roundifolia Yellow, orange 40"-72" Sun, average soil Resembles a sunflower. Start in place or indoors. Use in background plantings.

TORENIA torenia fourneri Blue, or violet and yellow 8"-12" Partial shade, average soil Also known as wishbone flower. Sow indoors or outdoors. Use massed; in shady garden.

TRANSVAAL DAISY gerbera jamesonii hybrida Several colors 18''-24''
full sun, sandy soil Grown in greenhouse for winter blooms and cut flowers.
Sow indoors in Jan. Put out after last frost. Use potted; massed; sandy
gardens; borders.

THUNBERGIA thunbergia Several colors Vine Full sun, well-drained soil
Climbs a trellis. Also used in hanging baskets, and as greenhouse plant. Sow
indoors. Sometimes called Black-eyed Susan vine.

VENDIDIUM vendidium fastuosum Orange and purple 14''-30'' Full sun,
well-drained soil Sow indoors, use potted, massed, in borders. Do not over-
water, may not do well during rainy summers. The flowers open in the morn-
ing and close at night.

VERBENA verbena nortensis Several colors 10''-20'' Sun, any soil Easily
grown, sow in place or indoors. Resists heat and poor soil. Use in rock
garden; borders; as ground cover.

VIPER'S BUGLOSS echium, several varieties Several colors 12''-18'' Sun,
average soil Grown in borders; massed. Easy to grow, sow in place or indoors.

VIRGINIA STOCK malcomia maritima Several colors 4''-10'' Sun, average
soil Sow in place and use massed; in edgings.

WALLFLOWER cheiranthus chieri Shades of red 10''-18'' Sun, well-drained
soil Use in rock gardens; beddings; borders. Does not tolerate heavy, wet
soil. Sow in cold frame or cool room.

WINGED EVERLASTING ammobium alatum White 18''-30'' Sun, average
soil Sow in place, in beddings or borders. Easily grown and used in dry flower
arrangements.

WAX BEGONIA begonia semiflorens White to red 10''-18'' Partial shade,
rich, well-drained soil Good house plants. Use potted indoors or out and in
shade gardens, or massed. Sow indoors. Don't let it dry out.

ZINNIA zinnia, in variety Several colors   15''-30'' Sun, any soil With-
stands heat, drought, heavy soil, or sandy soil and can tolerate partial shade.
Good cut flowers. Use massed; in borders. Sow in place or indoors.

33

PERENNIALS

ACHILLEA (Yarrow) achillea, in variety Flowers—white, shades of yellow or red foliage—green to white or grey 5"-30" Sun, average but well-drained soil The varieties range from ground covers to tall background plants. Usually used in rock gardens, borders, edgings or in place of grass in dry, sandy areas.

AGERATUM eupatorium coelestinum Shades of blue to purple flowers 12"-24" Sun, average soil Especially good in autumn gardens, massed or as a border. Propagated by division.

AGROSTEMMA lychnis coronaria Flowers—crimson foliage—silver-tinted 18" Sun, average soil Used massed or in borders.

AJUGA Ajuga reptans Flowers—shades of blue, purple, or red foliage—several colors low to 8" Sun to partial shade Any soil An easily grown, very tough, ground cover, used in sunny or shady areas. Propagated by division or seed, it may and often does escape into other areas.

ALYSSUM alyssum, in variety Flowers—shades of yellow or white 3"-15" Full sun, sandy soil A lovely low plant for borders, rock gardens, walkways, some of the varieties are fragrant, all are fairly tough.

ANCHUSA anchusa, azurea Flowers—shades of blue 30"-48" Sun, average but well-drained soil Usually used in borders, beddings, massed or as background. They are sensitive to cold and must be well mulched over winter. May not survive very cold winter. Propagated by division or seeds.

ASTER aster, in variety Several colors but none are yellow 10"-45" Sun to partial shade average soil Late blooming and used in autumn gardens, rock gardens, wild gardens, borders or beddings. Mulch well in winter. Propagated by seed.

ASTILBE (Spirea) astilbe, in variety Flowers—white or pink 10"-60" Sun, average soil Used as a greenhouse and florist plant, it is useful outside in borders, beddings, or potted.

BABY'S BREATH gypsophila White to pink flowers 5"-36" Full sun, any soil Delicate looking flowers that are used by florists with other cut flowers and alone. They like to be crowded and can be used massed, in borders, rock gardens or potted.

BALLOON FLOWER piatycodon, grandiflorum Flowers—white, pink, violet, blue 12"-24" Sun, average soil Grown in beddings or borders. Propagated by division.

ASTER

BEAR GRASS Yucca, giauca Blades—edged in white flowers—light green to white low Fully sun, sandy soil A hardy succulent, useful in rock gardens and wild gardens.

BEARD TONGUE penstemon, in variety Flowers—red, blue, yellow or purple 5"-48" Sun, average but well-drained soil Good bee attractors that must be well mulched in cold winter climates. Used in rock gardens and borders. Propagated by seed or division.

BEE BALM monarda, didyma Flowers—shades of white, pink, red 18"-30" Partial shade, average soil This aromatic plant usually grown in wild gardens, on stream banks, massed, or in shady gardens. Flowers used in bouquets. Propagated by division.

BLEEDING HEART dicentra Pink to white 10"-30" Partial shade, well-drained soil Grown in shade gardens, fern growings, and in edgings.

BUTTERFLY FLOWER ascelpias, tuberosa Orange flowers 15"-30" Full sun, sandy soil Used in sandy gardens, massed or in wild gardens.

CANDYTUFT Iberis, sempervirens Flowers—white foliage—dark green 6"-12" Ful sun, average soil Keep moist, used in rock gardens and in edgings. Propagated by division or seed.

CATNIP nepeta cataria Flowers—white, light purple foliage—greyish 18"-36" Sun, ordinary soil Very easily grown, cats love it dried or fresh. Grown in herb gardens, rock gardens, borders, or potted.

CAUCASIAN ROCK-CRESS arabis, caucasia Flowers—white to soft rose-tinted 6"-spreading Full sun, average soil Used as a ground cover in rock gardens or in borders.

CENTAUREA centaurea Foliage—white flowers—several colors 24" Sun, any soil Used in borders, or potted. Propagated by seeds or cuttings.

CHINESE LANTERNS physalis alkekengi Flowers—white fruit—orange-scarlet 20" Full sun, average soil Grown for the colorful fruit used in borders or potted. Flowers good for cutting. Propagated by seed or root division.

CHIVES allium schoenophrasum Flowers—mauve 15" Sun to light shade, average soil Leaves chopped as needed, and used as seasoning. Grown in herb gardens, edgings or potted.

36

CHINESE CHIVES allium tuberosum Flowers—white 15"-20" Sun to light shade, average soil Fragrant flowers that can be used dried. Grown usually in beddings or borders.

CHRYSANTHEMUM chrysamthemum Several colors 18"-36" Full sun, well-drained soil Popular cut flowers, may need to be staked. Use in borders, massed, or potted.

CINQUEFOIL potentilla, in variety Flowers—several colors 2"-36" Sun, average soil From ground covers to low shrubs they are used massed in borders and in rock [gardens. Propagated by seeds or division.

CLEMATIS clematis, in variety Flowers—several colors vine Sun to partial shade, rich, well-drained soil. Since this vine has tendrils it does not always need support. Grow on trellis, walls, under small shrubs and trees. Propagated by cuttings, grafting, layers.

COLUMBINE aquilegia vulgaris Several colors 18" Sun, well-drained soil Useful as cut flowers. Plant in borders, or massed or in wild gardens.

COMMON THRIFT armeria maritima Flowers—shades of white, pink, or purple 12" Sun, average well-drained soil Use in rock gardens, borders, or potted.

CONEFLOWER rudbeckia Shades of yellow, orange, red, brown, purple 24"-120" Full sun, average soil Easily grown, use in borders or as background, propagated by seeds or division of rootstocks.

CORAL BELLS heuchera sanguinea Shades of pink to red 15"-18" Partial shade, average soil Tolerates a variety of soil conditions, useful in rock gardens, wild gardens or as bedding plant.

COREOPSIS coreopsis lanceolata Yellow flowers 18"-30" Sun, average soil In borders, good cut flowers. Listed in annuals and often grown as annual.

CROWN VETCH coronilla varia Pinkish-white Low, spreading Full sun, average to poor soil Very fast growing ground cover, used to check soil erosion. Often grown on banks and hillsides.

CUPID'S DART cantananche coerula Blue, white 24" Sun, average soil Used as dried flowers, plant in masses. Often grown as annual, listed in annuals.

CHRYSANTHEMUMS

DELPHINIUM (Larkspur) delphinium Several colors 12''-24'' Sun to slight shade, average soil Popular cut flowers used in background borders, or massed. Cool weather important to seed germination. Listed in annuals.

ERIGERON erigeron, in variety Shades of red to blue with yellow centers 15''-18'' Sun, average soil Used in rock gardens and borders. Propagate by division.

EUPHORBIA (Cushion Spurge) euphorbia epithymoides Yellow to red flowers 12'' Full sun, sandy soil Grow in sandy gardens, rock gardens, or potted.

EVENING PRIMROSE oenothera Yellow, white, pink 18''-72'' Full sun, well-drained soil Backgrounds, massed; day-blooming and night-blooming types.

FEVERFEW chrysanthemum parthenium Yellow, white 6''-24'' Full sun, well-drained soil Use in beddings and borders.

FESTUCA festuca giaca Silver-grey grass low to 8'' Sun to partial shade, average, well-drained soil An ornamental grass used as edging, ground cover, and on banks.

FOXGLOVE digatalis White, yellow and brown 24''-36'' Sun to light shade, average soil In borders or massed, good cut flowers. Propagated by division.

FORGET-ME-NOT, TRUE myosotis scorpioides Blue 8''-20'' Partial shade, average soil Good bedding plant, likes to be crowded, keep moist.

FOUNTAIN GRASS eulalia gracillima Flowers mahogany tipped with white, changing to all white in fall low Sun, average well-drained soil An ornamental grass.

FLAX linum perenne Blue 18'' Sun, well-drained soil Use massed or in borders.

FLAX, GOLDEN linum flavum Yellow 10'' Sun, well-drained soil Plant in border or use massed.

GAILLARDIA (Blanket-flower) gaillardia aristata Shades of red and yellow 8''-16'' Full sun, well-drained soil Use in borders or massed.

DELPHINIUM

38

GERANIUM (Cranesbill) geranium, san guineum Red, white 10''-15'' Full sun to slight shade, well-drained soil Drought resistant and useful in rock gardens, borders, or potted.

GERMANDER teucrium Foliage—green flowers—shades of red 6''-12'' spreading Sun to partial shade A ground cover, useful as edging.

GEUM geum, in variety Shades of yellow to red 12''-24'' Sun, average soil A fine flower for bedding or borders. Propagate by division or seeds.

GLOBE THISTLE echinops, ritro Blue flowers, whitish foliage 24''-36'' Sun, average soil Needs space to grow, use in borders or beddings. Seeds or division.

GOLDEN MARGUERITE anthemis tinctoria shades of yellow, daisy-like 18'' Sun, average soil Use massed in borders, or wild gardens.

HELEN'S FLOWER helenium, autumnale Yellow, shades of red, yellow 24''-48'' Full sun, average soil Good cut flowers, use massed or in borders.

HENS AND CHICKS (Houseleek) sempervivum, tectorum Succulent rosette foliage, flowers shades of red Low, spreading Full sun, sandy soil Use in miniature gardens, rock gardens, sandy gardens, potted. Set out year-old clumps.

HIBISCUS hibiscus White, shades of pink to red 36''-120'' Full sun, well-drained soil Shrub, background, needs room to grow.

HOLLYHOCK althaea rosea Several colors 36''-48'' Full sun, average soil Cut flowers, use massed or in background plantings. Listed in annuals.

HOSTA (Funkia) hosta, in variety Flowers—violet, blue, white foliage— all green or varigated with white Low to 30'' Partial shade to sun, average soil Easily grown, usually in shady gardens but can be grown in sunny border. Propagate by division.

INCARVILLEA (Hardy gloxinia) incarvillea delavayi Pink, red 12'' Sun average, but well-drained soil Large trumpet shaped flowers used massed or in beddings. Does not tolerate wind, keep well mulched in winter. Propagate by seeds or division.

SCARLET AND ZONAL GERANIUMS

GERANIUM—"INCOMPARABLE"

GERANIUM—"MRS. POLLOCK"

40

JACOB'S LADDER polemonium caeruleum Blue 16'' Sun to partial shade, average soil Use massed, in shady gardens, or borders. Propagate by seeds, cuttings, or division.

LACE PLANT (Silver fleece) polygonum, aubertii Flowers—white, greenish-white (fragrant) Vine-to 30 ft. Sun to shade, any soil Chiefly grown to cover an area quickly, perfect for a chain-link fence trellis. Extremely hardy, blooms late in the summer, and a good bee attractor. Propagated by seeds, cuttings, division.

LAMIUM lamium, in variety Yellow, purple, or greenish-white flowers Low or up to 84'' Partial shade, average well-drained soil From background plantings to ground covers, in shade gardens or rock gardens. Propagated by seeds or division.

LAVENDER, SWEET lavendula, vera Flowers—lavender or purple foliage—white 12''-18'' Sun, average well-drained soil Like most herbs, lavender is happier in poor soils. Use in herb gardens, borders, circling evergreens, fragrant, in sachets.

LEOPARDBANE doronicum caucasicum Yellow flowers 15'' Sun, average soil Daisy-like flowers used in borders and beddings. Good cut flowers. Propagated by division.

LIATRIS liatris, in variety Flowers—white or shades of red, purple 24''-48'' Sun, any well-drained soil Resists drought and poor soil. Use in wild gardens or borders. Good cut flowers.

MONEY PLANT lunaria biennis Flowers—crimson, silver pods 16'' Sun, average soil A biennial, grow in borders or massed. Used in dry flower arrangements. Propagate by seed.

MOUNTAIN FLEECE polygonum, amplexicaule Flowers—rose, red, white 36'' Sun to shade, any soil A good border plant. Will attract bees. Propagated by seeds, cutting, division.

NEPETA nepeta mussini Blue flowers 18''-24'' Sun, ordinary soil The same family as catnip, but showier and also attractive to cats. Aromatic, use in borders, rock gardens, beddings. Propagate by seeds or division.

OBEDIENT PLANT (False dragonhead) dracocephalum virginianum Flowers—shades of pink, red, purple, and white 24''-72'' Partial shade, average soil Keep slightly moist, grow in shade gardens, borders, as background. Good cut flowers. Propagate by seeds, division.

41

PEONY

LUPINE lupinus, polyphyllus Several colors 36''-60'' Partial shade to sun, moist soil Use in shady gardens, borders. Propagated by seeds, division.

LYCHNIS lychnis Flowers—shades of red 12''-36'' Full sun, any soil Grown in rock garfdens, borders, massed. Propagated by seeds, division.

LYTHRUM (red sally) lythrum, salicaria Flowers—shades of pink, purple 18''-48'' Sun to partial shade, any soil, keep moist Grown near ponds or streams, or as a bedding plant. Does not withstand drought. Propagate by division.

MADEIRA VINE boussingaultia baselloides Flowers—white Vine (tendrils) Sun, rich well-drained soil Also called mignonette vine because of fragrance. Use in windowboxes, potted, on a trellis. Evergreen in mild climates. Southern perennial, not hardy in north.

MINT mentha, in variety Flowers—white, blue foliage—green, green variegated with white or yellow Low, and to 14'' Full sun, average soil Aromatic, grow in herb gardens, rock gardens, also ground cover, along walkways, or potted.

ORCHARD GRASS dactylis glomerata Foliage—green with silver on edges 18''-30'' Partial shade, ordinary soil Useful in shade garden beddings mixed with flowers or under trees as ground cover. Weedy and easily grown.

PACHYSANDRA pachysandra, in variety White, purple Low Partial shade to sun, average soil Popular ground cover for shady areas, banks and slopes.

PAINTED DAISY (pyrethrum) chrysanthemum coccineum Flowers—white, shades of pink, red, lavender 18'' Sun, average soil Use in borders, massed or potted.

PASQUE-FLOWER anemone pulsatilla Shades of violet, blue, red 8''-12'' Sun to slight shade, any well-drained soil Better in poor soil, grow in rock gardens, wild gardens, borders. Propagate by seed.

PEONY peony, herbaceous types Pink, red, white 18''-48'' Full sun, well-drained soil Use only organic fertilizers, massed or in borders. Propagate by division.

PEONY, TREE peony, suffruticosa Red, pink, purple, white 36''-72'' Full sun, well-drained soil Very beautiful, use as background planting, tree-form, only organic fertilizers, propagate by division.

PASQUE-FLOWER (ANEMONE PULSATILLA)

43

PHLOX, EARLY phlox carolina White, shades of red, purple Spreading 8''-12'' Full sun, average, but well-drained soil Fragrant, use in rock gardens and borders.

PHLOX, HARDY phlox Several colors 10''-45'' Full sun, average, but well-drained soil Favorite for rock gardens, borders.

PINKS, HARDY dianthus White, pink, red, purple 4''-24'' Sun, well-drained soil From low mat forming to tall types, use in rock gardens, beddings. Good cut flowers (includes sweet william).

PLUMBAGO (Leadwort) plumbago larpentiae Flowers—blue foliage—dark green 8''-12'' Sun, average soil Use in borders, rock gardens, or massed. Propagate by division.

PLUME POPPY bocconia cordata Huge plumes of feathery, small white blooms 72''-120'' Sun, rich, well-drained soil Grows quickly and needs room, grow as background, or in borders.

POKER PLANT kniphofia, uvaria Yellow, shades of orange, red 18''-40'' Sun, well-drained soil Mulch well with salt-hay over winter. Use massed, borders, background. Propagate by seeds, division, offsets.

POPPY, ORIENTAL papauer, orientale Shades of red 24''-40'' Sun, well-drained soil Other perennial poppies include Icelandic poppy, to 12'' in several colors. Beautiful flowers. Use massed, in borders, beddings. Propagate by seed.

PRICKLY PEAR opuntia, humifusa Yellow flowers Low Full sun, sandy soil Use in rock gardens, wild gardens, sandy gardens, potted.

PRIMROSE primula Several colors 8''-24'' Partial shade, average soil Keep slightly moist, use in shade gardens, edgings. Good cut flowers. Propagate by seed.

PURPLE ROCK-CRESS aubrieta, leichtlini Flowers—shades of purple Low to 6'' Partial shade to sun, average soil Use as ground cover, in rock gardens, edgings, borders, shady gardens.

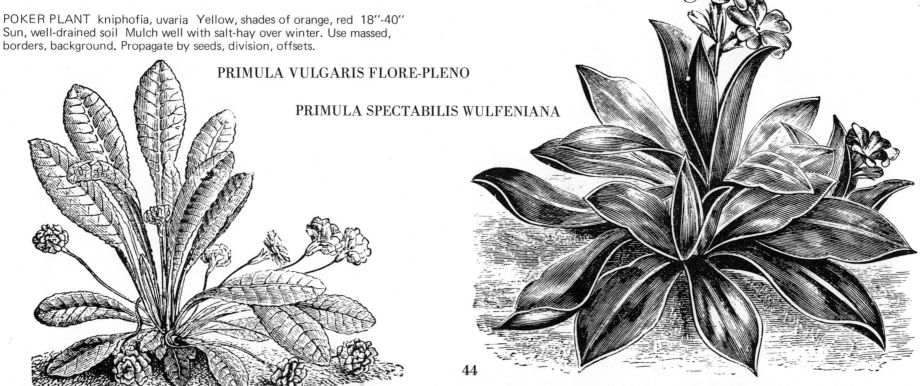

PRIMULA VULGARIS FLORE-PLENO

PRIMULA SPECTABILIS WULFENIANA

44

SALVIA (Sage) salvia Shades of red, purple, blue 10''-36'' Full sun, average soil Good bee attractors, use massed, in borders or background. Propagate by cuttings or division.

SANTOLINA (Lavender cotton) santolina chamaecyparissus Foliage—grey 12''-forms mounds Sun, average soil Ground cover for borders, rock gardens, herb gardens. Keep well mulched during winter in cold climates. Propagate by cuttings.

SCABOSIA scabosia Several colors 5''-36'' Sun, average soil Use as bedding plant, in borders, rock gardens. Propagate by seed, division.

SEDUM Sedum, in variety Flowers—several colors foliage—green to bronze Low to 10'' Full sun, sandy soil Traditional ground cover in rock gardens, also use in sandy gardens or potted.

SEDUM, SHOWY sedum, spectabile Flowers—white, shades of pink, red 15''-18'' Full sun, sandy soil Use in autumn gardens, rock gardens, potted.

SHASTA DAISY chrysanthemum, maximum White 18''-30'' Full sun, average soil Good cut flowers, late blooming. Use massed, in borders, potted.

SIBERIAN WALLFLOWER erysimum, asperum Orange 15'' Sun, any soil A biennial that will tolerate any soil but bloom more in richer soils. Blooms in May, sow indoors in late winter. Use massed.

SILVER MOUND artemisia, schmidtiana Flower—white foliage—fern-like and silvery grey Low, mound like to 10'' diameter Sun, sandy soil Ground cover for rockery, walkway, edging, autumn gardens.

SOAPWORT, ROCK saponaria ocymoides Pink flowers Spreading, to 8'' Full sun, average soil Another ground cover, useful in rock gardens, edgings.

SPANISH BAYONET yucca, filamentosa Bright green, sword-like foliage, white flowers 60''-72'' Full sun, sandy soil A dramatic succulent useful in rock gardens and sandy gardens.

SPIDERWORT, VIRGINIA tradescantia, virginica Foliage—variegated green and purple flowers—white, blue, purple 18''-36'' Partial shade, average soil Keep slightly moist, use in shady gardens, borders, wild gardens. Propagate by cutting, division.

AYONET

SEDUM SIEBOLDII

SNOW IN SUMMER cerastium tomentosum Foliage—grey to white Flowers—white Creeping low to 8" Full sun, any well-drained soil Ground cover, use in rock gardens, wild gardens, borders.

STATICE armeria, in variety White shades of red, pink, purple Low to 18" Full sun, any well-drained soil Grown in rock gardens, borders, and potted.

STOKES ASTER stokesia iaevis Dark blue 12"-18" Sun, average soil Use massed and in borders.

SUNFLOWER, FALSE heliopsis, in variety Shades of yellow, orange To 30" Full sun, any soil Borders, massed, wild gardens.

SUNFLOWER, PERENNIAL helianthus Yellow 36"-144" Full sun, moist soils Use as background, near wild gardens, on stream banks, or slopes.

SWEET PEA lathyrus White shades of pink, red, purple Vine to 110" Sun, sandy soils Grow on trellis, fences, sandy gardens, usually near coastlines in the wild.

THERMOPSIS thermopsis, caroliniana, or mollis Yellow 18"-48" Sun, well-drained soil Resists drought, grow in sunny areas, borders or massed.

THYME, CREEPING thymus, serpyllum Foliage—grey, green flowers—white, pink, red, purple Low Full sun, well-drained soil An aromatic ground cover used in rock gardens, walkway plantings, potted. Prefers limey soil.

VERBENA verbena, canadensis Flowers—white, shades of red, purple 8"-14" Sun, well-drained soil A ground cover for borders, edgings. Propagate by seeds, cuttings.

VERONICA veronica, herbaceous Several colors Low, from 2" to 20" Sun, average soil Fragrant and used in rock gardens, borders. Propagate by division.

VINCA MINOR (Periwinkle) vinca minor Foliage—evergreen flowers—several colors Low, trailing Shady, any well-drained soil Fragrant ground cover for shady gardens, banks, slopes, under trees. Propagate by division, cuttings.

VIOLET, SWEET viola, odorata Flowers—white and shades of purple Low, to 6" Partial shade, average to rich soil Fragrant and used in shade gardens, wild gardens, massed. Propagate by seed, division, cuttings.

VIOLA RENIFORMIS (NEW HOLLAND VIOLET)

TREES & SHRUBS

Trees planted around homes and along city and village streets fill a need. They fill a need for shade, a need for screening, a need for softening the harsh and stark lines of buildings, a need for adding beauty and graciousness and a feeling of welcome to streets that otherwise are purely functional.

For trees to do their intended job satisfactorily—and continue to do it—they must be selected carefully, then watched over until they become established. Once they are established, carefully selected trees require less attention.

SELECTING THE RIGHT TREE

When you plant a tree you also plant shade, or shape, or background, or screening, or color. The use that you intend for your tree and the location in which you will plant it should guide you in its selection.

In selecting a shade or ornamental tree—

Limit selection to trees of reliable HARDINESS in your area.

Select the FORM that is best for the intended use.

Determine the mature SIZE that is desirable; consider whether GROWTH RATE and LONGEVITY are limiting factors.

Avoid trees having UNDESIRABLE CHARACTERISTICS for the intended use.

Determine AVAILABILITY of suitable trees.

Hardiness

Start with a list of trees that are reliably hardy to the environment that they must grow in. Consider the total environment: The climate, the soil type, the available moisture, the contaminants in the atmosphere, and competition from the activities of human society.

When you consider hardiness to the climate of your area, remember the summer's heat as well as the winter's cold. Trees native to northern climates easily withstand southern winters but may be scorched beyond use by heat of a southern summer.

And be sure trees are RELIABLY hardy in your area; trees planted north of their adapted range may grow satisfactorily through a series of milder-than-normal winters, but when an especially severe winter comes along, they will be killed. Then the person who planted them will have lost money and labor and—most precious of all—time.

AMERICAN LINDEN. Tilia Americana

Soils in the city tend to be compacted and poorly drained. If you are selecting trees for city planting, therefore, you must either select trees that are tolerant of soil compaction or be prepared to invest time and labor in preventing these conditions.

Available moisture, too, can limit a tree's usefulness. In park plantings or specimen plantings in a yard, trees native to the area are not likely to suffer from lack of water during periods of normal rainfall. Near a street, however, trees can never receive their fair share of water. Rain flows off into gutters and storm drains and is carried away. For city plantings, select trees that can grow in reasonably dry soil, then see that they get enough water to keep them growing until their root systems adjust to the continuous subnormal soil moisture.

City air is filled with smoke and fumes and dust and soot. Some trees can grow successfully in this environment, others cannot. For example, ginkgo and London plane trees do well in downtown fumes and dirt; sugar maple does not.

Trees planted in the open—in parks or large yards—usually have less competition from the activities of human society than street trees. But many city trees must compete with automobiles and foot traffic, with lawnmowers, with sewer lines underground, and with utility lines overhead. To compete with human society successfully, a tree must be tough.

Form

Consider whether the mature form of a tree is appropriate to its intended use. A broad-spreading and low-hanging tree may be ideal as a park or yard tree, but it would be unsatisfactory along a driveway. A slim, upright tree may be perfect for lining driveways, but of little use for shading a patio.

If you are not familiar with the mature form of trees under consideration, study illustrations of them in books or nursery catalogs.

Size

Many homeowners have learned by experience that Norway spruce is not a suitable tree for foundation plantings. The 6-foot-tall evergreens that look so attractive beside the front steps can eventually grow to a height of 70 feet and a spread of 40 feet. And they seem to get out of hand before the homeowner does anything about it.

Size of Mature Trees

Small
(Up to 40 feet)

Arborvitae
Brazilian pepper
Cherry laurel
Desert willow
Green ash
Hemlock
Jacaranda
Mimosa
Wax

Medium
(40 to 75 feet)

American holly
Blue spruce
Goldrain tree
Hackberry
Honeylocust
Live oak
Norway maple
Red maple
Scotch pine
Valley oak

Large
(More than 75 feet)

American beech
Pecan
Southern magnolia
White oak
Willow oak

THUYA GIGANTEA.

50

GROWTH RATE of a potentially large tree, however, may be slow enough to allow the tree's use for many years before it gets too large. Tuliptree, for example, may grow to a height of 100 feet or more, which makes it much too large for a yard tree on the usual city or suburban lot. But tuliptree takes more than 100 years to mature. The tree may be of acceptable size for 40 or 50 years after planting. You must decide whether you care what happens 40 years hence.

LONGEVITY also is a matter for thought. Some trees grow rapidly, giving shade and screening soon after they are planted. They reach maturity quickly, then decline. How soon will they decline? Will their decline—and need for removal—affect you? If, when you are 25 years old, you plant a tree with a 40-year life expectancy, you may have to cut it down just as you are planning to spend some of your retirement time sitting under it. But if you plant the same tree when you are 45, you can sit under it in retirement years and you are not likely to care when it begins to decline. You have to decide whether you are planting trees for posterity or for yourself.

Useful Life Expectancy

Short (to 50 years)	Medium (to 75 or 100 years)	Long (100 or more years)
Arborvitae	American holly	American beech
Brazilian pepper	Blue spruce	Live oak
Desert willow	Goldrain tree	Pecan
Mimosa	Green ash	Southern magnolia
Redbud	Hackberry	White ash
Sydney wattle	Honeylocust	White oak
Umbrella tree	Jacaranda	Willow oak
	Norway maple	
	Red maple	
	Scotch pine	
	Valley oak	

Undesirable Characteristics

It is difficult to find a tree that has no undesirable characteristics. Some traits make a tree unsuited for any use. For example, the American elm—one of our favorite trees—is susceptible to Dutch elm disease, which makes the tree a poor risk in areas where the disease occurs.

AMERICAN ELM.
Ulmus Americana

Thornless honeylocust is subject to attack by the mimosa webworm, which ruins the appearance of the tree unless it is sprayed every year. White mulberry and the female ginkgo produce fruits that are so objectionable that these species may be considered garbage trees.

Some trees have traits that are nuisances, but may be tolerable. Oaks, hickorys, horse chestnuts, crabapples—all produce fruits that attract children who may use them for missiles. Sweetgum fruits—gum balls—are covered with thorny protuberances that make the fruits a nuisance in lawns. Poplars and mimosa produce an abundance of seeds that sprout in lawns and flowerbeds. If you like these trees otherwise, you may choose to overlook their undesirable characteristics.

Some trees have characteristics that are intolerable in one situation but not in another. Some maples, for example, have a tendency to raise and crack pavement with their roots. If they are planted where there is no nearby pavement, this is no problem. Some trees—red and silver maples, elm, willow, and poplar—are notorious sewer cloggers. If they are planted away from sewer lines, again this is no problem.

You must match the tree's characteristics with its intended use; decide if they are compatible.

Availability

When you have narrowed your list down to a few acceptable trees, you must find which of them are available. There is a good chance that the best tree for the purpose may be in such demand that it is not available locally. Then you must either settle for second best or shop around by mail to find the tree you want.

Many reputable nurseries do business by mail. You can feel secure in dealing with any of the old-line firms. But beware of firms that make fantastic claims for their nursery stock or promote common trees by giving them unusual names.

CARING FOR TREES

The city is a difficult, often hostile, environment for shade trees. Success in growing shade trees in the city depends most on selection of a tree that can survive in this unfavorable environment. Then the tree must be cared for until it has a chance to become established.

Planting; fertilizing; watering; mulching; pruning; protecting from insects, diseases, and mechanical injury—these are the steps in preparing a tree for survival in the city.

PIN OAK. Quercus palustris

Planting

The key to good tree planting is generosity: Be generous in digging a planting hole, in replacing poor soil with good, in expending energy to do the job right.

The right way to do the job depends on how good the soil is on the planting site:

In good soil—

Dig planting holes for bare-root trees large enough to receive the roots when they are spread in a natural position.

Dig planting holes for balled-and-burlapped trees 2 feet wider than the rootball.

Dig holes deep enough so you can set the trees at the same level at which they grew in the nursery.

In poor soil—

Dig holes for all trees as wide and deep as you can conveniently make them.

Replace the poor soil from the hole with good soil when you fill in around the newly set tree.

In soil with impossibly poor drainage—

Take all practical measures to improve drainage.

Limit tree selection to species having a mature height less than 50 feet.

Set the rootball in a shallow depression in the soil.

Fill in around the rootball with good soil, forming a slightly concave bed extending out as far from the trunk as you can manage. Topsoil is often removed in building operations. Subsoil is commonly unfavorable for trees. In such cases, the best procedure is to use as much topsoil as practicable in the planting hole.

Pack soil under the newly set tree until it sets at the level at which it grew in the nursery.

Before filling around the rootball, stake or guy the tree. If the trunk diameter of the tree is 3 inches or less, use one or two 6-foot poles or steel fenceposts to stake the tree. Set the poles vertically into the soil next to the rootball. Fasten the trunk to the poles with a loop of wire that is enclosed in a section of garden hose to prevent bark cutting.

If the tree trunk is larger than 3 inches in diameter, support it with three hose-covered guy wires. Loop the wires around the trunk about two-thirds up the main stem or trunk. Stake one guy wire to the ground in the direction of the prevailing wind. Stake the other two wires to the ground to form an equilateral triangle.

After the tree is set and the hole is filled with good soil, settle the soil around the roots by watering thoroughly. Then wrap the trunk with burlap or creped kraft paper to prevent sunscald. Start wrapping at the top and wrap toward the ground. Tie the wrapping material with stout cord, knotting it about every 18 inches. The wrapping should remain for 1 to 2 years.

Fertilizing

If you use plenty of good soil for backfilling newly planted trees, the trees are not likely to need fertilizer for the first year after planting. However, street trees, planted in the narrow parking between sidewalk and curb, may need earlier feeding.

If you think your trees need fertilizer—if the leaves are paler than normal and if growth is slower than normal—you can apply it in spring this way:

Measure the diameter of the trunk 3 feet above the ground; use 2 pounds of 5-10-5 for each inch of diameter (a 1-pound coffee can holds about 2 pounds of fertilizer).

Using a soil auger, if one is available, or a crowbar or posthold digger, make holes 15 to 24 inches deep and about 18 to 24 inches apart around the drip line of the tree (the area beneath the ends of the longest branches).

Distribute the fertilizer equally among the holes, then fill the holes with good soil. A mixture of equal parts topsoil, sand, and peatmoss is good for filling the holes; it provides aeration and water access as well as filling the space.

Watering

City trees often get too little water. Many trees grow in places where the area of soil exposed to rainfall is small. Lawn trees have to compete with grass and other plants for water. Drainpipes honeycomb the city and remove thousands of gallons of water every day.

Trees can become conditioned to this constantly low amount of water. But they have to be kept alive until they can adjust.

Water trees for the first two seasons after planting them. Water about once a week and let the water run for several hours. If you have one of the special needles that attaches to a garden hose for injecting water and water-soluble fertilizer into the root zone, you will find it to be useful, particularly for watering curbside trees.

If the soil in your area is tight clay or is underlain with hardpan, be careful that you do not overwater. Excess water will kill some kinds of trees faster than drought.

FLOWERING DOGWOOD. Cornus florida

Mulching

In the forest, decaying fallen leaves provide a protective mulch that conserves natural moisture, tempers summer's heat and winter's cold, and adds organic matter to the soil. In city or suburban yards, however, fallen leaves beneath lawn trees are more likely to be considered litter than mulch. And fallen leaves in public space along curbs clog gutters and drains; make streets slippery, and are fire hazards, so they must be removed. As a consequence, organic matter in the soil becomes depleted.

Yard trees can be mulched with materials more attractive than rotting leaves—pine bark, tanbark, ground corncobs, or peanut hulls, for example—and they will receive the organic matter they need. Trees can be supplied with soil organic matter as a result of fertilizer application; the peatmoss in the soil mixture that is used to fill fertilizing holes will help to keep the soil moist, aerated, and well drained.

Pruning

Inspect your shade trees regularly and prune them when needed. By following this procedure, you can improve their appearance, guard their health, and make them stronger. And by pruning as soon as the need becomes apparent, you can easily correct defects that would require major surgery if allowed to wait.

In your program of scheduled pruning, try to eliminate undesirable branches or shoots while they are small. Drastic, difficult, or expensive pruning may be avoided by early corrective pruning.

Here is a list of things to look for and prune:

Dead, dying, or unsightly parts of trees.

Sprouts growing at or near the base of the tree trunk.

Branches that grow toward the center of the tree.

Crossed branches. If branches cross and rub together, disease and decay fungi can enter the tree through the abraded parts.

V crotches. If it is possible to do so without ruining the appearance of the tree, remove one of the members forming a V crotch. V crotches split easily; their removal helps to prevent storm damage to the tree.

Multiple leaders. If several leaders develop on a tree that normally has only a single stem and you wish the tree to develop its typical shape, cut out all but one leader. This restores dominance to the remaining stem.

"Nuisance" growth. Cut out branches that are likely to interfere with

electric or telephone wires. Remove branches that shade street lights or block the view in streets so as to constitute a traffic hazard. Prune out branches that shut off breezes. Cut off lower limbs that shade the lawn excessively.

Do not leave stubs when you prune. Stubs usually die. They are points at which decay fungi can enter the tree.

Small pruning cuts heal quickly. Large cuts—more than 1 inch in diameter—should be treated with antiseptic tree dressing to prevent entrance of decay or disease while the wound is healing.

Protecting From Insects, Diseases, and Mechanical Injury

Most insects and diseases can be controlled by spraying. Your county agricultural agent, extension landscape specialist, or State agricultural experiment station can tell you what spray schedules to follow in protecting your trees from insects and diseases. When trees are small, you can spray them yourself. As they grow larger, however, spraying becomes a job for professional arborists, who have the equipment and knowledge required to do a thorough job.

Danger from mechanical injury by lawnmowers, bicycles, and foot traffic is reduced when stakes and guy wires are installed. If needed for protection, tree boxes can be made from snow fencing and placed around trees.

REPLACING LOST TREES

Trees fill a need—a need that remains after the tree is lost. You recognize that yard trees enhance the value of your home by providing shade, screening, color, or architectural balance. If yard trees die you replace them.

But what about trees on public space? How are you affected by loss of street or park trees? What can you do to insure that they are replaced?

How You Are Affected

Community beautification pays off economically as well as aesthetically. Residential property in an attractive part of town is worth more than residential property in an unattractive part of town. Trees on your streets add dollars to the value of your property. Conversely, your property loses value when trees are removed and not replaced.

What You Can Do

If you live in an incorporated city or town, let city authorities know that you think lost street and park trees should be replaced. Voters' associations, garden clubs, service clubs, parent-teacher groups—all should express their interest in having street trees properly cared for and, if necessary, replaced. They should also express their appreciation to city authorities who do a good job of street-tree maintenance and replacement.

If you live in an unincorporated community, replacing street trees is likely to be more of a do-it-yourself job. But you, together with other interested citizens, can insure that lost trees are replaced satisfactorily.

Help is available to citizens' groups through your city parks system, your State agricultural experiment station, your county agricultural agent, commercial nurserymen, and, in many areas, the local light and power company.

REGIONAL LIST OF TREES

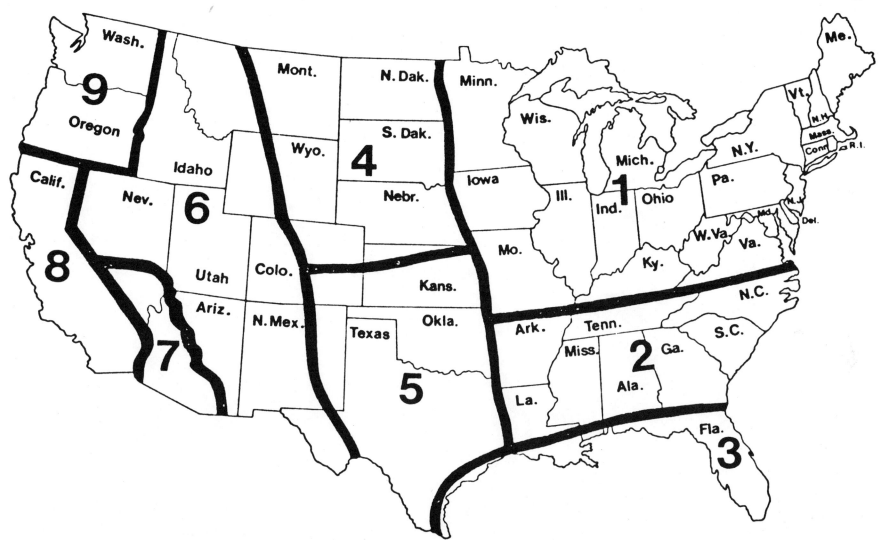

Wash.

9

Oregon

Calif.

8

7

Nev.

6

Idaho

Utah

Ariz.

N. Mex.

Mont.

Wyo.

Colo.

N. Dak.

S. Dak.

Nebr.

Kans.

Okla.

Texas

5

Minn.

Iowa

Mo.

Ark.

La.

Wis.

Mich.

Ill.

Ind.

1

Ohio

Ky.

Tenn.

Miss.

Ala.

2

Ga.

Fla.

3

Me.

Vt.

N.H.

Mass.

Conn.

R.I.

N.Y.

Pa.

N.J.

W.Va.

Va.

Md.

Del.

N.C.

S.C.

4

57

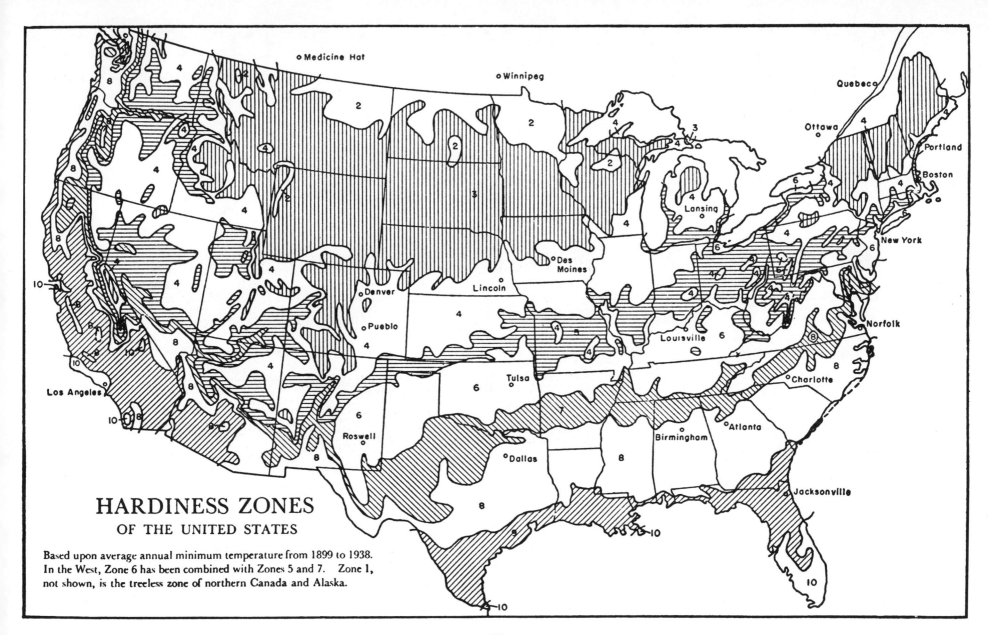

HARDINESS ZONES
OF THE UNITED STATES

Based upon average annual minimum temperature from 1899 to 1938.
In the West, Zone 6 has been combined with Zones 5 and 7.   Zone 1,
not shown, is the treeless zone of northern Canada and Alaska.

58

REGION 1

Evergreens, broadleaf
  Holly, American; Zone 6.
  Magnolia, Southern; Zone 7.
Evergreens, needle leaf and scale leaf
  Arborvitae, Eastern; Zone 2.
  Arborvitae, Japanese; Zone 6.
  Cedar, Deodar; Zone 7.
  Cedar, Eastern Red (Juniper); Zone 2.
  Cedar of Lebanon; Zone 6.
  Cryptomeria; Zone 6.
  Fir, White; Zone 5.
  Hemlock, Canadian; Zone 3.
  Lawson False Cypress; Zone 6.
  Pine, Eastern White; Zone 3.
  Pine, Red; Zone 2.
  Spruce, Colorado Blue; Zone 2.
  Spruce, White; Zone 2.
Deciduous
  Ash, Green; Zone 2.
  Ash, White; Zone 3.
  Aspen, Quaking; Zone 2.
  Baldcypress; Zone 5.
  Beech, American; Zone 3.
  Beech, European; Zone 5.
  Birch, Cutleaf European; Zone 2.
  Birch, Paper; Zone 2.
  Birch, White; Zone 2.
  Buckeye; Zone 4.
  Catalpa, Northern; Zone 3.
  Catalpa, Southern; Zone 5.
  Cork Tree, Phelledendron Amur; Zone 4.
  Cucumber Tree (Magnolia, Cucumber); Zone 5.
  Elm, American; Zone 3.
  Elm, English; Zone 6.
  Elm, European; Zone 5.
  Elm, Scotch; Zone 5.
  Ginkgo; Zone 5.
  Goldenrain Tree; Zone 5.
  Hackberry, Eastern; Zone 3.
  Hickory, Bitternut; Zone 5.
  Hickory, Mockernut; Zone 5.
  Hickory, Pignut (Pignut); Zone 5.
  Hickory, Shagbark; Zone 5.
  Honeylocust, Thornless; Zone 3.
  Hornbeam, Zmerican; Zone 3.
  Hornbeam, European; Zone 6.
  Hornbeam, Hop; Zone 5.
  Horsechestnut; Zone 3
  Horsechestnut, Red (Buckeye, Red and Horsechestnut, Ruby); Zone 3.
  Japanese Pagoda Tree; Zone 5.
  Katsura Tree; Zone 5.
  Kentucky Coffeetree; Zone 5.
  Larch, European; Zone 3.
  Linden, American; Zone 3.
  Linden, Littleleaf; Zone 3.
  Linden, Silver; Zone 5.
  Locust, Black; Zone 3.
  London Plane; Zone 6.
  Magnolia, Sweetbay; Zone 7
  Maple, Norway; Zone 4.
  Maple, Red; Zone 3.
  Maple, Sugar; Zone 3.
  Maple, Sycamore; Zone 6.
  Mimosa; Zone 7.
  Oak, Black; Zone 5.
  Oak, Bur; Zone 3.
  Oak, Chestnut; Zone 5.
  Oak, Northern Red; Zone 4.
  Oak, Pin; Zone 4.
  Oak, Scarlet; Zone 4.
  Oak, Shingle; Zone 6.
  Oak, Turkey; Zone 6.
  Oak, White; Zone 5.
  Oak, Willow; Zone 6.
  Oak, Yellow; Zone 5.
  Pear, Bradford; Zone 5.
  Sassafras; Zone 5.
  Silverbell; Zone 5.
  Sourgum; Zone 5.
  Sweetgum; Zone 5.
  Sycamore; Zone 5.
  Tamarack; Zone 2.
  Tulip Poplar; Zone 5.
  Willow, Weeping; Zone 6.
  Yellowwood; Zone 4.
  Zelkova; Zone 5.

NORWAY SPRUCE.

Picea excelsa

REGION 2

Evergreens, broadleaf
Bayberry; Zone 7.
Camphor Tree; Zone 9.
Holly, American; Zone 6.
Holly, Chinese; Zone 7.
Holly, English; Zone 7.
Laurelcherry; Zone 7.
Magnolia, Southern; Zone 7.
Oak, Laurel; Zone 9.
Oak, Live; Zone 8.
Wax Myrtle; Zone 9.
Evergreens, needle leaf and scale leaf
Arborvitae, Eastern; Zone 2.
Arborvitae, Oriental; Zone 3.
Cedar, Atlas; Zone 6.
Cedar, Deodar; Zone 7.
Cedar, Eastern Red; Zone 2.
Cedar, Incense; Zone 6.
Cedar of Lebanon; Zone 6.
Cryptomeria; Zone 6.
Hemlock, Carolina; Zone 7.
Pine, Eastern White; Zone 3.
Pine, Loblolly; Zone 7.
Pine, Longleaf; Zone 8.
Pine, Shortleaf; Zone 7.
Pine, Slash; Zone 8.
Spruce, Colorado Blue; Zone 2.
Spruce, Red; Zone 7.
Deciduous
Ash, White; Zone 3.
Baldcypress; Zone 5.
Beech, American; Zone 3.
Beech, European; Zone 5.
Birch, Cutleaf European; Zone 2.
Buckeye; Zone 4.
Catalpa, Northern; Zone 3.
Catalpa, Southern; Zone 5.
Cherry, Black; Zone 3.
Chinaberry (Umbrella Tree); Zone 7.
Chinese Tallow Tree; Zone 7.
Crape Myrtle; Zone 7.
Cucumber Tree (Magnolia, Cucumber); Zone 5.

Elm, American; Zone 3.
Elm, Cedar; Zone 7.
Elm, English; Zone 5.
Elm, Winged; Zone 7.
Ginkgo; Zone 5.
Goldenrain Tree; Zone 5.
Hackberry, Eastern; Zone 3.
Hickory, Bitternut; Zone 5.
Hickory, Mockernut; Zone 5.
Hickory, Pignut (Pignut); Zone 5.
Hickory, Shagbark; Zone 5.
Honeylocust, Thornless; Zone 3.
Hornbeam, American; Zone 3.
Hornbeam, Hop; Zone 5.
Japanese Pagoda Tree; Zone 5.
Katsura Tree; Zone 5.
Kentucky Coffeetree; Zone 5.
Linden, American; Zone 3.
Linden, Littleleaf; Zone 3.
London Plane; Zone 6.
Magnolia, Sweetbay; Zone 7.
Maple, Norway; Zone 4.
Maple, Red; Zone 3.
Maple, Silver; Zone 3.
Maple, Sycamore; Zone 6.
Mimosa; Zone 7.
Mulberry, Paper; Zone 6.
Oak, Black; Zone 5.
Oak, Bur; Zone 3.
Oak, Chestnut; Zone 5.
Oak, Pin; Zone 4.
Oak, Post; Zone 7.
Oak, Scarlet; Zone 4.
Oak, Southern Red; Zone 7.
Oak, Water; Zone 8.
Oak, White; Zone 5.
Oak, Willow; Zone 6.
Pear, Bradford; Zone 5.
Pecan; Zone 7.
Persimmon; Zone 7.
Redbud, Eastern; Zone 6.
Sassafras; Zone 5.
Silverbell; Zone 5.
Sourgum; Zone 5.
Sourwood; Zone 7.

Sweetgum; Zone 5.
Sycamore; Zone 5.
Tulip Poplar; Zone 5.
Yellowwood; Zone 4.
Palms
Palmetto, Cabbage; Zone 8.

WHITE OAK. *Quercus alba*

REGION 3

Evergreens, broadleaf
African Tuliptree (Bell
Flambeau); Zone 10.
Brazilian Pepper; Zone 9.
Cajeput; Zone 10.
Cocoplum; Zone 10.
Fig, Fiddle Leaf; Zone 10.
Fig, India Laurel; Zone 10.
Fig, Lofty; Zone 10.
Geiger Tree; Zone 10.
Holly, American; Zone 6.
Holly, Chinese; Zone 7.
Indian Rubber Tree; Zone 10.
Jacaranda; Zone 9.
Laurelcherry; Zone 7.
Magnolia, Southern; Zone 7.
Mahogany, West Indies (Mahogany,
Swamp); Zone 10.
Oak, Laurel; Zone 9.
Oak, Laurel; Zone 9.
Oxhorn Bucida; Zone 10.
Pigeon Plum; Zone 10.
Silk Oak; Zone 10.
Silver Trumpet; Zone 10.
Wax Myrtle; Zone 9.
Evergreens, needle leaf and scale leaf
Pine, Longleaf; Zone 8.
Pine, Slash; Zone 8.
Pine, Spruce; Zone 9.
Deciduous
Baldcypress; Zone 5.
Bo Tree; Zone 10.
Crape Myrtle; Zone 7.
Cucumber Tree (Magnolia,
Cucumber); Zone 5.
Fig, Benjamin; Zone 10.
Goldenrain Tree; Zone 5.
Linden, American; Zone 3.
Maple, Red; Zone 3.
Mimosa; Zone 7.
Mimosa, Lebbek; Zone 9.

Oak, Water; Zone 8.
Orchid Tree; Zone 9.
Pecan; Zone 7.
Redbud, Eastern; Zone 6.
Royal Poinciana; Zone 9.
Sweetgum; Zone 5.
Palms
Palm, Coconut; Zone 10.
Palm, Cuban Royal; Zone 10.
Palm, Fishtail; Zone 10.
Palm, Florida Royal; Zone 10.
Palm, Manilla; Zone 10.
Palm, Washington (Palm,
Mexican Fan); Zone 9.
Palmetto, Cabbage; Zone 8.
Leafless
Casuarina (Beefwood,
Horsetail); Zone 10.
Cunningham Beefwood;
Zone 10.
Scaly Bark Beefwood; Zone 9.

REGION 4

Evergreens, broadleaf
    None
Evergreens, needle leaf and scale leaf
    Arborvitae, Eastern; Zone 2.
    Arborvitae, Oriental; Zone 3.
    Cedar, Eastern Red (Juniper); Zone 2.
    Cedar, Incense; Zone 6.
    Douglas Fur; Zone 3.
    Hemlock, Canadian; Zone 3.
    Juniper, Rocky Mountain; Zone 3.
    Pine, Austrian; Zone 3.
    Pine, Ponderosa; Zone 3.
    Pine, Scotch; Zone 3.
    Spruce, Colorado Blue; Zone 2.
    Spruce, White; Zone 2.
Deciduous
    Ash, Black; Zone 3.
    Ash, Green; Zone 2.
    Ash, White; Zone 3.
    Birch, Cutleaf European; Zone 2.

Birch, Paper; Zone 2.
Birch, White; Zone 2.
Catalpa, Northern; Zone 3.
Cherry, Black; Zone 3.
Cottonwood, Plains (Poplar, Plains);
    Zone 3.
Elm, American; Zone 3.
Elm, Siberian; Zone 3.
Hackberry, Eastern; Zone 3.
Hackberry, Western
    (Sugarberry); Zone 5.
Honeylocust, Thornless; Zone 3.
Katsura Tree; Zone 5.
Larch, Siberian; Zone 3.
Linden, American; Zone 3.
Linden, Littleleaf; Zone 3.
Maple, Silver; Zone 3.
Oak, Bur; Zone 3.
Oak, Northern Red; Zone 4.
Oak, Pin; Zone 4.
Oak, Scarlet; Zone 4.
Zelkova; Zone 5.

STAGHORN SUMAC. Rhus hirta

WHITE MULBERRY. Morus alba

AMERICAN WHITE BIRCH. Betula populifolia

REGION 5

Evergreens, broadleaf
  Oak, Live; Zone 8.
Evergreens, needle leaf and scale leaf
  Arborvitae, Oriental; Zone 3.
  Cedar, Atlas; Zone 6.
  Cedar, Eastern Red (Juniper);
    Zone 2.
  Cryptomeria; Zone 6.
  Cypress, Arizona; Zone 7.
  Juniper, Rocky Mountain; Zone 3.
  Pine, Austrian; Zone 3.
  Pine, Loblolly; Zone 7.
  Pine, Ponderosa; Zone 3.
  Spruce, Colorado Blue; Zone 2.
Deciduous
  Ash, Green; Zone 2.
  Baldcypress; Zone 5.
  Beech, European; Zone 5.
  Buckeye; Zone 4.
  Catalpa, Northern; Zone 3.
  Catalpa, Southern; Zone 5.
  Chinaberry (Umbrella Tree); Zone 7.
  Desert Willow; Zone 7.
  Elm, American; Zone 3
  Elm, Chinese; Zone 5.
  Elm, English; Zone 6.
  Elm, European; Zone 5.
  Elm, Siberian, Zone 3.
  Goldenrain Tree; Zone 5.
  Hackberry, Eastern; Zone 3.
  Hackberry, Western
    (Sugarberry); Zone 5.
  Honeylocust, Thornless; Zone 3.
  Huisache; Zone 9.
  Japanese Pagoda Tree; Zone 5.
  Katsura; Zone 5.
  Kentucky Coffeetree; Zone 5.
  Maple, Silver; Zone 3.
  Maple, Sycamore; Zone 6.
  Mesquite; Zone 9.
  Mulberry, Paper; Zone 6.
  Mulberry, Russian; Zone 5.

Oak, Bur; Zone 3.
Oak, Chestnut; Zone 5.
Oak, Pin; Zone 4.
Oak, Post; Zone 7.
Oak, Scarlet; Zone 4.
Oak, Spanish; Zone 8.
Oak, Texas (Oak, Shumard); Zone 5.
Oak, Yellow; Zone 5.
Pecan; Zone 7.
Pistache, Chinese; Zone 8.
Redbud, Eastern; Zone 6.
Retama; Zone 9.
Sassafras; Zone 5.
Soapberry, Western; Zone 6.
Sycamore; Zone 5.
Zelkova; Zone 5.
Palms
  Palm, Washington (Palm,
    Mexican Fan); Zone 9.

BUTTON-WOOD. Platanus occidentalis

REGION 6

Evergreens, broadleaf
  Olive, Common; Zone 9.
  Olive, Russian; Zone 5.
Evergreens, needle leaf and scale leaf
  Arborvitae, Giant; Zone 6.
  Arborvitae, Oriental; Zone 3.
  Cedar, Atlas; Zone 6.
  Cedar, Eastern Red (Juniper); Zone 2.
  Cedar, Incense; Zone 6.
  Douglas Fur; Zone 3.
  Fir, White; Zone 5.
  Juniper, Rocky Mountain; Zone 3.
  Pine, Austrian; Zone 3.
  Pine, Ponderosa; Zone 3.
  Spruce, Colorado Blue; Zone 2.
Deciduous
  Ash, European; Zone 3.
  Ash, Green; Zone 2.
  Ash, Modesto (Ash, Arizona); Zone 7.
  Beech, European; Zone 5.
  Buckeye; Zone 4.
  Catalpa, Northern; Zone 3.
  Cottonwood, Plains (Poplar Plains);
    Zone 3.
  Elm, American; Zone 3.
  Elm, Chinese; Zone 5.
  Elm, European; Zone 5.
  Elm, Siberian; Zone 3.
  Ginkgo; Zone 5.
  Goldenrain Tree; Zone 5.
  Hackberry, Eastern; Zone 3.
  Honeylocust, Thornless; Zone 3.
  Horsechestnut; Zone 3.
  Horsechestnut, Red (Buckeye, Red
    and Horsechestnut, Ruby); Zone 3.
  Japanese Pagoda Tree; Zone 5.
  Katsura Tree; Zone 5.

Kentucky Coffeetree; Zone 5.
Linden, American; Zone 3.
Linden, Littleleaf; Zone 3.
London Plane; Zone 6.
Maple, Bigleaf; Zone 8.
Maple, Norway; Zone 4.
Maple, Sugar; Zone 3.
Mulberry, Russian; Zone 5.
Oak, Bur; Zone 3.
Oak, Northern Red; Zone 4.
Oak, Pin; Zone 4.
Oak, White; Zone 5.
Sweetgum; Zone 5.
Zelkova; Zone 5.

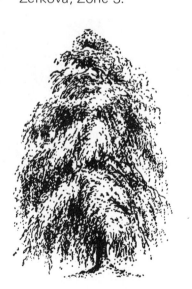

BALSAM FIR. Abies balsamea

64

REGION 7

Evergreens, broadleaf
    Carob; Zone 9.
    Eucalyptus (Gum); Zone 10.
    Olive, Common; Zone 9.
    Olive, Russian; Zone 5.
    Palo Verde, Blue; Zone 7.

Evergreens, needle leaf and scale leaf
    Cedar, Atlas; Zone 6.
    Cedar, Deodar; Zone 7.
    Cedar, Eastern Red (Juniper); Zone 2.
    Cypress, Arizona; Zone 7.
    Cypress, Italian; Zone 7.
    Douglas Fur; Zone 3.
    Fir, Silver; Zone 5.
    Juniper, Rocky Mountain; Zone 3.
    Pine, Aleppo; Zone 9.
    Pine, Austrian; Zone 3.
    Pine, Canary Island; Zone 8.

Deciduous
    Acacia, Baileys (Baileys Wattle); Zone 9.
    Ailanthus (Tree of Heaven); Zone 5.
    Ash, Green; Zone 2.
    Ash, Modesto (Ash, Arizona); Zone 7.
    Chinaberry (Umbrella Tree); Zone 7.
    Cottonwood, Fremont; Zone 5.
    Cottonwood, Plains (Poplar, Plains); Zone 3.
    Desert Willow; Zone 7.
    Elm, Chinese; Zone 5.
    Elm, Siberian; Zone 3.
    Ginkgo; Zone 5.
    Goldenrain Tree; Zone 5.
    Hackberry, Eastern; Zone 3.
    Hackberry, Western (Sugarberry); Zone 5.
    Honeylocust, Thornless; Zone 3.
    Huisache; Zone 9.
    Linden, Littleleaf; Zone 3.
    Locust, Black; Zone 3.
    London Plane; Zone 6.
    Maple, Silver; Zone 3.
    Mesquite; Zone 9.
    Mulberry, Russian; Zone 5.
    Oak, Pin; Zone 4.
    Oak, Southern Red; Zone 7.
    Pecan; Zone 7.
    Pistache, Chinese; Zone 8.
    Poplar, Bolleana; Zone 5.
    Poplar, Carolina; Zone 5.
    Sweetgum; Zone 5.
    Wattle, Sydney; Zone 10.

Palms
    Palm, Canary Date; Zone 9.

SUGAR MAPLE. Acer Saccharum

REGION 8

Evergreens, broadleaf
  Cajeput; Zone 10.
  Camphor Tree; Zone 9.
  Carob; Zone 9.
  Cherry, Australian Brush; Zone 8.
  Coral Tree; Zone 10.
  Eucalyptus (Gum); Zone 10.
  Fig, India Laurel; Zone 10.
  Fig, Moreton Bay; Zone 10.
  Jacaranda; Zone 9.
  Laurel, California; Zone 7.
  Laurelcherry; Zone 7.
  Laurel, Grecian; Zone 6.
  Magnolia, Southern; Zone 7.
  Oak, Canyon Live; Zone 7.
  Oak, Coast Live; Zone 9.
  Oak, Holly; Zone 9.
  Oak, Live; Zone 8.
  Palo Verde, Blue; Zone 7.
  Tanoak; Zone 8.
Evergreens, needle leaf and scale leaf
  Arborvitae, Oriental; Zone 3.
  Cedar, Atlas; Zone 6.
  Cedar, Deodar; Zone 7.
  Cedar, Incense; Zone 6.
  Cedar of Lebanon; Zone 6.
  Cryptomeria; Zone 6.
  Cypress, Arizona; Zone 7.
  Lawson False Cypress; Zone 6.
  Norfolk Island Pine; Zone 10.
  Pine, Aleppo; Zone 9.
  Pine, Canary Island; Zone 8.
  Spruce, Colorado Blue; Zone 2.
Deciduous
  Ash, Modesto (Ash, Arizona); Zone 7.
  Chinaberry (Umbrella Tree); Zone 7.
  Chinese Lantern Tree; Zone 6.
  Cottonwood, Fremont; Zone 5.
  Desert Willow; Zone 7.
  Elm, American; Zone 3.
  Elm, Chinese; Zone 5.

Elm, Siberian; Zone 3.
Ginkgo; Zone 5.
Goldenrain Tree; Zone 5.
Hackberry, Eastern; Zone 3.
Honeylocust, Thornless; Zone 3.
Japanese Pagoda Tree; Zone 5.
Locust, Black; Zone 3.
London Plane; Zone 6.
Maple, Bigleaf; Zone 8.
Maple, Norway; Zone 4.

Maple, Red; Zone 3.
Mimosa; Zone 7.
Mulberry, Russian; Zone 5.
Oak, Bur; Zone 3.
Oak, English; Zone 5.
Oak, Northern Red; Zone 4.
Oak, Pin; Zone 4.
Oak, Scarlet; Zone 4.
Oak, Valley; Zone 9.
Orchid Tree; Zone 9.

Pistache, Chinese; Zone 8.
Sweetgum; Zone 5.
Tulip Poplar; Zone 5.
Palms
  Palm, Canary Date; Zone 9.
  Palm, Washington (Palm, Mexican
    Fan); Zone 9.
Leafless
  Casuarina (Beefwood, Horsetail);
    Zone 10.

Evergreens, broadleaf
  Holly, English; Zone 7.
  Madrone; Zone 7.
  Magnolia, Southern; Zone 7.
  Tanoak; Zone 8.
Evergreens, needle leaf and scale leaf
  Arborvitae, Giant; Zone 6.
  Arborvitae, Oriental; Zone 3.
  Cedar, Atlas; Zone 3.
  Cedar, Deodar; Zone 7.
  Cedar, Incense; Zone 6.
  Cryptomeria; Zone 6.
  Lawson False Cypress; Zone 6.
  Pine, Austrian; Zone 3.
  Pine, Ponderosa; Zone 3.
  Spruce, Colorado Blue; Zone 2.
Deciduous
  Ash, European; Zone 3.
  Ash, Green; Zone 2.
  Ash, White; Zone 3.
  Beech, European; Zone 5.
  Birch, White; Zone 2.
  Cork Tree, Phelledendron Amur;
    Zone 4.
  Dogwood, Pacific; Zone 7.
  Elm, American; Zone 3.
  Elm, Chinese; Zone 5.
  Elm, English; Zone 6.
  Elm, Scotch; Zone 5.
  Elm, Siberian; Zone 3.
  Ginkgo; Zone 5.
  Golden Chain Tree; Zone 7.
  Goldenrain Tree; Zone 5.
  Honeylocust, Thornless; Zone 3.
  Hornbeam, American; Zone 3.
  Horsechestnut; Zone 3.
  Horsechestnut, Red (Buckeye, Red and
    Horsechestnut, Ruby); Zone 3.
  Japanese Pagoda Tree; Zone 5.
  Kentucky Coffeetree; Zone 5.
  Linden, American; Zone 3.
  Linden, Littleleaf; Zone 3.

  London Plane; Zone 6.
  Maple, Bigleaf; Zone 8.
  Maple, Norway; Zone 4.
  Maple, Red; Zone 3.
  Maple, Sugar; Zone 3.
  Mimosa; Zone 7.
  Oak, Northern Red; Zone 4.
  Oak, Oregon White; Zone 6.
  Oak, Pin; Zone 4.
  Oak, Scarlet; Zone 4.
  Oak, White; Zone 5.
  Silverbell; Zone 5.
  Sourwood; Zone 7.
  Sweetgum; Zone 5.
  Tulip Poplar; Zone 5.
  Yellowwood; Zone 4.

WEEPING BIRCH. Betula pendula

TRANSPLANTING TREES AND SHRUBS

You might need to move a plant because it is too crowded, because it gets too much or too little shade, or simply because it may be more appealing or useful in another place. Whatever the reason, you begin to dig up that tree or shrub you want to move.

If, at this point, you tell yourself that transplanting is nothing more than digging up and planting again, you may be disappointed when your newly transplanted tree or shrub doesn't grow well or when it dies during the first year. There are, however, many things you can do to help insure successful transplanting.

WHAT TO TRANSPLANT

Successful transplanting can depend entirely on the individual plant you select to move. The kind of tree or shrub, however, isn't always as important as its age, size, and condition. For instance, young plants and small plants can be transplanted with less risk than older or larger ones. Also, healthy plants are more likely to survive the shock of transplanting than unhealthy ones.

In some cases, you might want to move an unhealthy plant to a more suitable location. Transplanting for this reason may be especially helpful for plants that manage to survive in their present environment but lack vigor. A change of environment more suited to the needs of the plant often can restore its vitality.

BEFORE MOVING ANY PLANT INTO ANOTHER STATE, CHECK STATE PLANT QUARANTINE REGULATIONS.

Healthy Plants

Good indicators of a plant's health and vigor are the length of annual twig growth, the condition of buds and flowers, the number of dead branches, and the size and color of the leaves. Wilting, stunted growth, malformation, and disease spots are signs of poor health.

Hardy Plants

Plants are considered hardy when they can withstand various extremes of environmental conditions, such as very low winter temperatures and extreme summer heat and drought.

Moving a plant from one part of your property to another should not affect its hardiness unless there are extreme changes in wind and sun exposure.

If you wish to move a plant from one part of the country to another, make sure that the plant will be hardy in its new location. If temperature differences are too extreme at the new location, the plant will not survive.

Perhaps the best way to tell whether your plant will survive in a certain area of the country is to consult the nurseries in that area. The trees and shrubs nurserymen raise and sell should be hardy for their areas.

WHEN TO TRANSPLANT

The best time for transplanting is when plants are still dormant in early spring or after they have become dormant in the fall. How long they are dormant depends upon the climate as well as the kind of plant.

In the spring, deciduous trees and shrubs should be moved before the buds start to grow. In the fall, they should be moved only after their leaves turn color and drop off. Transplant only when the ground is not frozen and is workable.

TULIP TREE. Liriodendron Tulipifera

Spring planting is advisable in areas that have severe winters. Transplant in the spring if you live in an area with strong, drying winter winds, deficient soil moisture, or deeply frozen ground during the winter months. This applies to evergreens as well as to deciduous plants.

Evergreens can be transplanted earlier in the fall and later in the spring than deciduous plants. They may be moved from early September to June if the weather is not too severe.

If you transplant in the summer, make sure that the rootball is kept moist while it is out of the ground. Because of high temperatures in summer, plants have a greater tendency to lose too much moisture through evaporation.

You can cut down this water loss by using a transpiration inhibiting chemical. Antitranspirants can be purchased at nurseries or garden supply stores. When sprayed onto the plant, the chemical coats the leaves and reduces moisture loss.

Another method of reducing water loss is to shade the plant for the first few days after replanting. One way of shading is to cover the plant with burlap.

WHERE TO TRANSPLANT

Select the planting site carefully. Consider not only where a plant would look good, but also where it will grow most successfully. Make sure that your plant can adapt to any changes in sun, shade, wind exposure, and soil moisture. In addition, avoid these common mistakes: placing plants too close together in an effort to get quick screening effects, setting young trees under windows, and crowding the walls of buildings.

At the new site, provide enough space above and below the ground to allow for future spreading and growth of the top and roots of the plant. Later crowding may deform it, stunt its growth, or eventually kill it.

HOW TO TRANSPLANT

Digging

When digging up a deciduous tree or shrub, avoid injuring as many roots as possible. Start digging from the outer edge of the crown, and carefully remove the soil while working toward the trunk until the main roots are found.

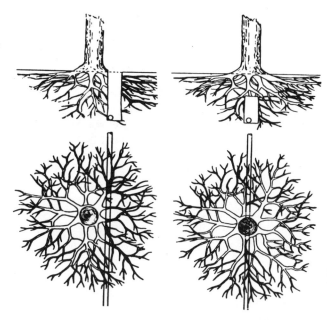

Tunnel beneath root systems. Drawings at left show trenching that would probably kill the tree. Drawings at right show how tunneling under the tree will preserve many of the important feeder roots.

WEEPING WILLOW. Salix Babylonica

CARE AFTER TRANSPLANTING

Pruning

Transplanting deciduous trees and shrubs often results in root damage and some root loss. For trees, prune one-third of the lateral growth to counterbalance this loss. You can also "top" the tree by cutting off a small portion of the top of the main stem. For shrubs, cut back one-third of the branches.

When replanting, you should prune off diseased branches, cross branches that rub, and any branches that detract from the shape and appearance of the plant. Be careful not to overprune. If overprouned, the plant will be set back since you are removing the foliage which produces its food. Plant growth is then slowed down depending on how many leaves you prune off.

Not all trees and shrubs must be pruned after transplanting. Evergreens, for example, may not need it because the rootball normally protects the roots from injury. Deciduous plants may not need pruning if they are planted in humid areas of the country. Where it is humid, new roots usually will be formed within a few weeks and will restore adequate water absorption from the soil.

Watering

Be careful to avoid extremes in watering. Too little water will cause the roots to dry up and die, and too much water may rot them away.

Newly transplanted trees and shrubs need regular watering during the spring, summer, and fall of the first year, unless you plant in an area where rainfull is abundant.

In winter, evergreens retain their leaves and continue to lose water through them. For this reason, evergreens should be watered during dry winter periods. Deciduous plants do not need watering in the winter since they are dormant and will not lose any moisture.

Do not water plants every day. Allow the soil to dry at the surface before you water again. Test the soil for dryness by crumbling it through your fingers. The amount of water needed is the amount that the soil can absorb. Stop watering when water no longer seeps rapidly into the soil.

Mulching

After planting, mulch the soil beneath the branches with a 3-inch layer of peat moss, leafy mold, or forest litter. Use only well-decayed material because the decomposition of such material as fresh manure, green plants, or fresh grass clippings releases by-products that can be harmful to the roots.

To reduce damage by mice and decay, keep the mulch about a foot away from the trunk or stem of larger plants. Make sure that the mulch covers the area occupied by the roots. For small or young trees, reduce the depth of the mulch near to the trunk or stem.

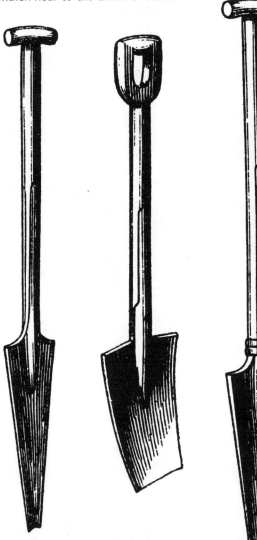

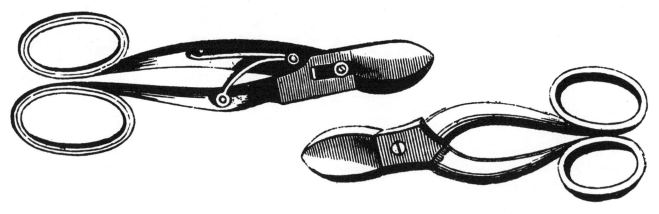

70

Fertilizing

If you use plenty of rich soil for back-filling, newly transplanted trees and shrubs are not likely to need fertilizer for the first year. However, if immediate growth seems stunted or leaves are paled, fertilizing is advisable.

Apply fertilizer in fall or early spring in the following way:

For Trees.—Measure the diameter of the trunk 3 feet above the ground; use 2 pounds of 5-10-5 fertilizer for each inch of diameter. For trunks with a diameter of less than 3 inches, use ½ pound for each inch.

Using a soil auger, crowbar, or posthole digger, make holes 15 to 24 inches deep and 18 to 24 inches apart around the drip line of the tree (the area beneath the ends of the longest branches). Also, fertilize a few feet beyond the drip line especially for young trees.

Distribute the fertilizer equally among the holes, using ¼ cup per hole. Then fill the holes with soil. A mixture of equal parts of topsoil, sand, and peatmoss is a good filling.

For Shrubs.—Scatter fertilizer on the surface over the root area, then scratch it in. Use one or two handfuls of fertilizer depending on the size of the shrub.

Protecting From Sun and Wind Damage

Young trees or those dug from shady areas may easily be damaged by sudden exposure to the sun. If you replant them in an open area, protect them by wrapping the trunks with strips of burlap or durable paper.

To protect trees and shrubs from wind damage, install guy wires to hold them in place until the root system regenerates.

The number of guy wires needed depends on the size of the plant. You may wish to use wires with a turnbuckle so you can adjust the pull of the wires and can tighten them when they become loose.

Guy wires should be placed high enough so that leverage of the top does not loosen them. A crotch is a good place to anchor the wires.

Use a short length of rubber hose around each wire to protect the bark from injury. Do not wrap the loop so tightly that the growth of the bark is restricted.

Fasten the wires securely to sturdy stakes or other solid anchors. If you use 3 guy wires, space anchors evenly. Place one anchor against the prevailing winds.

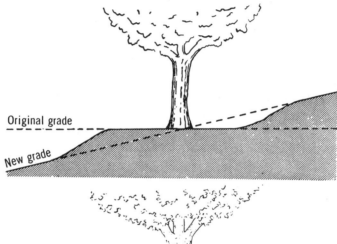

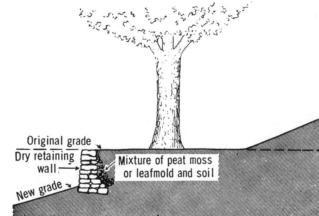

A retaining wall protects a tree from a lowered grade.

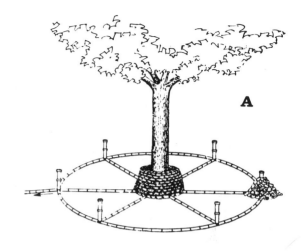

A tile system protects a tree from a raised grade. A, the tile is laid out on the original grade, leading from a dry well around the tree trunk. B, the tile system is covered with small stones to allow air to circulate over the root area.

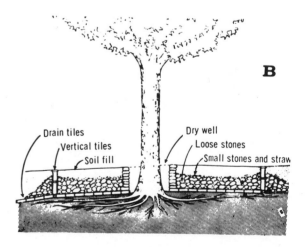

TRANSPLANTING FROM THE WILD

With amateur handling, such plants as dogwoods, oaks, and maples will usually die when moved from the woods. The key to successfully moving wild trees and shrubs is root pruning.

To root prune, cut all roots with a sharp spade at the same distance from the trunk as when you are digging a rootball. Go out from the trunk one foot for each inch diameter of the trunk before you start cutting the roots. Next, make sure that the roots beneath the plant are also cut. Then, lift the plant slightly to make sure all the roots are free. Drop the plant back into position, firm the soil around it, and see that it is watered during dry periods. Though most plants can be successfully transplanted this way, plants that have very dominant top roots, such as hickory and sassafras, may not survive.

If you intend to move your wild plant in the fall, then root prune the previous spring. Likewise, if you intend to move the plant in the spring, root prune the previous fall.

Remember also that when you move a plant from a wild to a cultivated environment as your lawn, you may be changing its environment to such an extent that the plant may lose its hardiness and die. For example, if you move a plant that is adapted to a lot of shade and shelter in the woods to an open, sunlit spot, the tree may die through overexposure. If it is necessary to move the wild tree to a more exposed place, protect the trunk by wrapping it with a strip of burlap.

PLANTING AND SPACING STANDARDS

The following recommendations for planting and spacing are usually followed in private and institutional landscape work.

PLANTING HOLE SUGGESTIONS

Size of Shrub	Diameter and Depth of Planting Holes
1 to 2 ft.	16 in. by 10 in.
2 to 3 ft.	18 in. by 12 in.
3 to 4 ft.	20 in. by 14 in.
4 to 6 ft.	24 in. by 18 in.

Size of Trees	Diameter and Depth of Planting Holes
6 to 8 ft.	30 in. by 19 in.
1 to 1½ in. cal.	34 in. by 21 in.
1½ to 2 in. cal.	36 in. by 22 in.
2 to 2½ in. cal.	40 in. by 25 in.
2½ to 3 in. cal.	44 in. by 26 in.
3 to 4 in. cal.	52 in. by 30 in.
4 to 5 in. cal.	56 in. by 32 in.

GROUND COVER SPACING

Type of Ground Cover	Suggested Spacing
Cotoneaster, spreading varieties	18 in. on Center
Euonymus radicans and varieties	12 in. on Center
Hedera helix and varieties	8 in. on Center
Juniperus horizontalis and varieties	18 in. on Center
Rosa wichuraiana hybrids	18 in. on Center
Vinca minor and varieties	8 in. on Center

HEDGE PLANTING SPACING

Type of Hedge	Suggested Spacing
Berberis thunbergi and other Barberry	16 in. apart
Buxus suffruticosa	12 in. apart
Euonymus alatus and compactus	18 in. apart
Ilex crenata varieties	24 in. apart
Ligustrum ovalifolium and other Privet	18 in. apart
Pyracantha coccinea lalandi	24 in. apart
Taxus, upright varieties	24 in. apart
Thuja occidentalis nigra	24 in. apart

TREE SPACING

Type of Tree	Suggested Spacing
Small flowering and minor shade trees	20 ft. apart
Medium sized and columnar shade trees	30 ft. apart
Major shade trees	40 to 60 ft. apart
Screening trees	6 ft. apart

PLANTING SUGGESTIONS

To assist you in quickly choosing plant material suitable for various conditions and uses we have endeavored to classify into the following groupings the varieties we produce.

You will note that some varieties are recommended for several types of uses. This is achieved through pruning methods. For example, Ilex Opaca and its named female varieties can be kept pruned as a foundation plant, clipped as a hedge or allowed to grow into a tree.

COLORFUL AUTUMN FOLIAGE

Acer palmatum atropurpureum, Red
Acer platanoides Crimson King, Purple
Acer platanoides, Yellow
Acer rubrum, Red
Berberis chenauti, Red
Berberis julianae, Red
Berberis julianae nana, Red
Berberis thunbergi, Red
Berberis thunbergi atropurpurea, Red
Berberis verruculosa, Red
Cercidiphyllum japonicum, Orange to Red
Chionanthus virginicus, Yellow
Cornus florida, Bronze to Red
Cornus florida rubra, Bronze to Red
Cornus kousa, Bronze to Red
Cotoneaster horizontalis, Red
Cryptomeria japonica lobbi, Bronze
Euonymus alatus varieties, Red
Euonymus radicans colorata, Purple
Fagus grandiflora, Golden
Gleditsia tricanthos Sunburst, Golden-bronze
Nandina domestica, Red
Nyssa sylvatica, Red
Ostrya virginica, Yellow
Oxydendrum arboreum, Bronze to Red
Prunus thundercloud, Purple
Pyrus caleryana Bradford, Red
Quercus borealis, Red

Quercus coccinea, Scarlet
Rosa rugosa, Orange
Viburnum prunifolium, Red to Purple
Viburnum sieboldi, Red

ATTRACTIVE FRUITS

Amelanchier canadensis, Red, Spring
Aucuba japonica, Red, Winter
Aucuba japonica variegata, Red, Winter
Berberis julianae, Blue, Fall
Berberis thunbergi, Red, Fall and Winter
Berberis thunbergi atropurpurea, Red, Fall and Winter
Berberis triacanthophora, Blue-black, Fall
Berberis verruculosa, Black, Fall
Chionanthus virginicus, Blue, Summer
Citrus trifoliata, Yellow, Fall
Cotoneaster varieties, Red, Fall
Cornus florida, Red Fall
Cornus kousa, Red, Fall
Crataegus cordata, Red, Winter
Elaeagnus angustifolia, Yellow to Orange
Euonymus alatus varieties, Red, Fall
Ilex aquifolium, Red, Fall and Winter
Ilex cornuta burfordi, Red, Fall and Winter
Ilex crenata convexa, Black, Summer
Ilex glabra, Blue-black, Fall
Ilex opaca femina, Red, Fall and Winter
Ligustrum lucidum, Blue-black, Fall and Winter
Lonicera morrowi, Red, Summer
Lonicera tatarica rosea, Red, July
Magnolia grandiflora, Red, Sept.
Magnolia glauca, Red, Fall
Mahonia bealei, Blue, Summer
Malus varieties, Yellow to Red, July to Fall
Myrica cerifera, Gray, Fall
Myrica pensylvanica, Gray, Fall
Nandina domestica, Red, Fall and Winter
Osmanthus varieties, Blue-black, Fall
Pyracantha, ata, aurea, Yellow, Fall
Pyracantha cocco. Ialandi, Orange, Fall
Pyracantha Ingleside Crimson, Red, Fall
Pyracantha loboy, Orange, Fall
Rosa rugosa, Red, Fall
Sorbus aucuparia, Red, Fall

Viburnum dilatatum, Red, Fall
Viburnum prunifolium, Blue-black, Fall
Viburnum rhytidophyllum, Red, Aug.
Viburnum sieboldi, Black, Fall
Viburnum tomentosum varieties, Red to black, Summer

FORMAL HEDGE, DECIDUOUS

Berberis thunbergi, 7'
Berberis thunbergi atropurpurea, 7'
Euonymus alatus varieties
Forsythia varieties, 8'
Ligustrum obtus. regelianum, 5-6'
Ligustrum ovalifolium, 15'
Lonicera fragrantissima, 6'
Lonicera tatarica rosea, 10'
Pyracantha varieties, 12'
Rosa rugosa, 6'
Spirae vanhouttei, 7'

FORMAL HEDGE, EVERGREEN

Abelia grandiflora, 8'
Berberis chenaulti, 5'
Berberis julianae, 8'
Berberis julianae nana, 5'
Buxus sempervirens, 12'-15'
Buxus suffruticosa, 6'
Elaeagnus pungens, 10'
Ilex cornuta burbordi, 25'
Ilex crenata, 20'
Ilex crenata convexa, 5'
Ilex crenata rotundifolia, 8'
Ilex opaca, 50'
Ligustrum lucidum, 15'
Ligustrum Suwannee River P. P. 1402
Linicera (bush forms)
Lonicera nitida, 6'
Osmanthus ilicifolius, 15'
Osmathus ilic. Gulftide, 15'
Taxus varieties

FOUNDATION USE—Low Growth Habit

Abelia Edwarfd Goucher
Abelia grandiflora prostrata
Azalea
Berberis chenaulti
Berberis julianae nana
Berberis thunbergi
Berberis thunbergi atropurpurea
Berberis tricanthophora
Berberis verruculosa
Buxus suffruticosa
Cotoneaster, spreading varieties
Deutzia gracilis
Euonymus radicans coloratus
Hydrangea otaksa
Ilex cor. burfordi, dwarf
Ilex cor. rotunda
Ilex crenata compacta
Ilex crenata convexa
Ilex crenata helleri
Ilex crenata hetzi
Ilex glabra compacta
Jasminum nudiflorum
Juniperus chinensis pfitzer
Juniperus chinensis pfitzeriana compacta
Juniperus horiz. (depressa) plumosa
Ligustrum Suwannee River
Lonicera nitida
Lonicera pileata
Picea glauca conica
Pyracantha loboy
Spirea bumalda A. W.
Taxus spreading varieties

FOUNDATION USE—Medium Growth Habit

Abelia grandiflora
Berberis julianae
Buxus sempervirens
Deutzia Pride of Rochester
Elaeagnus pungens
Ilex aquifolium
Ilex cornuta burfordi
Ilex crenata
Ilex crenata rotundifolia
Ilex glabra
Ilex opaca
Juniper glauca hetzi
Kalmia latifolia
Ligustrum lucidum
Lonicera tatarica rosea
Mahonia bealei
Nandina domestica
Osmanthus ilicifolius
Osmanthus ilic. Gulftide
Prunus lauro schipkaensis
Prunus lauroc. schipkaensis marcrophylla
Pyracantha
Syringa hybrids
Thuja nigra
Thuja occ. compacta
Taxus, upright varieties
Viburnum rhytidophyllum
Weigela rosea
Weigela vaniceki

Flowers of
Azalea mollis.

EVERGREENS WITH STRIKING FLOWERS

Abelia Edward Goucher, Deep Pink
Abelia grandiflora, Light Pink
Azalea varieties, White-Pink-Red-Lavender
Berberis julianae, Yellow
Berberis julianae nana, Yellow
Berberis verruculosa, Yellow
Camellia varieties, White-Pink-Rose
Kalmia latifolia, White to Pink
Magnolia grandiflora, White
Mahonia bealei, Yellow

QUICK GROWING SCREEN

Abelia grandiflora, 8'
Acer platanoides, 60'
Amelanchier canadensis, 20-30'
Cedrus deodara, 150'
Crataegus phaen. cardata, 30'
Elaeagnus angustifolia, 20'
Forsythia varieties, 8'
Halesia tetraptera, 12-15'
Ilex opaca, 50'
Ligustrum lucidum, 15'
Ligustrum ovalifolium, 15'
Lonicera tartarica rosea, 10'
Osmanthus ilic. Gulftide, 15'
Phyllostachys aurea, 15-20'
Picea excelsa, 80'
Pinus strobus, 100'
Populus nigra italica, 90'
Pyracantha Ingleside crimson, 12'
Salix babylonica, 60'
Salix niobe, 60'
Syringa vulgaris, 20'
Syringa vulgaris alba, 20'
Thuja nigra, 20'

FRAGRANT FLOWERS

Berberis julianae
Berberis julianae nana
Berberis triacanthophora
Berberis verruculosa
Elaeagnus pungens
Magnolia grandiflora
Magnolia macrophylla
Mahonia bealei
Osmanthus ilicifolius
Syringa varieties

AZALEAS

SHRUBS FOR SHADY GARDENS

When you have shady areas in your garden, select shade-tolerant plants. Some plants that will grow in shade are as follows.

Deciduous shrubs
Abelia grandiflora (Glossy Abelia)
Amelanchier (Juneberry)
Berberis thunbergii (Japanese Barberry)
Calycanthus floridus (Carolina Allspice)
Cercis canadensis (Redbud)
Cornus (Dogwood)
Hydrangea quercifolia (Oakleaf Hydrangea)
Ilex verticillata (Winterberry)
Ligustrum (Privet)
Symphoricarpos (Snowberry)
Viburnum

Evergreen shrubs
Aucuba japonica (Gold Dust Tree)
Berberis julianae (Barberry)
Buxus (Boxwood)
Camellia
Euonymus fortunei vegetus
Fatsia japonica
Ilex (Holly)
Kalmia latifolia (Mountain Laurel)
Leucothoe
Mahonia aquifolium (Holly Mahonia)
Nandina domestica
Photinia serrulata
Pieris
Taxus (Yew)

Vines
Aristolochia durier (Dutchman's Pipe)
Gelsemium sempervirens (Carolina
    Yellow Jessamine)
Hedera canariensis (Algerian Ivy)
Hedera helix (English Ivy)
Lonicera (Honeysuckle)
Pathenocissus (Boston Ivy)
Vitis labrusca (Fox Grape)

Flowering annuals
Begonia semperflorens (Wax Begonia)
Coleus
Impatiens holstii
Lobelia ermus
Nicotiana (Flowering Tobacco)
Torenia fournieri (Wishbone Flower)
Vinca rosea (Madagascar Periwinkle)

79

Flowering perennials
Ajuga (Bugleweed)
Anemone japonica
Aquilegia (Columbine)
Astilbe (Spirea)
Campanula (Bellflower)
Convallaria majalis (Lily of the Valley)
Dicentra (Bleeding Heart)
Digitalis (Foxglove)
Helleborus
Heuchera (Coralbells)
Hosta (Plantain Lily)
Hypericum calycinum (St. Johnswort)
Lunaria biennis (Honesty)
Mertensia virginica (Virginia Bluebell)
Myosotis (Forget Me Not)
Trollius (Globeflower)
Viola (Violet)

Bulbs
Begonia
Caladium
Chionodoxa luciliae (Glory of the Snow)
Colchicum (Autumn Crocus)
Colocasia antiquorum (Elephant's Ear)
Galanthus nivalis (Snowdrop)
Leucojum aestivum (Summer Snowflake)
Lilium (Lily)
Muscari (Grape Hyacinth)
Narcissus
Ornithogalum (Star of Bethlehem)
Scilla hispanica (Spanish Bluebell)

BULBS

GROWING AND SELECTING SPRING FLOWERING BULBS

Spring flowering bulbs are hardy plants that require little care. They provide early color in your garden or yard at a time when few other plants are in bloom.

Among the more popular spring flowering bulbs are tulip, narcissus, hyacinth, iris, and crocus. Some that are not so well known are scilla, chionodoxa, muscari, and galanthus.

You can use bulbs anywhere in your garden. Some are best as border plants. Others are best when grouped in large masses of color. And many kinds can be scattered in lawns or planted among shrubs as ground cover.

To grow spring flowering bulbs successfully—

Select healthy, mature bulbs and store them in a cool, dry place until planting time.

Prepare the soil in the planting beds thoroughly.

Plant at depths, distances apart, and planting times recommended for each kind of bulb.

Maintain a winter mulch to prevent damage from alternate freezing and thawing.

The following alphabetical list gives a brief description of how to plant and manage the more commonly grown spring flowering bulbs.

ALLIUM

Allium (flowering onion) varies in height from 9 inches to 5 feet. It lives many years and grows well throughout the United States.

Many varieties are grown. Allium blooms in May, June, and July. Flowers are white, yellow, red, or pink.

Some commonly grown kinds of spring flowering allium and their characteristics are as folows:

Christophi—Purple flowers, 12 inches in diameter; grows 2 feet tall; blooms in June.

Cowanii—White flowers; grows 2 feet tall; blooms in early spring.

Moly—Yellow flowers, 12 inches in diameter; blooms in June.

Ostrowskianum—Reddish pink flowers, 6 inches in diameter; blooms in June.

Plant bulbs 2 or 3 inches deep in late fall. Space them 6 to 15 inches apart in clumps of 6 to 12 bulbs. The distance between bulbs depends on the height of the plant at flowering time.

You can leave the bulbs in place for many years. Dig, separate, and replant them when they become crowded or produce small flowers.

AMARYLLIS

Amaryllis (Hippeastrum) is grown as a potted plant indoors for spring flowering. It blooms from February to April. Flowers are red, pink, rose, white, or salmon. The plants grow about 3 feet tall.

Plant bulbs in early December in an 8-inch pot. Use a mixture of sandy soil and peat moss with an inch of small gravel in the bottom of the pot. Plant only half of the bulb beneath the soil. Water thoroughly after planting and each time the soil becomes moderately dry.

When the flower begins to form, water and fertilize at weekly intervals; continue for 3 months after flowering. Fertilize with a mixture of 1 teaspoon of 20-20-20 soluble fertilizer per gallon of water.

Keep the potted bulb in a cool room (60 to 65 degrees F.) and away from direct sunlight until May when it may be put outside.

When the leaves turn yellow, decrease watering until the soil becomes very dry. Store the potted plant on its side in a cool, dry place (40 to 55 degrees F.). Leave the bulb in the same pot for 3 years.

82

ANEMONE

Anemone (windflower) varies in height from 5 to 12 inches. It grows from tubers and blooms in March or April. Flowers are purple, red, blue, white, or pink. Anemone is a good source of cut flowers.

Select a planting site that is sheltered from the wind and lightly shaded. Soak tubers in water for 48 hours before planting. Plant them in October, 2 inches deep and 4 inches apart in clumps of 12 tubers. Leave tubers in place 2 or 3 years.

CHIONODOXA

Chionodoxa (glory -of-the-snow) grows 3 or 4 inches tall. It blooms very early as the snow is melting. Flowers are silvery pink, or blue and white. Use chionodoxa in groups under deciduous trees or in lawns.

Plant bulbs 3 inches deep in the fall. Space them 2 inches apart in clumps of 12 to 25 bulbs. Leave bulbs in place until they become crowded, often 5 to 8 years.

CROCUS

Many varieties of crocus are grown. Bulbs are usually sold by variety and graded by size. The largest bulbs produce the largest flowers.

The varieties generally recommended for planting are:

Yellow Mammoth (yellow); Snowstorm, Remembrance, Mont Blanc (white); King of the Striped (white, striped blue); and Purpurea Grandiflora (purple).

Crocus grows 4 or 5 inches high from corms planted in October or early November. It blooms in late February or early March. Use crocus in a rock garden, border, or scattered in the garden.

Crocus speciosus

Select a planting site that is sheltered from the wind for early flowering. Plant in an exposed area for late flowering.

Plant corms 3 inches deep and 3 to 6 inches apart in clumps of 25. Leave them in place for many years.

83

ERANTHIS

Eranthis (winter aconite) grows 2 to 8 inches high. It blooms in early spring and produces a yellow flower cushioned on green leaves. Use eranthis in rock gardens.

Plant tubers 2 inches deep in the fall. Space them 2 to 6 inches apart in clumps of 12 tubers. Leave them in place for many years. They are too small to dig.

FRITILLARIA

Fritillaria includes both meleagris (snakes-head fritillaria) and imperialis (crown imperial).

Meleagris

Melagris produces bell-shaped flowers in April and May. They are white, grayish purple, or pink. Use meleagris in rock gardens, as borders, or scattered as ground cover.

Plant the bulbs 3 or 4 inches deep, and put a handful of sand around each bulb. Space them 3 or 4 inches apart in clumps of 12 bulbs. Plant them in the fall. Leave the bulbs in place for many years; they are too small to dig.

Imperialis

Imperialis produces large flowers that hang in a circle from the top of the stem. Flowers are coppery red, orange, or yellow. Use imperialis in borders.

Plant these bulbs 6 to 8 inches deep and 12 inches apart in the fall. Use at least three bulbs on their sides to keep water from settling in the centers of the bulbs and rotting them.

Fertilize the plants three or four times during the growing season with a mixture of 1 teaspoon of 20-20-20 fertilizer per gallon of water. Leave the bulbs in place for many years.

GALANTHUS

Galanthus (snowdrop) grows 6 inches tall. It blooms at the end of January. Flowers are snow-white. Use galanthus in flowerbeds, as borders, or scattered in lawns and gardens.

Select a planting site that is shaded. Plant bulbs 6 inches deep in light sandy soil and 4 inches deep in heavy clay soil. If you wish, you may plant galanthus with other small bulbs such as muscari or chionodoxa.

Plant galanthus in September or October in clumps of at least 25 bulbs. Plant bulbs so they almost touch each other. Leave them in place until they become crowded.

HYACINTH

Hyacinth is showy and formal. It produces many small flowers close together along the stem.

These bulbs are sold by variety and usually are graded by size. Size of bulb indicates size of flower. Top-grade bulbs produce the largest flowers.

Some well known and dependable varieties are:

City of Haarlem (yellow), L'Innocence (white), Gertrude (rose), and Bismarck, King of the Blues (blue).

You can buy hyacinth plants that are specially grown and potted for indoor flowering at Christmas.

Hyacinth grows 6 to 12 inches high. It usually blooms in April when narcissi fade and before tall tulips blossom. Flowers are all colors. Use hyacinth in formal plantings among shrubs and as borders.

The bulbs of some varieties are larger than others. Plant small bulbs 3 or 4 inches deep and 4 to 6 inches apart; plant large bulbs 5 or 6 inches deep and 6 to 8 inches apart. Plant bulbs in October.

Handle these bulbs carefully because they bruise easily. Leave them in place for several years. Flowers become smaller each year; dig and discard the bulbs when flowers become too small for good display.

CLIVIA MINIATA

85

IRIS

Two kinds of iris are grown. Tall iris grows 2 to 2½ feet high. Dwarf iris varies in height from 3 to 12 inches.

Some varieties of both kinds of iris are grown from bulbs and some from rhizomes (underground stems). Both bulbs and rhizomes are called bulbs here.

Tall iris

Tall iris produces flowers that are erect on firm, straight stems. The most common types are Dutch, Spanish, and English. Blooming time varies among the types, but the difference is slight.

Some commonly grown varieties are: Golden Harvest, Pacific Gold, Yellow Queen (yellow); White Excelsior, White Superior (white); Wedgewood (light blue); and Imperator (dark blue).

Tall iris blooms in May, June, and July. Flowers make excellent indoor arrangements; cut when a blue or yellow slit appears down the side of the opening flower.

Plant bulbs 3 inches deep and 6 to 8 inches apart in October. If flowers appear before the danger of freezing has passed in the spring, protect them by placing cut branches over the plants. Leave bulbs in place 2 or 3 years.

Dwarf iris

The flowers of dwarf iris are small; some, as iris reticulata, are very fragrant. Dwarf iris should be planted in masses for best display.

Dwarf iris blooms from January to March. Flowers are yellow, purple, violet, or blue. Use dwarf iris in rock gardens.

Select a planting site in the rock garden that is protected from the wind. Plant 2 to 4 inches deep in October or November. Space 1 or 2 inches apart in drifts of 25 to 50 bulbs. Leave bulbs in place for many years. They are too small to dig and replant.

86

LEUCOJUM

Leucojum (snowflake) grows 16 inches tall. It blooms in April and May. Flowers are white like those of galanthus, but much larger.

Select a planting site that is well drained and lightly shaded. Plant bulbs 4 inches deep in the fall. Space them 4 inches apart in clumps of 12 bulbs. Leave them in place for many years.

LILY-OF-THE-VALLEY

Lily-of-the-valley grows 12 to 15 inches high from pips (underground stems). It produces white, bell-shaped flowers in May. Use lily-of-the-valley as bedding plants in lightly shaded areas, among shrubs as ground cover, and in rock gardens.

Plant pips in late summer. Plant them so their tops are level with the ground. Space them 6 to 12 inches apart in clumps of 12 pips. Leave them in place for many years. Dig and divide pips only when they become crowded.

MUSCARI

Muscari (grape hyacinth) grows 6 to 8 inches tall. It blooms in mid-April. Its flowers generally are shades of blue or white. Starch muscari, however, has large black flowers, 5 inches in diameter; ostrich feather produces violet blue flowers in a feathery plume.

Use muscari in rock gardens or scattered among shrubs as ground cover.

Plant the bulbs 3 or 4 inches deep and 3 or 4 inches apart in October. Leave them in place until they become crowded. These bulbs seldom are dug and replanted because they are too small to handle.

NARCISSUS

The narcissus family includes the narcissus and the daffodil. They are classified by the length of the crown—the center of the flower that forms either a cup or a trumpet. Flowers are white, cream, yellow, orange, red, or peach.

Narcissi grow 3 to 20 inches high. They bloom in March and April. Use them in flowerbeds or scatter them in lawns and gardens. Narcissi make good cut flowers.

Bulb size determines the number of flowers. Double-nose bulbs produce two flowers and smaller, round bulbs produce one flower. Bulbs with old and new growth on them may produce three or four flowers.

Plant bulbs 4 to 6 inches deep and 4 to 8 inches apart in September and October. If you plant them scattered in lawns, you may replace the sod over them. Leave the grass uncut at least until July.

Narcissus bulbs may be left in place until they become crowded, usually 3 or 4 years.

ORNITHOGALUM

Ornithogalum (star of Bethlehem) grows 8 to 18 inches tall. It blooms in May and June; flowers are white or silvery gray. You may scatter ornithogalum wherever you like throughout the garden. Cut flowers last a long time.

Plant bulbs 3 inches deep and 4 inches apart from September to November. Leave them in place for many years. Do not dig and replant the old bulbs; use new ones.

OXALIS

Oxalis grows 3 to 4 inches high. Flowers are lilac pink or coppery red. Lilac-pink oxalis blooms from May to July and coppery-red oxalis in mid-August.

In warm climates, use oxalis in rock gardens. Plant the bulbs in October,, 3 inches deep and 3 to 6 inches apart in clumps of 12 bulbs.

Oxalis will not grow outdoors in cold climates; use it indoors as a potted plant. Plant eight or nine bulbs ½ inch deep in a 5-inch pot in October. Keep the potted bulbs in a cool, dark place until buds appear; then move them to a bright room for flowering.

PUSCHKINIA

Puschkinia (Lebanon squill) grows 6 inches high. It blooms in March and April. Flowers are pale blue or white. Use puschkinia in clumps in rock gardens, and in drifts or clumps in lightly shaded areas.

Plant the bulbs 3 inches deep and 3 inches apart in the fall. Use 12 to 25 bulbs in each clump or drift. Leave them in place for many years. The bulbs are too small to dig and replant.

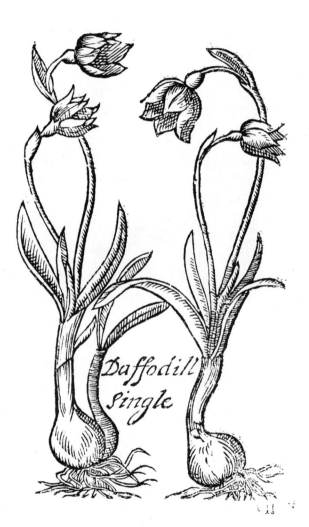

Daffodil single

TULIP

Tulips are sold by type, variety, or species. Common types of tulips and some of their characteristics are as follows:

Breeder—Bronzed, almost muddy appearance; colors are not bright and clear.

Cottage—Bloom later than other tulips; petals form a deep cup.

Darwin—Tallest tulips; flower is as wide as it is deep.

Lily Flowered—Petals curve outward and form a bell-shaped flower.

Parrot—Twisted, ruffled petals.

Double—Two or more rows of petals.

Many new types of tulips are being developed. Some have ruffled petals with lace edges. Others have mottled petals and foliage. Most of the new forms are similar to the varieties from which they were developed.

Tulips that do not belong to the common types are sold by species. Some well known species are greigii, kaufmanniana, fosteriana, tarda, praestans, and eichleri.

Tulips vary in height from 3 inches to almost 3½ feet. Most varieties have one cup-shaped flower to a stem. Tulips bloom in April and May. Flowers are red, pink, yellow, white, or blue. Use tulips for landscaping and as cut flowers.

Plant tulip bulbs 4 to 6 inches deep in late October or early November. Space them 6 to 12 inches apart in clumps of at least 8 to 10 bulbs.

Flowers become smaller each year. Dig and discard bulbs after about 3 years or when flowers become too small for good display. Use new bulbs for replanting. Bulbs that you dig from the garden and replant often fail to bloom.

Select varieties and colors that will blend with the rest of your garden. You can get ideas from local garden clubs, public parks, and botanical gardens.

Buy bulbs of named varieties that flower together and grow to about the same height. Be sure to buy enough of each color and type for a good display in your garden. You can buy mixtures of colors and types, but they are often unsatisfactory because they fail to give enough of each color.

If you buy bulbs before planting time, keep them in a cool, dry area. A temperature of 60 to 65 degrees F. is cool enough to prevent bulbs from drying out until you plant them. Temperatures higher than 70 degrees F. will damage the flower buds inside the bulbs.

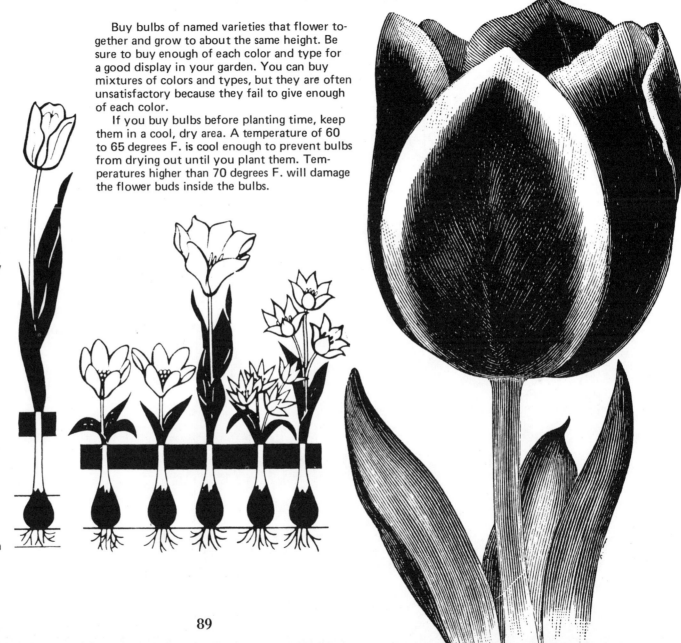

RANUNCULUS

Ranunculus grows 10 to 14 inches high. It produces flowers of all colors from May to July. Use ranunculus as color masses in gardens and as cut flowers.

Select a sunny, well-drained planting site. Plant the bulbs 2 inches deep and put a handful of sand around each bulb. Space them 6 to 8 inches apart in clumps of 12 bulbs. Mulch the ground with 2 or 3 inches of peat moss to keep the soil and bulbs from drying.

In warm climates, plant the bulbs any time from December until mid-April. In cold climates, plant them after the danger of freezing has passed in spring. These bulbs will not overwinter.

SCILLA

Scilla includes squill and bluebells. Squill grows 3 to 6 inches high and bluebells, 12 inches. Use either kind in beds, as borders, in rock gardens, or scattered in lawns.

Squill blooms in March and April and bluebells in May and June. Flowers are blue, white, or pink.

Plant squill bulbs three times their diameter in depth and bluebell bulbs 3 or 4 inches deep. Space both kinds 3 or 4 inches apart in clumps of 12 bulbs. Plant them in October and November. Leave the bulbs in place for many years. Do not dig and replant these bulbs; use new ones.

FLOWERS INDOORS

Many spring flowering bulbs make excellent flowers for indoor arrangements. You may use the whole plants of tulips and other small bulbs, or you may use cut flowers of all kinds. If you dig the whole plant, the flower lasts much longer.

Dig the plants when flowers appear, wash the soil from the roots, and plant the bulbs in coarse sphagnum moss or vermiculite in waterproof containers. Water lightly to keep the plants alive. When the flowers fade, discard the plants.

Cut flowers last only a few days. After you cut the flowers, put them in water. Be sure to wash the containers with soap and water before you use them.

Although spring flowering bulbs are primarily cold-weather plants, some will grow and produce flowers in warm areas. Tulip, hyacinth, crocus, and narcissi grow well in the Deep South and other hot areas.

When you buy bulbs in hot climates, be sure the bulbs have been stored in reliable commercial storage at 40 degrees F. and are kept at that temperature until planting time in mid-January. When bulbs are left in the ground in hot climates or stored in warm temperatures, they will not produce good flowers.

FORCING BULBS

Bulbs can be forced to bloom indoors earlier than they normally would outdoors in the garden or yard. The easiest bulbs to force are crocus, galanthus, hyacinth, narcissus, scilla, and tulip. A nurseryman can tell you the varieties that are best suited for forcing.

Forcing bulbs includes two phases. The bulbs develop buds and roots in the first phase and bloom in the second.

You should begin the first phase in October or early November. Plant the bulbs in pots and keep them at a temperature of 40 degrees F. for 8 to 12 weeks. During this phase, you can keep the potted bulbs outdoors or in a cold room indoors.

If you keep your bulbs indoors, the room must be dark and kept at 40 degrees F. Do not let the soil in the pots dry out; water the bulbs every day.

The second phase begins about mid-January after shoots have appeared on the bulbs. When the shoots are well out of the necks of the bulbs, bring the bulbs into a cool, bright room that can be kept at 55 degrees F. They will bloom in about 1 month.

You may refrigerate crocus, hyacinth, narcissus, and tulip bulbs at 40 degrees F. for 2 months instead of planting them in pots. At the end of 2 months, plant the bulbs in bowls and start them in the second phase of development.

You should discard bulbs that you force. They seldom grow and flower well when replanted in the garden.

91

SUMMER BULBS

GROWING SUMMER BULBS

Summer flowering bulbs are easy to grow, and do well in all parts of the United States. Most of them are grown for their flowers, some for their foliage.

Among the more popular summer flowering bulbs are tuberous rooted begonia, canna, dahlia, gladiolus, lily, and caladium.

Some bulbs may be grown as pot plants, some as pot or garden plants, and others as garden plants only. In the garden, various kinds of bulbs may be used as foundation plantings, as borders, in front of shrubs, or in groups for masses of color.

To grow summer flowering bulbs successfully—

Select healthy, mature bulbs and store them in a cool, dry place until planting time.

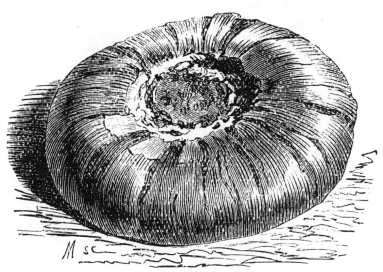

**BULB OR CORM OF GLADIOLUS
(UNDER PART)**

Prepare the soil in the planting site thoroughly.

Plant at depths, distances apart, and planting times recommended for each kind of bulb.

Water the plants at regular intervals.

PLANTING

Some kinds of summer flowering bulbs are grown in the garden outdoors and others in pots indoors. You can start many bulbs in flats or pots indoors in winter or early spring and replant them outdoors when the danger of frost has passed in the spring. Specific planting times are given in the list of bulbs.

Most bulbs need full sunshine. Try to select a planting site that will provide at least 6 to 10 hours of direct sunlight a day. Bulbs planted in a southern exposure near a building or wall bloom earlier than bulbs planted in a northern exposure.

Before preparing news flowerbeds, test the drainage of the soil. Dig a hole about a foot deep and fill it with water. The next day, fill the hole with water again and see how long it remains. If the water drains away in 8 to 10 hours, the soil is sufficiently well drained.

If water remains in the hole after 10 hours, it will be necessary to improve the drainage of the planting site. Dig furrows along the sides of the bed and add soil from the furrows to the bed. This raises the level of the bed above the level of the ground.

Dig and plant your flowerbeds when the soil is fairly dry. Wet soil packs tightly and retards plant growth. If you can crumble the soil between your fingers, it is dry enough for digging and planting.

Spade the soil 8 to 12 inches deep. As you dig, remove large stones and building trash, but turn under all leaves, grass, stems, roots, and anything else that will decay easily.

Add fertilizer, sand, and coarse peat moss to the soil. Use ½ pound (1 rounded cup) of 10-6-4 fertilizer for a 5- by 10-foot area, or a small handful for a cluster of bulbs. Place a 1-inch layer of sand and a 1- to 2-inch layer of peat moss over the bed. Thoroughly mix the fertilizer, sand, and peat moss with the soil.

Use a small handful of 10-6-4 fertilizer and equal parts of garden soil, peat moss, and sand for each pot plant. All bulbs require low levels of fertilizer. Avoid frequent applications of high nitrogen fertilizers; this will promote rotting in the bulbs.

Plant bulbs upright, and press the soil firmly over them to prevent air pockets underneath. Water the planted beds thoroughly to help settle the bulbs in the soil.

ACHIMENES

Achimes (nut orchid) grows 8 to 12 inches high and blooms in summer.
The flowers are almost every color. Use achimenes in shady flowerbeds, as
borders, or as pot plants.

ALLIUM

Allium (flowering onion) varies in height from 9 inches to 5 feet. Many vari-
eties bloom in June and July. Flowers are white, red, yellow, blue, or pink.
Use allium in borders.

AMARYLLIS

Amaryllis (hippeastrum) grows about 3 feet tall. It blooms in June and July.
Flowers are red, pink, rose, white, or salmon. Use amaryllis in borders or as pot
plants.

BEGONIA

Begonia that is grown for summer and fall flowering is tuberous rooted. It
grows 1 to 2 feet tall. Flowers are red, pink, orange, salmon, yellow, or white
and they grow up to 13 inches in diameter. Use begonia as a pot plant, for cut
flowers, and in lightly shaded flowerbeds. It blooms throughout the summer.

CALADIUM

Caladium is grown for its showy, colorful leaves. The flower buds should
be removed as soon as they appear so the leaves can develop fully.

CALLA

Call is a large plant and may grow 4 to 5 feet tall. It blooms almost anytime.
Flowers are white, red, pink, and yellow. Use calla as a pot plant.

CANNA

Many types of canna are grown. Tall types grow 5 to 7 feet high and dwaft types, 18 to 30 inches. Canna blooms for many weeks in summer. Flowers are red, pink, orange, yellow, and cream. Use canna in flowerbeds.

DAHLIA

Dahlia varies in height from less than 1 foot to more than 6 feet. It blooms in summer and fall. The flowers are white, yellow, red, orange, or purple. Use dahlia in borders and flowerbeds, or as cut flowers.

DAYLILY

Daylily (hemerocallis) varies in height from 6 inches to 6 feet. By selecting varieties that bloom at different times, you can have flowers all summer. The flowers are red, pink, orange, yellow, or cream. Use daylily in borders and flowerbeds, or as foundation plants.

GLADIOLUS

Gladiolus grows 2 to 4 feet high. It blooms in summer and fall and produces flowers of all colors. The kinds of gladiolus that are commonly grown are grandiflora, primulinus, primulinus hybrids, and colvilleii. Use gladiolus for cut flowers or in flowerbeds.

GLOXINIA

Gloxinia grows 12 inches tall. It produces both single and double flowers in many colors. Use gloxinia as a pot plant.

IRIS

Iris grows in both tall and dwarf forms. Some kinds of tall iris are summer flowering; they grow 2 to 2½ feet high and have white, blue, purple, orange, or yellow flowers. Dwarf iris blooms in early spring.

GLADIOLUS

94

ISMENE

Ismene (Peruvian daffodil) grows 2 feet high and produces large, funnel-shaped, white flowers that have green stripes down the funnel. Use ismene in front of shrubs, as foundation plantings around the home, and as pot plants.

LILIUM HYBRID

Lilium hybrids are among the most beautiful plants grown from bulbs. They have many forms, heights, flowering times, and colors.

LYCORIS

Lycoris (spider lily) grows 15 to 18 inches tall. It blooms from late July to October, depending on season and variety. Flowers are creamy white or red. Use lycoris as a pot plant in areas where the ground freezes in winter. In warm areas, it may be grown in the garden and used in flowerbeds in light shade.

MONTBRETIA

Montbretia grows 3 feet tall. It blooms in August and September and produces flowers 4 inches in diameter. Colors of the flowers are orange, gold, red, or yellow. Use montbretia in borders and as cut flowers.

PEONY

Peony grows 2 to 4 feet tall. It blooms in late spring and early summer. The flowers are white, yellow, cream, pink, and red. Use peony in borders and for cut flowers.

TIGRIDIA

Tigridia (Mexican shell flower) grows 2 feet tall and blooms in mid-summer. The tripetaled flowers are a mixture of white, red, yellow, and rose colors.

TUBEROSE

Tuberose (polianthes) grows 2 feet high and blooms in late fall. Its waxy, white, double flowers are very fragrant. Use tuberose in flowerbeds and as cut flowers.

ROSES

KINDS OF ROSES

Roses are separated into two main classes—bush roses and climbing roses—by their habits of growth. Full-grown bush roses are 1 to 6 feet high and require no support. Climbing roses produce long canes and must be provided with some kind of support.

BUSH ROSES

The bush roses are grouped into types according to their flowering habit, winter hardiness, and other traits. The types of bush roses are hybrid tea, floribunda, grandiflora, polyantha, hybrid perpetual, shrub, old fashioned, tree or standard, and miniature.

HYBRID TEAS

Hybrid teas are the so-called monthly or everblooming roses. They are more widely grown than all other types of roses combined. When the word "rose" is used, it generally suggests a hybrid tea variety.

Mature hybrid tea rose bushes are 2 to 6 feet high, the height depending on variety. The flowers vary from singles, which have but one row of petals, to doubles with many rows. In general, the buds are pointed and long, and the flowers are borne one to a stem or in clusters of three to five. Hybrid tea varieties are available in a wide range of colors, including pure white, and many shades of red, yellow, pink, and orange. All varieties are good for cutting, although some have short stems.

Most hybrid teas have some fragrance. This characteristic, however, is variable. When fragrance is present it is usually most intense in the early morning before the fragrant oil has evaporated from the base of the petals.

Most hybrid teas are winter hardy in area where the winter temperatures do not often go below zero, but varieties differ in cold resistance. In sections where winters are severe, practically all varieties need some protection.

FLORIBUNDAS

Floribunda roses bear their flowers in clusters, and the individual blooms of many of them closely resemble hybrid teas. They are increasing in popularity, especially for bed plantings where large numbers of flowers are wanted. Floribundas will tolerate more neglect than any other type of rose, with the possible exception of some of the shrub species.

GRANDIFLORAS

Grandiflora roses resemble hybrid teas in type of bloom—single on long stems—and in hardiness. Though the flowers are somewhat smaller than those of hybrid teas, grandifloras bloom more abundantly. The flowers are good for cutting.

POLYANTHAS

Flowers of polyantha roses are smaller than those of the grandifloras and are borne in rather large clusters. The clusters are similar in form and in size of individual flowers to many of the climbing roses, to which the polyanthas are closely related. The polyanthas are hardy and may be grown in many areas where hybrid teas are difficult to grow. Their chief use is in bed plantings or in borders with perennials. They are excellent for mass plantings.

HYBRID PERPETUALS

Hybrid perpetuals are the June roses of grandmother's garden. Their flowers are large. Generally they lack the refinement of hybrid teas; an exception is the white-flowered variety Frau Karl Kruschki, which many consider the finest white rose in existence.

Prior to the development of modern hybrid teas, hybrid perpetual roses were very popular. As their name indicates, they are considered as ever-blooming types, although most of them do not bear continuously through the growing season as do hybrid teas. They usually develop large, vigorous bushes if given good cultural care and proper pruning. They are very hardy and stand low winter temperatures without protection.

SHRUB ROSES

Shrub roses are actually a miscellaneous group of wild species, hybrids, and varieties that develop a large, dense, type of growth that is useful in general landscape work. They are hardy in all sections of the country. While their flowers do not equal in size or form those of other types of roses, many bear very attractive seed pods in the fall. They have fine-textured foliage and some are quite useful for hedges or screen plantings.

98

OLD-FASHIONED ROSES

Old-fashioned roses include the varieties and species that were popular in Colonial gardens. Though the flowers of old-fashioned roses are not as attractive as those of newer varieties, they usually are much more fragrant. These roses are all very hardy. require little care, and furnish an abundance of flowers in June.

Among the varieties occasionally found in gardens are:
Rosa centifolia (cabbage rose), light pink
Moss roses, pink
Cardinal de Richelieu, purplish red
Rosa mundi, striped white and red
York and Lancaster, Pink and white and variegated

TREE, OR STANDARD, ROSES

Tree, or standard, roses are distinctive because of the form of the plant rather than the type of flower. They are made by grafting any of the bush-type roses on upright trunks. Many of the better-known varieties of bush roses are available as tree roses. Tree roses are used in formal plantings or are used to accent a particular part of the garden. In sections where winters are severe the plants need special protection.

MINIATURE ROSES

Miniature rose plants, including leaves and flowers, are very small; for some varieties the maximum height is about 6 inches. Miniatures are used mostly for rock gardens, edging beds, and borders.

Long-leaved China.

Bramble-leaved.

Double Glossy.

R. sinica.

R. alba.

Marsh.

Yellow Brier.

Hybrid China.

Japanese.

Damask.

Musk.

Evergreen.

R. Lawrenciana.

Many-flowered.

99

CLIMBING ROSES

Climbing roses include all varieties that produce long canes and require some sort of support to hold the plants up off the ground. They are often trained on fences or trellises, and some are used without support to cover banks and aid in holding the soil in place. Climbing roses are rather hardy. They are becoming more popular with the development of finer varieties.

Climbing roses, like bush roses, are grouped into several types. There is much overlapping among types, and some varieties could qualify under several. Most rose catalogs list the following types: Ramblers, large-flowered climbers, everblooming climbers, climbing hybrid teas, climbing polyanthas, climbing floribundas, and trailing roses.

RAMBLERS

Rambler roses are very rapid growers. They sometimes develop canes as long as 20 feet in one season. The flowers are small—less than 2 inches across—and are borne in dense clusters. The plants flower only once during a season and on wood that was produced the preceding year. The foliage is glossy and the plants are very hardy; but, unfortunately, many varieties are very susceptible to mildew. They are being replaced by other climbing types that bear larger flowers during a long growing season and are less subject to mildew.

LARGE-FLOWERED CLIMBERS

Large-flowered climbers grow slowly in comparison with ramblers. They are often trained on posts or some other type of support, and may require rather heavy annual pruning to keep them in bounds. These roses are well adapted to small gardens where they may be trained against a wall, fence, or small trellis. When the plants are grown well, the flowers are rather large and are useful for cutting. Many varieties do not bloom as freely when the canes are trained vertically as they do when canes are trained horizontally.

EVERBLOOMING CLIMBERS

Everblooming climbers usually bear an abundance of flowers in early summer. After this period of heavy bloom, the plants produce a few scattered flowers until fall. Then if growing conditions are favorable, the plants again may bear heavily.

Plant breeders are improving this type of rose rapidly. Some everblooming climbers are available that bloom as continuously as hybrid teas and are more winter hardy.

CLIMBING HYBRID TEAS

Climbing hybrid tea roses have originated as seedlings and as chance sports of bush varieties.

When a bush hybrid tea produces a cane that has the climbing character, the new type of plant is usually given the same name as the bush variety from which it originated—for example, Climbing Crimson Glory.

The climbing forms of hybrid teas, in general, do not bloom as continuously as their bush parents. The flowers, foliage, and other characters, however, are usually identical. The climbing hybrid teas are just as susceptible to winter injury as the bush forms.

CLIMBING POLYANTHAS AND FLORIBUNDAS

These types, like the climbing hybrid teas, originated as sports and seedlings from polyanthas and floribundas. The flowers of these sports are generally identical with the bush forms from which they originated, and they also are fairly continuous in blooming. They are hardier than the climbing hybrid teas, but not hardy enough to withstand severe winter climates unless protected.

TRAILING ROSES

Trailing roses are climbers adapted to planting on banks or walls. They produce long canes that creep along the ground, making a pleasing ground cover. Their flowers are not so attractive as other types, but they are hardy and have a place in some gardens.

Small fruit.

Alpine.

Caucasian.

INDOOR HOUSE PLANTS

ALUMINUM PLANT pilea cadierei Thin, fleshy, quilted leaves with unusual silver markings. Indirect sun (bright light); well-drained potting soil; keep slightly moist. Low to medium humidity. Propagate by cuttings. Good in dish gardens, terrariums.

ANTHURIUM anthurium, in variety Some anthuriums are grown for their long-lasting cut flowers, others for their foliage. A. andreanum has brilliant red, white, coral, or pink flowers that look like patent leather. A. crystalinum has leaves that are velvety green with silver veins; its flowers are inconspicuous. Pot in well-drained potting soil, keep soil moist. Keep warm, 60 degrees minimum at night. High humidity and indirect sunlight.

ARALIA, FALSE dizygotheca, in variety Thread-like, drooping, dark greenish-brown leaves, arranged finger-fashion. D. veitchii has reddish leaves. Both types grow on a single trunk. Bright light. Medium to high humidity. Well-drained potting soil kept evenly moist. Mist often. Propagate by cuttings. A tree form that can range to fifteen feet.

ARALIA, MING polyscias, several varieties Beautiful, delicate looking but fairly sturdy tree form to twenty feet tall. Densely branched leaves roundish or long finger shapes. All are toothed; it is a fern-like foliage on a sturdy stem. Family includes shrubs and trees. High humidity important, well drained potting soil; bright light to partial shade; keep soil evenly moist. Propagate by cuttings.

ARROWHEAD syngonium All green or variegated arrow-shaped leaves to thirty inches. Long-time favorite houseplant because it is so amenable to different situations. Bright light to low light; well-drained potting soil; keep slightly moist; propagate by cuttings; humidity low to high. Can also be grown in water.

ARTILLERY PLANT pilea microphylla Small green leaves on fleshy stems to 10 inches long. Greenish flowers discharge a cloud of pollen when shaken, hence the common name; requires clipping to promote branching. Well-drained potting soil; keep slightly moist. Indirect sun (bright light); medium humidity. Propagate by cuttings. Good in dish gardens, terrariums.

ARDISIA ardisia crispa Graceful small tree form, useful in dish gardens and terrariums. Dark green leaves borne in clusters. Well-drained potting soil; keep evenly moist; medium to high humidity. Bright to low light; prefers slightly cooler temperatures. Propagate by cuttings.

ASPARAGUS FERN asparagus sprengeri Lovely light green feathery foliage. Popular plant for hanging baskets. Bright light. Fresh air; mdium humidity; well-drained putting soil; frequent misting in dryer conditions; keep slightly moist. It bears small, white flowers. Propagate by division or seed.

ASPARAGUS PLUMOSA asparagus plumosa More erect than sprengeri with delicate fern-like foliage that is amazingly sturdy. Same culture as sprengeri but can stand lower light conditions. A favorite with florists in rose bouquets. Other asparagus that are grown are a. meyeri, a. falcatus, a. asparagoides.

ASPIDISTRA (CAST-IRON PLANT) aspidistra Endures heat, dust, low light, and lack of water better than most houseplants. When it is well cared for produces a mass of broad glossy green leaves and bears flowers close to the ground. Grow in low light to filtered sun. Water when dry.

AVOCADO persea americana Start with the seed of a ripe avocado, preferably one that's already begun to split. Place over a glass of water inserting three toothpicks in seed so that only the lower, larger end of seed touches the water. After roots form and top growth appears, transplant into well-drained potting soil and put in a sunny location. Use an 8 to 12 inch pot because avocados don't like being transplanted. Keep slightly moist.

BABY'S TEARS helxine soleiroli Beautiful little creeping plant used potted alone or as ground cover in dish gardens or terrariums. Needs moist, cool atmosphere with some fresh air. Water by misting often. Well-drained potting soil. Easily propagated by division or cuttings.

BAMBOO, CHINESE bambusa multiflex A large bamboo to twelve feet tall. This one has reddish-green leaves. Bamboo is difficult to grow unless there's plant of fresh air and high humidity; but well worth the effort because they are veautiful, evocative plants. Full sun; well-drained potting soil; keep evenly moist. Propagate by division of clumps. B. nana is slightly smaller to 10 feet; with bluish leaves that are more profuse than the multiflex. A beautiful plant.

BAMBOO, GOLDEN phylbstachys aurea A bamboo-like grass that grows to twelve feet on a yellow stem with green leaves that have grey undersides. Cuture the same as bamboo. Both bambus and phyllostachs do best if summered outdoors. Be sure to protect from wind, especially on a high terrace.

BANANA musa, several types Banana trees to six feet tall, with huge green leaves and red and yellow flowers. Some species, e.g. m. velutina, produce edible fruit; others like m. rosacea do not. But all are showy background plants. Well-drained potting soil; fresh air; medium to high humidity; Bright light. Propagate by suckers that appear at the base of the plant.

BEGONIA, FIBROUS ROOTED begonia, fibrous rooted, in variety Many types with multicolored or all-green leaves in varying shapes. Really useful low-light plants, all with small flowers.

BOXWOOD (LITTLE-LEAF BOXWOOD) buxus microphylla Well-drained potting soil; bright light; keep slightly moist. Good in dish gardens as tree forms or simply potted. Needs cool atmospheres with medium to high humidity. Propagate by cuttings.

BEGONIA begonia, fibrous rooted in variety A big family of popular houseplants and summer annuals. Big variety in size (from miniature types good in terrariums and dish gardens, to huge, bushy plants to five feet tall. All have interesting and often spectacular foliage; in a great variety of shapes and sizes and colors. Flowers much smaller than tuberous begonias, but reliable, and sun shades of white, pink, or red. Types include wax begonia that flowers regularly all year long. Angel-wing begonias, with leaves wing shaped; shades of green or variegated with silver, blooms all year round. Well-drained potting soil. Bright light to direct sun. Water when dry; keep growing tips pinched out and prune back when plants get leggy. Propagate by cuttings or seed.

BEGONIA REX begonia rex Extraordinary foliage, full of color and pattern. These begonias are grown for their foliage. They are mostly rhizomatous rooted , which means a thick stem (rhizome) that skims the top of the soil and sends down shallow roots. They demand more humidity and warmth than their fibrous brothers, but like lower light intensities. Use shallow pots and water when dry. Propagate by cuttings or seeds. Try this plant, it is really beautiful! Be sure to let rest for several weeks during winter.

BEGONIA REX

BAMBOO

BROMELIADS bromeliads The bromeliads (aechmea, billbergia, crypt-anthus, neoregelia, vriesia, etc.) are the most adaptable of all foliage plants. Their leaves hold water and the plants grow well under dry indoor conditions in high or low light. Mostly epiphytic (meaning plants that are tree-perchers instead of growing on the ground). Mostly they root into the debris or moss found at the fork of a branch and derive their food from the air around them (they are sometimes called air plants). They are not parasites. Leaves are stiff, all green, or brightly colored. When plants are mature, a brilliantly colored flower spike grows from the center of the plant. This flower spike can last for several months and in some varieties changes color as it matures. It is an elegant show. In most varieties the leaves arrange a vase-like form; it is the center of this vase or cup that you keep filled with water. Keep leaves clean by frequent misting or syringing. Propagate from lateral shoots (offsets) that grow from the main plant after the flower withers. Potting medium should be extremely light and rich in organic material. Use wood chips, osmunda fiber, sand, soil, in equal parts. Or check with your local bromeliad society for specific instructions on the particular plant or plants you are growing. Keep your growing medium barely moist or water when dry. Exceptions to these rules among commonly grown bromeliads are: Cryptanthus, commonly called the star plant, whose leaves form a rosette and whose small white flowers are hidden by the leaves. Small, low growing, there is no cup to water, water the medium when dry. Neoregelia, commonly called the living vase plant, that demands a higher humidity than most. Uriesia splendens, called flaming-sword plant, propagated by removing new plant that appears in the center of the old one after flowering.

105

CALADIUM caladium, hybrid varieties The leaves of caladium are large and arrow shaped. Some kinds have pink leaves, some have variegated green and white leaves, and there are several other combinations. Grown from tubers potted in the spring. Caladiums like indirect sunlight, well-drained rich soil that's kept moist (avoid overwatering, caladiums rot easily). They are particularly sensitive to drafts. At the end of summer, gradually prolong periods between waterings until plants become dormant. Then store tubers without removing from soil in cool place (60 degrees) until spring. Repot in spring.

CALATHEA calathea, in variety Leaves various shades of green. Veined in contrasting green or white with red or purple underside. Striking and similar in appearance to prayer plant (maranta), but needing higher humidity. Good in terrariums. Indirect sunlight; rich well-drained soil; keep slightly moist. Lack of humidity usual reason it fails in the house. Propagate by division.

CHINESE EVERGREEN aglaonema Dark green leaves growing at the end of canelike stems. This plant will flourish in low light, dry areas where most other houseplants would suffer or die. Grow in water or in well-drained potting mixture. Water when dry. When the stems become too long, cut off the tops and reroot them.

COFFEE PLANT coffea arabica Dark shiny green leaves, similar in appearance to a gardenia. White flowers that are fragrant, followed by red coffee beans, although it may not flower in the home. Keep well pruned. Useful in containers and dish gardens. Bright light; well-drained potting soil; keep slightly moist; medium humidity. Propagate by tip cuttings or seed.

COLEUS coleus Direct sun, well-drained potting soil, keep soil slightly moist. Can survive some chilling and overwatering. Foliage is a wide variety of different colors and patterns. Propagate by cuttings; seed. Keep pinched back to avoid legginess. Will not withstand very dry air.

CORDYLINE (TI PLANT) cordyline terminalis Leaves in many combinations of colors and lance-shaped (palm-like) and crown the top of the cane; can grow to eight feet. Similar in appearance and culture to the draceana. Well-drained potting soil; bright light to direct sun; high humidity; keep slightly moist. Propagate by stem cuttings or root division.

CREEPING CHARLIE pilea nummularifolia Creeping plant, with small round leaves. Propagate by cuttings. Indirect sunlight; well-drained potting soil; keep slightly moist. Good in dish gardens, terrariums.

CROTON codiaeum Colorful container plants, with leaves variegated in several colors. All must have bright light to direct sun, fresh air, and medium to high humidity. Watch for spider mites. Plant in well-drained potting soil and keep evenly moist. Propagate from cuttings.

CYPERUS (UMBRELLA PLANT) cyperus A semi-aquatic plant that must be kept wet. Well-drined potting soil, bright light, fresh air, and medium to high humidity. Watch for red spider mites. Graceful drooping foliage borne in an umbrella-like cluster. Very nice near an aquarium, around bathtub, or indoor pool if you happen to have one. Varieties that range in size from eighteen inches to eight feet.

DIEFFENBACHIA (DUMB CANE) dieffenbachia, in variety One of the most popular large houseplants. Best as a foliage backdrop to smaller plants. Any humididty level except for very low; well-drained potting soil. Bright to low light. Huge green and white or yellow leaves snaking up a stout cane. Water when dry; keep leaves clean and out of the way of people as they easily bend and tear.

DRACAENA dracaena, in variety Many different types. All have sword-like leaves of varying width. All green or variegated in yellow, white, or red. They top a green-brownish cane that ranges from very thin to thick, depending on genus. The smallest is d. godseffiana, best potted in a group on eye-level shelf, to two feet. The d. marginata can grow to 20 feet and more. Other varieties include d. sanderiana, d. fragrons, and several more. Use well-drained potting soil. Water when dry to slightly moist. Bright light to direct sun. Propagate by stem cuttings or root division.

FATSHEDERA fatshedera lizei Fatshederas are evergreen shrubs. They produce leathery five-lobed leaves that are lustrous dark green. Well-drained potting soil, keep slightly moist. Grow on support in full sun, cool temperatures, medium humidity. Propagate by stem tip cuttings.

FIG, CREEPING ficus, pumila Indirect light to full sun; high humidity; well-drained potting soil. Keep slightly moist. Beautiful, delicate-looking small green leaves. Useful in dish gardens as ground cover; in hanging baskets. Good in small pots arranged in tiers, or hanging over a bathroom shelf. Propagate by stem tip cuttings.

FIG, FIDDLE-LEAF Ficus lyrata Large, thick, shiny green leaves. Shaped, as is described by its common name, like a fiddle. Bright light to direct sun; well-drained potting soil. Grows to 40 feet in its native habitat. Propagate by air layering or stem tip cuttings.

DRACAENA

FIG, WEEPING ficus bejamina Beautiful tree form, looks like a citrus tree. Bright light to direct sun; well-drained potting soil; medium to high humidity. Can grow to 50 feet. A good street tree in mild (frostless) areas. Propagate by cuttings or air-layering. Mist regularly.

FITTONIA fittonia, several varieties Bright light; well-drained potting soil; keep evenly moist. Useful in terrariums. Also used in hanging baskets. Ovalish thin green leaves with white, pink or red veins. Medium to high humidity. Propagate by tip cuttings.

FRECKLE FACE (POLKA-DOT PLANT) hypoestes sanguinolenta Green leaves with light to dark pink spots. Grows to 24" and has purple flowers. Keep pinched back. Direct sun to bright light; well-drained potting soil; keep slightly moist. Propagate by cuttings or seed.

FRIENDSHIP PLANT pilea pubescens Quilted reddish-brown leaves; greenish flowers. Low-growing; good in dish garden; terrarium. Bright light; well drained potting soil; keep slightly moist. Propagate by cuttings.

CITRUS citrus Citrus are trees or shrubs that are grown for their fruit and foliage. They all flower and often the flowers are very fragrant. Otaheite orange, ponderosa lemon, and Meyer lemon are the kinds most likely to flower and fruit indoors. The fruit on the otaheite orange is inedible, but is attractive and can appear on a very young plant. Fruit on the ponderosa and the Meyer is edible. You can **also** grow kumquats, citrus japonica, calomondin or miniature orange, citrus mitis, mandarin orange, citrus nobilis deliciosa. Or you can plant the seeds from breakfast including grapefruit seeds, which form a mass of foliage from the crowded seedlings, good in a shallow pot. The citrus are all good tub plants, the foliage is green and glossy. Plant in well-drained potting soil, keep evenly moist. Full sun to bright light, cool (not over 75 degrees), lots of fresh air and medium to high humidity. Mist regularly, prune in spring, move outside to a sheltered spot in summer, watch for scale. Propagate by cuttings or seeds.

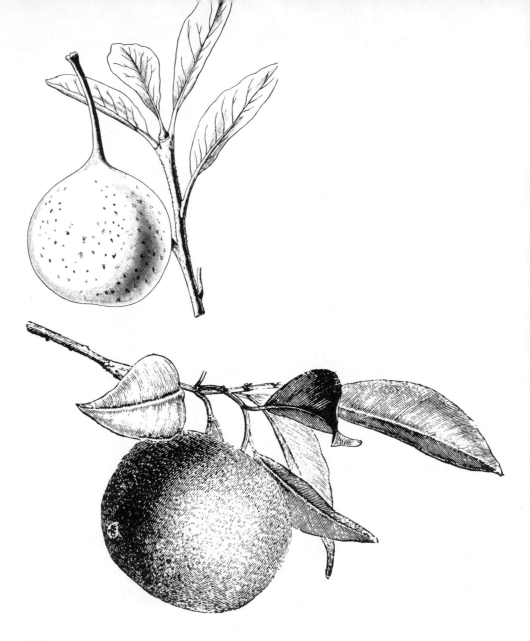

FERNS Ferns are feathery, lush plants. None of them flower, all reproduce by spores. Most can also be propagated by division or offsets. They are good low light plants, their major requirement being a high humidity level (50% or more) and it's the lack of humidity that is the usual reason for failure in the house. Keep soil evenly moist; use a rich (high humus) but wel-drained soil. Mist regularly. The smaller ferns are perfect for terrariums. The Victorians were especially fond of ferns and often grew them in "fern cases" which are just large, square, terrariums (like a fishtank with a lid). Fern cases contained arrangements of ferns and masses that echoed the lsh, green forest floor. Many ferns, for example the Boston fern, are grown in hanging baskets. Remember that hot air rises and the higher you hang the plant the lower the humidity (in winter) will be; in general experiment with different areas in your home until you find the best spot; it is well worth the effort. When the word sturdy is used in reference to a fern it means that it can withstand a drier atmosphere than most other ferns. The following is a list of commonly grown ferns, with mention of culture when it varies from the general rules stated above.

FERN, BIRD'S NEST asplenium nidus Particularly durable, good in dish gardens, not usually in terrariums because of its size (to 3 feet).

FERN, BOSTON nephrolepis exaltata A sturdy fern, a favorite in hanging baskets. Likes slightly brighter light than most ferns.

FERN, BRAKE pellaea viridis Pellaeas have roundish leaves and don't look like ferns. They are particularly sturdy. The brake fern will climb a support. Good in hanging baskets.

FERN, RIBBON BRAKE (CRETAN BRAKE FERN) pteris cretica, FERN SPIDER BRAKE pteris (serrulata or multifida), FERN, SWORD BRAKE Pteris ensiformis Pteris ferns are good in dish gardens or terrariums. Some are variegated with white.

FERN, FLUFFY RUFFLES nephrolepis A bit sturdier than its sister, the Boston fern, used the same way. Nephrolepsis ferns are all rather fast growing.

FERN, HARE'S FOOT polypodium aureum glaucum These have hairy, creeping reddish-brown rhizomes similar to the davallia. They are extra-ordinarily sturdy for ferns; although they should be kept evenly moist they can handle drying out occasionally, especially under very low light intensities. Propagated by division, but often go into shock when its done —be patient, they usually recover.

ORNAMENTAL FERN CASE AND STAND

109

FERN, HART'S TONGUE phyllitis scolopendrium cristatum Foliage looks like a tongue, keep cool (not over 70 degrees), lots of fresh air.

FERN, HEDGE polystichum aculeatum Fronds to 2 feet. Like the leather-leaf fern **can** take very low light.

FERN, HOLLY cyrtomium falcatum A holly-like leaflet. Use in a terrarium or dish garden.

FERN, JAPANESE PAINTED athyrium iseanum Provide ample fresh air and slightly cool temperatures (not over 70 degrees).

FERN, LEATHER-LEAF polystichum adiantiforme Can stand very low light intensities. A medium size fern.

FERN, MAIDENHAIR adiantum, several varieties Hard to grow outside of a terrarium or greenhouse since it requires constantly high humidity and wet soil. The most delicate of this group and perhaps the most beautiful. Be sure the soil is well aerated.

FERN, MEXICAN TREE cibotium schiedei A tree fern, sturdy with graceful drooping fronds. Can grow to twelve feet but usually much shorter in the house.

FERN, MOTHER SPLEENWORT asplenium bulbiferum Plantlets grow on surface of leaves. Cut off along with piece of old frond and repot, with old frond just below the surface.

FERN, PELLAEA pellaea rotundifolia Small sturdy ferns with roundish leaves, can take low light intensities and can even manage slight neglect and slightly drier air.

FERN, RABBIT'S FOOT davallia fejeensis Davallia have curious hairy, brown (hence the rabbit's foot common name) creeping rhizomes that eventually grow over the side of the pots. The fronds grow along these rhizomes. Fasten these rhizomes to the surface of the soil when potting. Use a copper wire fashioned into a hairpin shape. Be careful but firm. Good in hanging baskets.

FERN, SQUIRREL'S FOOT davallia bullata See above.

FERN, STAG HORN platycerium bifurcatum An epiphitic fern grown in osmunda fiber on slabs of wood. Must be kept constantly moist and in high humidity atmosphere, and be misted regularly. Fronds are thick, leathery, long and wide. Propagate by plantlets. Platycerium is a strange, primitive looking plant.

DICKSONIA BERTEROANA, showing Habit and Upper Portion of Detached Frond

110

FERN, TREE blechnum brasiliense Very sturdy tree form. The trunk can grow to 3 feet and the fronds that top it are up to two feet long.

FERN

IRESINE (BLOOD LEAF) iresine lindeni Well-drained potting soil; direct sun; medium humidity; keep slightly moist. Dark crimson red leaves; plinted and slender. Plants to one foot tall and good accent plants in groupings or dish gardens. Propagate by cuttings.

IVY, ENGLISH hedera helix Direct sun; well-drained potting soil; water when dry; fresh air; medium to high humidity and slightly cool temperatures essential for good bug-free growth. Watch for spider mites and aphids. Wash occasionally with non-detergent soap and water. Several different varieties, some all green; some variegated; waxy or pleated leaves. Great in hanging baskets or potted on over-hanging shelves. Keep well pruned.

IVY, GRAPE cissus rhombifolia A sturdy, beautiful low-light vine. Water when dry. Plant in well-drained potting soil. Dark green leaves; relatively slow growing but one of the best (if not the best) plants for the house. Grow in hanging basket. Propagate by cuttings.

IVY, SWEDISH plectranthus, several varieties Direct sun; well-drained potting soil; water when dry. Easily propagated by cutting. Keep pinched back to avoid legginess. Shiny green leaves; grow in hanging basket. Can tolerate indirect sun but best in full sun and medium humidity. There's a variegated Swedish ivy that's spotched with white.

IVY, CURLY hedera helix cristata Same culture as English ivy, deep green, leathery leaves that are curled and veined in light pink. Same uses as English ivy. This variety seems a bit more adaptable to neglect and dry air than most hedera's.

IVY, PARLOR (GERMAN IVY) senecio mikaniodes Very popular, with green, ivy-like leaves. Good in hanging baskets; potted on overhanging shelf. Bright light to direct sun; fresh air; slightly cool (not over 70 degrees); medium to high humidity; well-drained potting soil; keep slightly moist. Propagate by cuttings.

IVY, KENILWORTH cymbalaria muralis A creeper, with small green kidney-bean shaped leaves. Small flowers, lilac with yellow throats. Good in hanging baskets or in pots on overhanging shelf. Direct sun to bright light; well-drained potting soil; keep slightly moist; medium to high humidity; fresh air and cool atmosphere (not over 70 degrees); prune and mist regularly. Propagate by stem cuttings or seed.

IVY, HAHN'S (MAPLE IVY) hedera, var. helix, "Maple Queen" Perhaps the best of the hederas for indoors. Dark green, waxy leaves that overlap. Very lush looking when well grown, usually sold as simply "Ivy." The culture and uses are the same as the other hederas but can stand slightly lower light conditions. Propagate this and all the hederas by cuttings.

111

JAPANESE ARALIS fatsia japonica Leaves maple-looking and green or variegated with white. Can grow to twelve feet and used as specimen plant in cool, sunny rooms. Well drained potting soil; good humidity. Keep slightly moist. Propagate by cuttings.

JAPANESE FLAG acorus gramineus Grass-like tufts of all green leaves (acorus gramineus pusillus) or green variegated with white (acorus gramineus variegatus). Good in terrariums, dish gardens or potted alone. Need a moist well drained soil and high humidity, can tolerate chilly window sills. Low light. Propagate by division. From 4"–8" tall, use slow-acting organic fertilizer.

KANGAROO VINE cissus antarctica Dramatic green-toothed foliage, brother to the grape ivy. Beautiful plant for a hanging basket. Medium to high humidity. Well-drained potting soil; bright to low light; water when dry. Propagate from cuttings or division. Repot every year or so.

MOSES-IN-THE-CRADLE rhoeo spathacea To 10", green leaves with purple undersides, and white flowers nestled within two bracts. Good light; well-drained potting soil; water when dry to slightly moist. Propagate by offsets or seedlings that sprout up around the parent plant. R. spathacea vittata has purple leaves with yellow stripes.

NEPETA (CATNIP) nepeta cataria Flowers; white to light purple; foliage greyish. Cats love it. Full sun; well-drained potting soil; water when dry. Propagate by seed; cut back regularly, especially after summer growing season. Good in kitchen windowsill herb garden or anywhere it gets enough light; fresh air and low to medium humidity.

NEPHTYTHIS syngonium podophyllum Low to medium light foliage plants that are justly popular because they are so well suited to average home conditions. Leaves arrowhead shaped, green or variegated, on long stalks. In older plants leaves are lobed. Withstands all but driest conditions; well-drained potting soil; propagate by cutting; keep slightly moist. Useful as trailer or growing on a support or in terrariums.

NEW ZEALAND FLAX phormium tenax Long (to 50") sword-shaped green leaves edged in red. There are also varieties with leaves marked in bronze. Direct sun to bright light; fresh air, keep cool not over 70 degrees. Slightly moist; well-drained potting soil. Propagate by offsets. Good as a background plant surrounded by smaller plantings.

NORFOLK ISLAND PINE araucaria excelsa Branches are borne in symmetrical tiers; this formal symmetry makes it a useful decorative plant. Good light but indirect sunlight. Water when dry. Propagate by air-layering. Also makes a good Christmas tree. Medium to high humidity and some fresh air important to healthy growth.

WINDOW FERN CASE

112

PALM' CHINESE FAN livistona chinensis Huge leaves in a fan shape growing on a lone trunk, very dramatic looking; grows to eight feet. Bright light to direct sun; keep slightly moist. Well-drained potting soil; fresh air; mist regularly; medium to high humidity. Propagate by suckers or seeds.

PALM, DATE phoenix dactylifera Large date palm, with bluish-green foliage to eight feet. Culture the same as p. roebelenii.

PALM, ARECA chrysalidocarpus lutescens Densely-growing cones, a particularly lush looking palm. Well-drained potting soil. Water when dry, mist regularly; medium to high humidity; bright light; propagate by division or seed.

PALM, CHAMAEDOREA collinia, several varieties Very popular, graceful palms; they can take slightly lower light intensities than most other palms. Small types to 2 ft. tall, large ones to 6 ft. tall. Same environment as the areca palm. Propagate by seed or suckers.

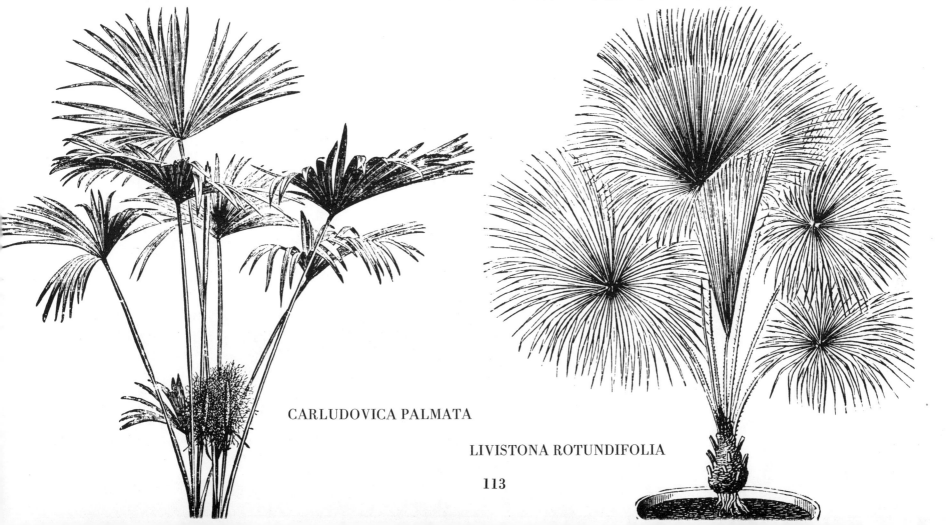

CARLUDOVICA PALMATA

LIVISTONA ROTUNDIFOLIA

PALM, DWARF DATE phoenix roebelenii A small plant with very graceful fronds to three feet tall. Mist regularly; well-drained potting soil; water when dry; bright light to direct sun. Propagate by seeds or suckers. Medium to high humidity.

PALM, FISHTAIL caryota (mitis, or plumosa) Called "fishtail" because the leaves look like fishtails. They can grow to be enormous, too big for your house or a container. While they are young, though, they are adaptable. Direct sun; well-drained to sandy potting soil; medium-to high humidity, water when dry. Porpagate seed. Mist regularly.

PALM, LADY rhapis, (excelsa and humilis) Very adaptable plants, one of the easiest palms to grow indoors. Canes look like bamboo, the leaves look like fans. Bright light to low light; water when dry; well-drained potting soil; fresh air; keep a bit cool (not over 70 degrees). Low to medium humidity. Propagate by seeds or suckers.

PALM, PARADISE (KENTIA PALM) howea fosteriana Perhaps the best of all palms for indoors. They are tough and slow-growing to six feet. Well-drained potting soil; water when dry. Bright to low light; mist regularly. Propagate by suckers or seeds. Low to medium humidity.

PALM, SAGO cycas revoluta Not a true palm, but an ancient palmlike evergreen shrub. Leaves frondlike and stiff topping a stout trunk-like stem. Very slow growing to 10 feet high with drooping fronds to feet feet long. Dramatic, well worth growing, and usually quite expensive. Full sun to bright light; medium to high humidity, slightly moist; well-drained potting soil. Propagated by suckers. Removed when plant is not issuing a new crop of leaves.

COCOS WEDDELIANA

JUBAEA SPECTABILIS

114

PANDANUS (SCREW-PINE) pandanus (utillis or veitchi) Long sword-like arched leaves with spiny margins. All green or banded in white or grey. Prop roots that hang down into soil (in older specimens) and seem to be holding the plant up. Striking potted plants that require high humidity; and that requirement must be the only reason why they are not as popular as others. Can grow to be enormous, up to 60 feet in the tropics. Bright light to low light, well-drained potting soil; keep slightly moist. Propagate by suckers.

PHILODENDRON philodendron, in variety The most popular houseplants; they live in a number of conditions and withstand neglect. There are vine or self-heading types. Leaves in various shapes, all green, dark red, variegated in different colors. Any light conditions; well-drained potting soil. Water when dry; low to high humidity. Propagate vines by stem cuttings; self-headers by offsets.

PIGGY-BACK PLANT (PICKABACK PLANT) tolmiea menziesii A relative of the strawberry-begonia; it has green, slightly hairy leaves that are heart-shaped and almost parchment thin. Used in hanging baskets or in pots on overhanging shelves. Propagated by the plantlets that appear at the base of the mature leaves. Humidity and fresh air important, lack of these is the usual reason for failure in the house. Use well-drained potting soil; keep evenly moist; bright light.

PEPEROMIA peperomia, in variety An old favorite of a houseplant. Useful in dish gardens, terrariums, or potted. Leaves ovalish in many different colors or combinations of colors. Many different varieties in cultivation. Can survive any but the direst atmospheres; well-drained potting soil; water when dry; bright to low light. Propagate by stem or leaf cuttings.

PITTOSPORUM pittosporum tobira Clusters of thick, shiny leaves; either all green or variegated with white. Flowers borne in clusters; small, white and fragrant. Good subject for bonsai or as shrub or tree form. Keep well pruned. They like cool rooms with fresh air and good humidity. Direct sun to bright light; water when dry and mist regularly; well-drained potting soil, propagate by cuttings.

PLEOMELE pleomele reflexa Leaves green or green with yellow stripes; cane stems; resembles a dracaena except leaves surround the stem. Can grow to 10 feet. Bright light; well-drained potting soil; keep slightly moist. Low to medium humidity. Propagate by stem cuttings or root division.

PODOCARPUS podocarpus, several varieties Evergreen trees, with thin, almost pine-like leaves except they are soft in texture. Slow growing. Useful for bonsai, dish-garden, or as a tree-form. Popular outdoor potted tree in

115

CUT LOAF PHILODENDRON

California. Medium to high humidity; fresh air; well-drained potting soil; direct sun to bright light. Propagate by cuttings or seeds.

POTHOS (DEVIL'S IVY) scindapsus aureus A lovely vine with heart-shaped leaves similar in appearance and culture to philodendron oxycardium, except pothos leaves are splashed with yellow or white. Good in hanging basket or overhanging shelf. Any light conditions; water when dry, well-drained potting soil; low to high humidity; propagate by cuttings.

PRAYER PLANT maranta Green leaves with brown, green, silver, or pink splotches fanning out symmetrically from the midrib. Called "prayer plant" because the leaves fold up at night like a pair of hands praying. Bright light to slight shade; well-drained potting soil; slightly moist; medium humidities. Propagate by division.

PURPLE PASSION (VELVET PLANT) gynura aurantiaca Hairy, purple leaves, on thick, much-branched stems. Need medium to high humidity; direct sun; well-drained potting soil; keep slightly moist. Keep cut back to avoid legginess. Propagate by cuttings. Grows to 18'' or more, good as a color accent among other plants. Watch for mealy bugs.

PUSSY EARS cyanotis somaliensis Related to tradescantia, and sometimes called wandering jew. It has fleshy leaves covered with white hairs; trailing stems. Useful in hanging baskets. Well-drained (sandy) potting soil; water when dry. Cuttings root easily in sand and should be taken regularly. Good light to direct sun.

RUBBER PLANT ficus elastica The rubber plant has large oval leaves that are leathery and dark green. Propagate by air layering or leaf cuttings. Bright light to direct sun; keep slightly moist; well-drained potting soil. A favorite house plant that can grow to 10 feet. It is durable and dramatic. Watch for scale and mealy bug. F. elastica decora is variegated with white splotches.

SCHEFFLERA (UMBRELLA PLANT) brassaia actinophylla Really useful low-light tree form; at its best it should be about as wide as it is tall. Densely branched; compound leaves that are dark green. The common name, umbrella plant, refers to that arrangement. Low to medium light; well-drained potting soil; water when dry; medium humidity. Propagate from cuttings.

SELAGINELLA (BLUE SELAGINELLA) selaginella uncinata A low-growing creeping plant that demands high humidity and is a good terrarium plant. Well drained potting soil. Keep slightly moist. Low light brings out more of bluish foliage color. Avoid water on foliage. Propagate by cuttings. Really magnificent in a hanging basket if the air is moist enough.

SELLOUM philodendron selloum Like all philadendrons an amazingly sturdy and reliable houseplant. This one has huge dark green leaves that fan out. A large container plant perfect for a low light living room. Use well-drained potting soil. Water when dry. Bright to low light. Low to high humidity; keep leaves clean by frequent syringing. Propagate by offsets.

SENSITIVE PLANT mimosa pudica Small leaflets that close when you touch them, this plant is grown mainly because of that phenomenon. The leaflets may also close on cloudy days. Give it bright light to full sun, keep slightly moist. Use well drained potting mixture. Good in dish gardens, terrariums, or for children. Needs medium to high humidity. Propagate by seed.

SILK OAK grevillea robusta Delicate looking fernlike foliage on a tree that is quick growing and quite beautiful. It demands a medium to high humidity. Well-drained potting soil. Slightly moist. Direct sun. Mist regularly. Propagate by seed. The silk oak has orange flowers that appear in clusters.

SPIDER PLANT chlorophytum, several varieties Tuft forming, grassy leaves, green or variegated with white or yellow stripes, small white flowers. The "spiders" are new plants that can be cut away after a few weeks and rooted in water or sand. Bright light to direct sun; water when dry; medium to low humidity. Propagate by "spiders" or division.

SPLIT-LEAF PHILODENDRON (SWISS CHEESE PLANT) monstrosa deliciosa Sturdy, large vines that climb a pole. Leaves dark-green, leathery, cut and perforated. Use well-drained potting soil; low to high humidity; water when dry; low light to bright light. Popular and easily grown; withstands some neglect. Propagate by stem cuttings.

SPATHIPHYLLUM spathiphyllum, several varieties Narrow green foliage with white flowers. Easily grown except under very dry conditions. Bright light to low light; well-drained potting soil; keep evenly moist; medium to high humidity. Propagate by division of rootstocks. A good potted plant just about anywhere.

STRAWBERRY BEGONIA (MOTHER-OF-THOUSANDS or STRAWBERRY-GERANIUM) saxifraga sarmentosa Beautiful little house plant with rounded, slightly hair leaves that are green veined with white and have reddish undersides. They send out runners like a strawberry. Useful in hanging baskets, dish gardens, or simply potted. Bright light to low light; prefers cool room; well-drained potting soil; medium to high humidity; keep slightly moist. Propagate from plantlets at the end of the runners.

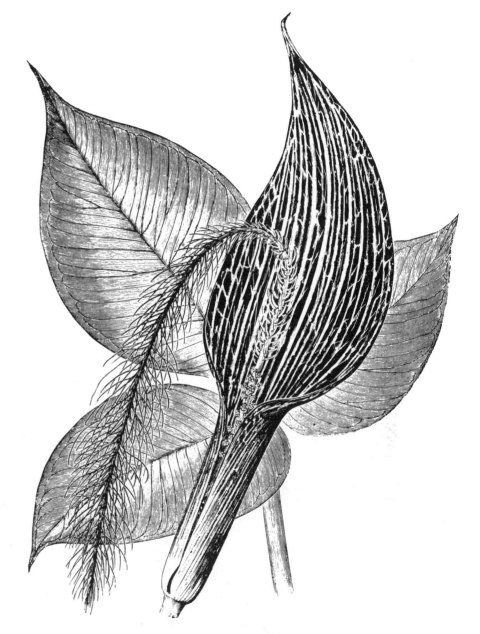

117

TEDDY-BEAR PLANT cyanotis kewensis Trailing leaves and stems covered with brown hairs. Sometimes called wandering jew and a relative of tradescantia. Good in hanging baskets. Well-drained sandy soil; good light to direct sun; water when dry. Easily propagated by cuttings, which should be taken regularly to prevent legginess and replace older plant.

TRADESCANTIA (WANDERING JEW) tradescantia fluminensis Often confused with zebrina and also known as wandering jew. Leaves green or green with yellow or white markings; flowers white; bluish-purple or pink. Very popular for hanging baskets and window boxes. Good light; well-drained potting soil; water when dry to slightly moist; keep pinched back. Cuttings root easily in water or sand and should be taken regularly to replace old plant.

WAX PLANT hoya carnosa Fleshy leaves, all green or variegated with white, growing along a vining stem. Nice on a low overhanging shelf or in hanging baskets. Flowers light pink and fragrant. Direct sun, low to medium humidity; water when dry; well drained potting soil. Propagate by cuttings or layering.

ZEBRA PLANT aphelandra squarrosa louisae Rich green shiny leaves veined in white on an upright stem with a terminal spike of yellow or dark orange flowers. Grown for foliage and flowers. Bright light; well-drained potting soil, slightly moist. Good humidity very important. Lack of humidity and light usual reason for failure. Do not like draughts or great fluctuation of temperature. Propagate by tip cuttings.

ZEBRINA (WANDERING JEW) zebrina pendula Vine, leaves green with purple undersides and purple flowers. The variety quadricolor has leaves striped green, red, and white. One of the most popular houseplants for hanging baskets; often confused with transcantia. Use well-drained potting soil; good light; water when dry to slightly moist. Keep pinched back. Cuttings root easily in water or sand and should be taken regularly to replace older plant.

BULBS, for forcing Several kinds of spring-flowering bulbs are easily forced indoors for winter flowers. Forcing is a process of literally speeding up time and convincing the bulb it has just experienced the winter and the coming of spring. Buy the dormant bulbs in the fall and plant in well-drained potting soil, mix small amount of bone meal (a teaspoon or so per pot) into the soil mixture. Plant leaving the top of the bulb above soil line. Place in an unheated but sheltered spot, somewhere where the temperature won't go above 45 degrees or so and won't constantly dip below freezing. A coldframe is perfect, or use a trench, unheated garage or toolshed, in the city you may have only a fire-escape, you can improvise a cold frame providing it still leaves you easy access to the fire-escape. Cover the pots with at least 6 inches of mulching material, anything will do, peat moss or sand are commonly used. You want the bulbs to be in complete darkness and at fairly constant temperatures. Keep bulbs constantly moist but not wet. Root systems take five to ten weeks to form, then you move pots indoors to warm, sunny room gradually, over the period of a week or so, move pots from indirect light (i.e. the floor, back from the window) to direct sun (i.e. the window sill). And, of course, you have removed the mulch when you brought them indoors. The flowers can last for up to two weeks, depending on variety and the conditions in your home. The cooler, sunnier, and more humid the air the longer the bloom will last. Bulbs that are forced cannot be forced again, you either discard them or plant them in the garden in the spring. If you plan ahead and start bulbs at intervals you can have flowers all winter long. See the bulb list in this book for specific information on particular bulbs.

HYACINTHS

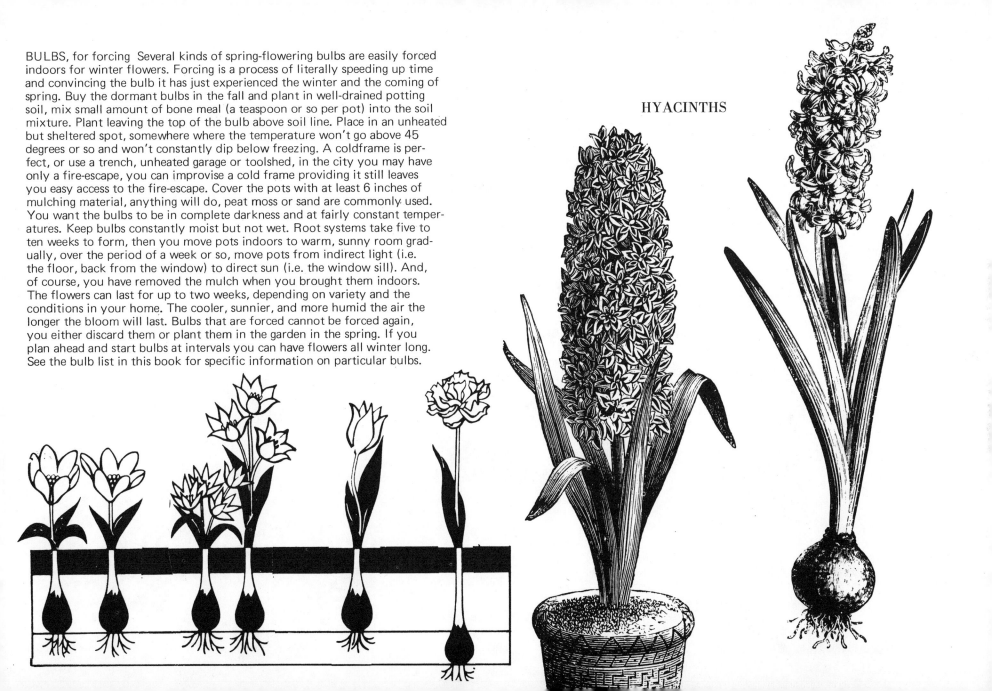

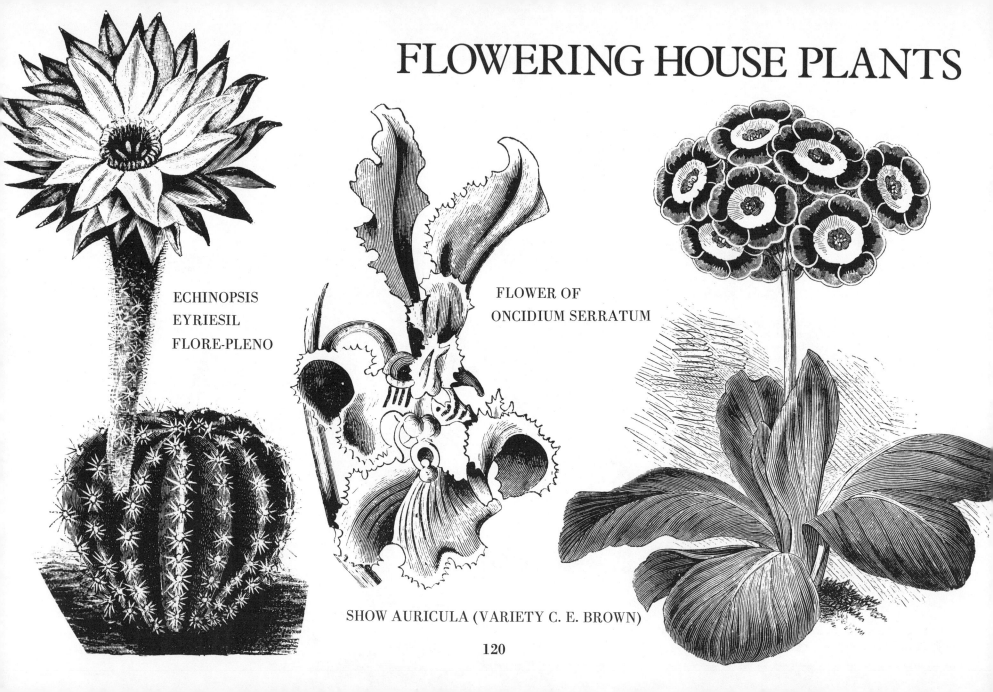

FLOWERING HOUSE PLANTS

ECHINOPSIS
EYRIESIL
FLORE-PLENO

FLOWER OF
ONCIDIUM SERRATUM

SHOW AURICULA (VARIETY C. E. BROWN)

120

ACHIMENES achimenes, several varieties A gesneriad to 3 feet usually trailing with flowers in one of a variety of different colors or in two contrasting colors. Good in hanging baskets, overhanging shelves. Bright light, keep soil evenly moist (especially during flowering) rich but well-drained potting soil. Propagate by leaf or stem cuttings, seed, or division. Medium to high humidity.

AESCHYNANTHUS (Lipstick Plant) aeschynanthus, several varieties (used to be called trichosporum) Another gesneriad, similar in culture to the achimenes except it demands a high humidity. Trailing, green leaves, red flowers, good for hanging baskets. This like all the gesneriads does well with artificial light. Propagate by stem or tip cuttings.

AFRICAN VIOLET saintpaulia, several varieties The most popular of the gesneriads and of all flowering house plants because of its year-round bloom and relative ease of culture. Much hybridized with a great variety of leaf and flower types. Most have hairy green leaves in a rosette formation. The flowers are profuse and arrive in any number of colors or in two shades of the same color or in two or more different colors. The colors range from white to blue to pink, red and purple. Bright light to direct sun, medium to high humidity, rich, well-drained potting soil, keep evenly moist, water with warm water. Propagate by leaf cuttings, division, or seed.

AMARYLLIS hippeastrum vittatum Huge, colorful flowers on thick, rigid scarps to 2½ feet tall, the plant looks like a big jungle lily. It grows from a bulb potted anytime between fall and spring. Pot in well-drained potting soil with half of the bulb exposed, keep moist after growing season and store bulb in pot until the next year.

AZALEA rhododendron Beautiful bush forms covered with flowers that range in a variety of colors. Coolness is a must, best in a room that just receives residual heat from the rest of the house. Mist regularly, keep slightly moist, bright light, well-drained potting soil, feed throughout spring and summer. These are usually Christmas and Easter gift plants, and since they require temperatures between 50 and 60 degrees during the winter, they usually don't last past their initial bloom.

BEGONIA begonia, tuberous rooted Large variety of flowers in different shapes, sizes, and colors, several echoing other types of flowers (e.g. carnation begonia). Most require cool temperatures. Use well-drained potting soil, keep moist, bright light to sun, medium to high humidity. Plant bulbs with concave side up and level with soil, hanging types seem better suited to homes than the more elaborate flowering varieties.

BELLFLOWER (Star of Bethlehem) campanula, several varieties Profuse, star shaped flowers in white or blue on trailing stems. Good for hanging baskets. Well-drained potting soil, keep slightly moist. Direct sun to bright light. Plenty of fresh air. Keep cool, medium to high humidity. Prune in fall and spring, can take temperatures down to 40 degrees in winter. Propagate by spring cuttings.

AZALEAS

BIRD OF PARADISE strelitzia reginae Big, banana-like leaves to 3 feet. Flower bracts are boat shaped, green with red margins, they hold flowers that have orange petals and a blue tongue. Direct sun, cool (not over 70 degrees), well-drained potting soil, slightly moist, medium to high humidity. Propagate by offsets or division of the rhizomes.

BLOOD LILY haemanthus, several varieties Quite small but profuse flowers in white or shades of red, leaves are green. Plant grows from a bulb and can grow to 12" high. Direct sun to bright light, medium to high humidity, well-drained potting soil, keep slightly moist. Water only when dry during resting period from autumn through winter. Repot every few years, propagate by offsets when repotting.

BOUGAINVILLEA (Paper-Flower) bougainvillea, several varieties Long, graceful vines, with colorful flower bracts that are red or purple or multi-colored in a metallic reddish brown with pink and yellow, the flowers themselves are very small and inconspicuous. This is a rampant grower, keep well pruned, some types (e.g. "Temple Fire") are more compact and can be trained into a bushy form. Full sun, well-drained potting soil, medium to high humidity, fresh air, mist regularly. Propagate by seed or cuttings.

BRIDE'S FLOWER (Madagascar jasmine) stephanotis floribunda A vine with dark green leaves, with small waxy, white flowers borne in clusters. The flowers are very fragrant. Well-drained potting soil, keep slightly moist; direct sun, medium to high humidity. Propagate from spring cuttings.

BROWALLIA (Night Shade) browallia, speciosa major Bushy, semi-trailing plant with dark-green leaves and violet-blue flowers. Grows to 16". There are also types with white, light purple or blue flowers. Direct sun to bright light, well-drained potting soil, keep slightly moist, medium to high humidity, mist regularly, keep cool (not over 70 degrees), plenty of fresh air, prune autumn and spring. Propagate by seed or cuttings.

CAMELLIA camellia japonica Evergreen, asiatic shrubs, with shiny green foliage, and large long lasting waxy flowers that may be of a variety of colors ranging from white to keep red, or variegated. They are single, double or semi-double. Coolness (not over 65 degrees), fresh air, and sun are most important to success in growing camellias. Use well-drained potting soil. Mist regularly, medium to high humidity, keep slightly moist, an acid plant food during spring and summer. Prune and disbud. Root cuttings taken in late summer to early fall.

FLOWERING BRANCH OF

CAMELLIA JAPONICA

CLIVIA (Kaffir Lily) clivia miniata Lily-like thick green leaves; a thick flower spike rises from the center of the leaves, flowers yellow to red, borne in clusters on top of the spike. Well-drained potting soil, keep slightly moist, direct sun to bright light, medium humidity. Propagate by division, when growth slows (in the fall) water sparingly until the winter or early spring when growth rate increases again.

CINNERARIA senecio cruentus A popular gift plant, cinnerarias have a profuse bloom of daisy-like flowers that appear in one of a variety of colors. Must have coolness (not over 65 degrees) and lots of fresh air. Use well-drained potting soil, keep slightly moist, direct sun, medium to high humidity, watch for aphids. Propagate by seed.

CHRYSANTHEMUM chrysanthemum Another gift plant, should be kept cool, but not quite as fussy as the cinneraria. Bright light to direct sun, keep slightly moist, medium humidity. After blooms die, cut back severely to an inch or two, put in cool, dark place until spring, watering only when dry. Plant in garden, you can take cuttings from the garden growth for a pot plant that will flower in autumn.

COLUMNEA columnea, several varieties Yet another gesneraid, a vine very good in hanging baskets, tubular red to orange flowers. Greenish-brown or all green, usually hairy leaves. Same culture as African violets. Propagate by tip cuttings or seed.

CORAL PLANT jatropha multifida Flowers are red-coral, foliage narrow, deeply cut, borne in a circular cluster. Blooms year-round. Direct sun, medium to high humidity, fresh air, keep slightly moist, mist regularly, well-drained potting soil, prune as needed. Propagate by seed or cuttings.

CRAPE MYRTLE lagerstroemia indica Small dark-green leaves, flowers in clusters in one of a variety of colors. Prune back each spring. Can be kept as a large tub plant or used as a bonsai specimen. Well-drained potting soil, keep slightly moist, mist regularly, medium to high humidity, fresh air, keep cool (not over 70 degrees). Propagate by spring cuttings.

CROSSANDRA crossandra infundibuli formis Shiny dark-green leaves with orange flowers on a bushy, branched plant to three feet high. Under good conditions flowers can bloom at intervals all year long. Direct sun, medium to high humidity, well-drained potting soil, keep slightly moist, mist regularly, prune as needed. Propagate by seed or tip cuttings.

CUPHEA cuphea hyssopifolia Small green leaves crowded along the stems, much-branched flowers profuse and violet. Good small shrubs or bonsai

subjects. Direct sun, well-drained potting soil, keep slightly moist, medium to high humidity, keep well-pruned, provide fresh air. Propagate from spring cuttings or seed.

CYCLAMEN cyclamen indicum Cyclamen grows from a tuber. You can buy the tuber and start from that but usually you start with a full grown plant, it is a very popular gift plant. There are several different varieties, some with very large flowers or double flowers or fringed petals. Flower colors from white to shades of pink, red, or orange. The leaves are dark green. Both leaves and flower petals are heart-shaped. It is a woodsy-looking plant. Flowers appear one to a stem, there are many stems to a plant. They must be kept cool (not over 70 degrees), in high humidity, with lots of fresh air and in bright light but not direct sun. Use well-drained potting soil, keep evenly moist, except during summer when you water when dry. Repot in the autumn.

CHRYSANTHEMUMS

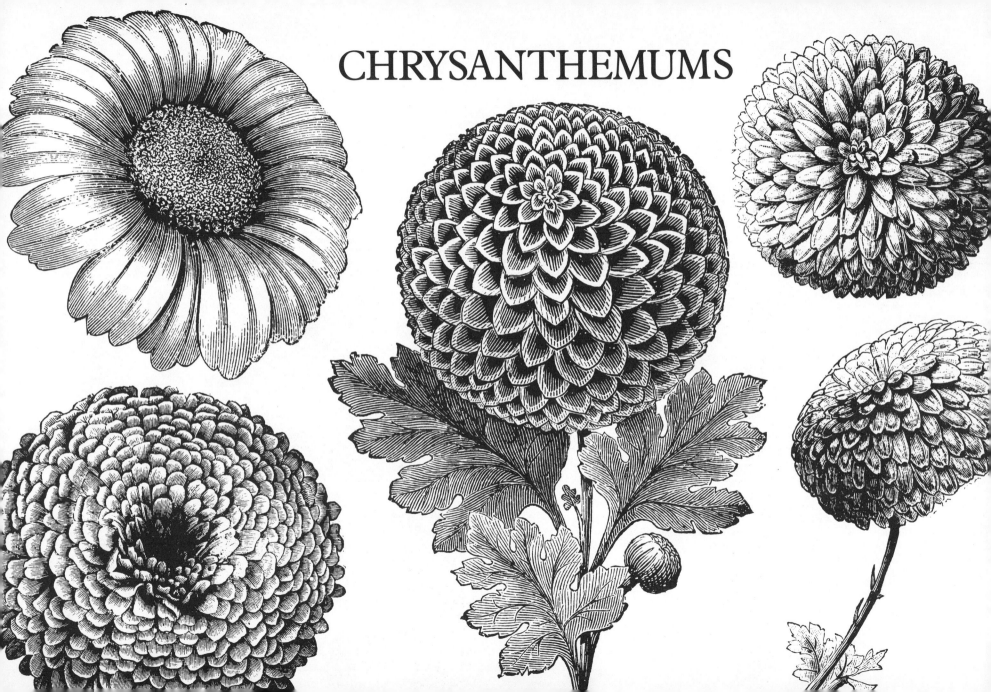

CHRYSANTHEMUMS

GARDENIA gardenia Beautiful, very fragrant white flowers with shiny dark-green foliage. They are not easy to grow but well worth the effort. Most fail in houses from a combination of dry air, low light, and high nighttime temperatures. Use a well-drained acid potting mixture, be sure to use peat moss and not vermiculite. Direct sun, medium to high humidity, keep evenly moist, mist regularly, provide fresh air and temperatures that do not exceed 70 degrees at night nor drop below 60 degrees. Watch for red spider. Feed from spring to fall with an acid fertilizer. Prune in spring and propagate from the cuttings.

GERANIUM pelagorium, in variety A large variety of shapes, sizes, and scents. The most familiar, pelagorium hortorum, has red flowers borne in cluster on top of the spike. Ivy geranium p. pelatum, is trailing and good for hanging baskets. It has small white flowers with a touch of pink. Scented geraniums can smell something like lemon, nutmeg, roses, etc. They are all fairly easy houseplants since they can resist the dry air of the house better than most plants. Full sun, keep cool (not above 65-70 degrees), provide fresh air, low to medium humidity, water when dry, use a well-drained to sandy potting mixture. Use a teaspoon of bone meal per 5" pot. Feed a slow-acting organic fertilizer from spring to fall. Prune back in spring and fall, low to medium humidity. Propagate by seed or spring cuttings.

GLOXINIA sinningia Large, hairy leaves, with huge flowers that are patterned and richly colored. Same culture as the African violet. Gloxinias have the most spectacular flowers of the gesneriads. Grow from bulbs, leaf cuttings, stem cuttings or seed.

HIBISCUS (Rose of China) hibiscus rosa sinensis Usually large red, pink, or dark yellow flowers, that can be single or double. Foliage either shiny green or variegated. A shrub that can bloom at intervals all year round. Prune back severely in spring. Use well-drained potting soil, keep evenly moist, medium to high humidity, fresh air, full sun. Propagate by spring cuttings. Watch for insects.

HYDRANGEA hydrangea macrophylla Small flowers borne in clusters, either white, pink or blue. Several of the pink turn blue and vice versa by upping the acidity in the soil for blue color and lowering for pink. Most are received as Easter gift plants. They must be kept evenly moist, you can soak them in a tub once a day. Bright light to direct sun medium to high humidity, fresh air, prune back after flowering. Repot and set outside for the summer in a shady spot, bring in in fall, put in cool, dark spot, bring into cool, sunny room in January, mist regularly, begin feeding again.

GLOXINIA

HYPOCRYRTA allopectus nummularia A trailing gesneriad, good for hanging baskets, potted on overhanging shelves. Flowers are red. Same culture as African violets. Propagate by seed or tip cuttings.

IMPATIENS (Busy Lizzie) impatiens, several varieties The best low light flowering plant, will bloom at intervals all year long in a cool north window. Flowers in a variety of colors. It is a prime target for any number of insect pests, but is also capable of making remarkable recoveries when well cared for. Keep well pruned and pinched out. Careful pruning will not only help plant's health but will reveal an interesting much-branched form. Use a well-drained potting soil, keep slightly moist, mist regularly, fresh air and cool temperatures (not over 70 degrees). Easily propagated by cuttings, bright light.

JASMINE jasminum, several varieties Fragrant, clusted white or yellow flowers with shiny green foliage. Some are shrubby and some are trailing. Most are large to 6 feet. J. parkeri is small to one foot with small yellow flowers. Direct sun, high humidity, mist regularly, fresh air, use well-drained potting soil, keep evenly most, prune, propgate by cuttings of almost mature wood.

JASMINE, STAR trachelospermum jasminoides Fragrant white or yellow flowers with shiny green foliage, this is a vine with star-shaped flowers. Grow in hanging basket or potted on overhanging shelf. Keep growing tips pinched out. Direct sun, keep a bit cool, medium to high humidity, fresh air, mist regularly. Well-drained potting soil, keep slightly moist. Propagate by cuttings in spring.

JERUSALEM CHERRY solanum pseudo-capsicum Bushy with pointed oval leaves, the fruit is its claim to fame. It is round and red and inedible. These plants are particularly sensitive to natural gas fumes, so don't put it near a stove. Keep in cool (not over 70 degrees) but not drafty, sunny window. Use well-drained potting soil, water when dry to barely moist, medium to high humidity, prune back each spring. Propagate by seed. Watch for insects.

JESSAMINE, NIGHT cestrum nocturnum A shrub to 6 feet high with green foliage and star-shaped heavily-scented white flowers that open in the evening; blooms at intervals all year long. Keep inched back and well pruned. Use well-drained potting-soil, keep slightly moist, mist regularly, medium humidity. Propagate by cuttings in the spring.

MORNING GLORY VINE ipomoea tricolor Really nice growing up a trellis on the window frame. Keep cool (but not drafty), use a sunny window, well-drained potting soil, keep slightly moist, prune back occasionally, mist regularly, medium to high humidity. Try to use hybrid seeds for best results.

LANTANA lantana camara and montevidensis Shrubby or trailing, with clusters of small flowers in a variety of colors, some changing color as they mature. Watch for white fly. Well-drained potting soil, water when dry, medium to high humidity, mist regularly, fresh air, keep cool (not over 70 degrees), prune back in spring and late fall.

NATAL PLUM carissa grandiflora A shrub to 6 or 7 feet high with shiny green leaves, large fragrant white flowers. Well-drained potting soil, slightly moist, mist regularly, direct sun. Propagate by cuttings or seed. C. grandiflora nana compacta, grows to 2 or 3 feet and is a good bonsai subject.

OLEANDER nerium oleander A profusion of colorful flowers, in red, white, rose, pink, peach. Flowers are single or double. Plants bloom when they are young, flowers are more profuse in older plants. These can grow to 8 feet and larger. A good shrub form. Prune after flowering or in fall, the sap in the stem is poisonous as is the fruit. Direct sun, well-drained potting soil, keep slightly moist, medium to high humidity, very cool in winter but frost free and water only when dry. Propagate by seeds or cuttings of tip growth in the spring or summer.

OXALIS (wood-sorrel) oxalis, several varieties Clover-like leaves and small delicate flowers in a variety of colors. Some bloom all year round, others only in specific seasons. They grow from small tubers that are planted in a 6" pot. They are also a good addition to a dish garden. Full sun, well-drained potting soil, keep barely moist until growth begins, then keep slightly moist. Cool (not over 75 degrees), fresh air, medium to high humidity. Keep dry when not in growing season. Flowing types go dormant in summer and summer flowering types go dormant in winter. Keep specially cool (around 50 degrees). Propagate by offsets or division of rhizomes on those with fleshy rhizomes.

PASSION FLOWER passiflora Big flowing vines to 6 feet with flowers in summer or fall. Flowers in two colors, blue and white, blue and pink, or all red or blue. Colors are very deep and rich. It is spectacular in a hanging basket. Direct sun, medium to high humidity, mist regularly, keep growing tips pinched out, and prune as needed, well-drained potting soil, give roots some extra room, keep slightly moist and rest for a few months after blooming by withholding fertilizer, watering when dry, then prune as growth begins anew. Propagate by seed or cuttings.

POMEGRANATE punica granatum nana A dwarf tree form to one foot high. Good potted alone, or in dish gardens, or as a subject for bonsai. Shiny green foliage, red or orange flowers. P. granatum has small edible dark red fruit. Full sun, water when dry, medium humidity, fresh air, and cool (not over 70 degrees). Propagate by seeds or cuttings.

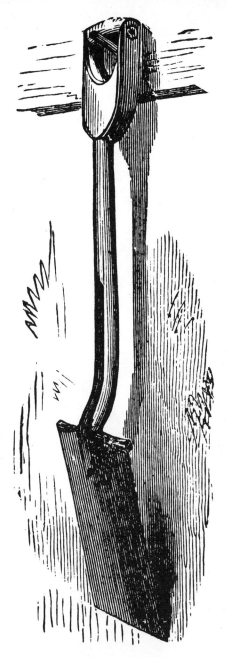
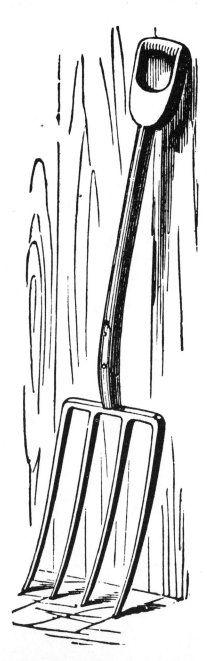

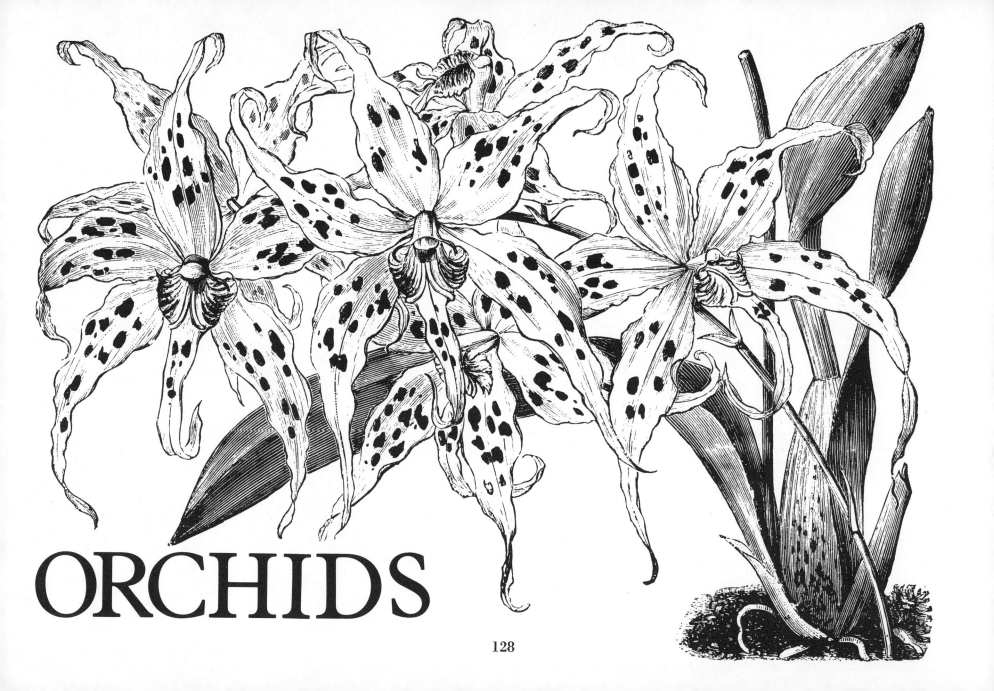

ORCHIDS

ORCHID An enormous family of epiphytic and land-growing plants. As a rule they need high humidity, good light to direct sun but always slightly shaded, never in full south sun. The soil mixture should be very light and full of organic material. Mixtures vary with variety. Use a well-drained potting soil on terrestrial types and osmunda fiber or shedded bark for the epiphytic types. The flowers range a big variety of color, size and shape. The foliage is likewise variable. The following is a short and just glancing look at some of the more common types. If you decide to grow orchids your local orchid society will be a great help. Brassavola—very fragrant pale green flowers, epiphytic. Cattaleya—the orchids used most in corsages, epiphytic. Cypripediums—lady-slipper orchid, also used in corsages, terrestrial. Cymbidium—large and miniature types available, clusters of flowers, epiphytic. Phaleanopsis—beautiful cascades of flowers, one of the best, epiphytic.

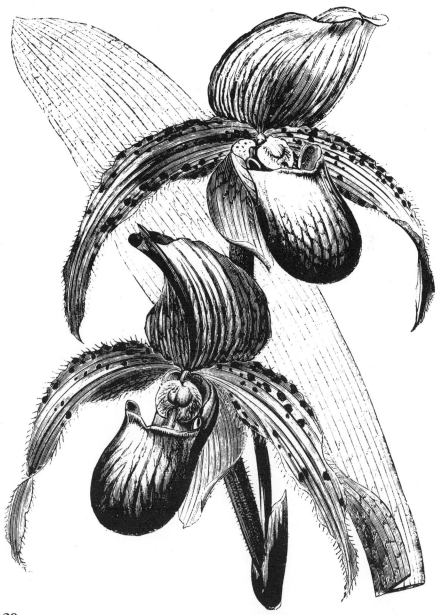

ROSE, MINIATURE rosa, several varieties Miniature roses are small-scale duplicates of hybrid tea roses. They need direct sun, preferably a south window with cool temperatures (not over 70 degrees), medium to high humidity. Use a well aerated and drained soil, kept slighly moist and lightly mulched. Mist regularly. Feed often spring through fall with a very dilute mixture of rose food. Prune back in early fall, and keep in a very cool (not over 50 degrees) room until January or February, then move into warmer, sunnier spot mentioned above. Propagate by seeds or cuttings.

SHRIMP PLANT beloperone guttata Very popular for hanging baskets, especially in California. Trailing stems with red overlapping flower bracts. These look (if you stretch your imagination a bit) like shrimp. The flowers are white, small, and hard to see. Direct sun, fresh air, mist and prune regularly and use well-drained potting soil, water when dry, medium to high humidity. Propagate by cuttings.

STREPTOCARPUS streptocarpus, several varieties A wide variety of shapes and sizes (from plants with one or two leaves to many small leaves borne in a rosette pattern). Flowers in a variety of colors and profusely. A gesneriad culture, same as African violets. Propagate by seed, division, stem or leaf cuttings.

SWEET POTATO VINE ipomoea batatas An old-fashioned house plant that is easy and cheap, culture same as morning glory (which see). Plant only a sweet potato that is beginning to sprout. You can plant it half submerged in water, use charcoal in the water to keep it sweeter longer, or use a light, water retentive medium like vermiculite or perlite, again half-submerging. It probably will not flower, but it is really nice in a hanging basket.

SWEET OLIVE osmanthus fragrans A shrub to two feet high, with shiny green leaves and clusters of small fragrant white flowers that bloom at intervals all year round. Direct sun, cool (not over 70 degrees), fresh air, medium to high humidity, well-drained potting soil, keep slightly moist. Prune in late summer or early fall. Propagate by cuttings.

THUNBERGIA thunbergia alata and grandiflora Vines with large, showy flowers. T. grandiflora has light blue flowers, t. alata has light salmon or white flowers. Good in hanging baskets. Well-drained potting soil, keep slightly moist, spring through fall, water when dry in winter. Medium to high humidity and mist regularly, fresh air, direct sun. Prune in fall and spring. Propagate from seeds or cuttings.

VOODOO LILY (sacred lily of India) hydrosme rivieri A strange looking plant, the spathe is a purplish color and from its center rises a spadix that is white and purple, the flowers themselves are minute. It all grows on a single brown and white spotted thick stem. The spadix has an awful odor, like rotten meat. It is grown because of its oddness. If you put it outside in the summer in a protected spot it forms a green leafy plant, again rising on a single stalk. Inside, keep it in direct sun, medium humidity, use well-drained potting soil, water when dry to slightly moist, provide fresh air for you and the plant. Feed often with a heavily diluted organic fertilizer from spring to fall. Keep soil drier in the winter. Propagate from offsets of the parent tuber.

CACTI AS FLOWERING HOUSE PLANTS

TERRARIUM PLANTS

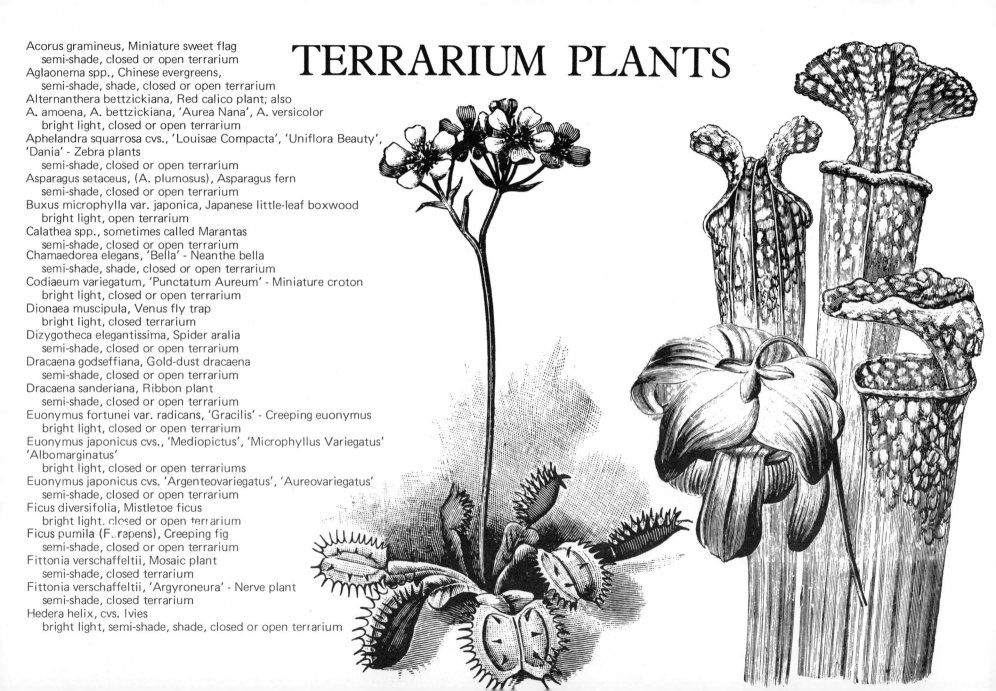

Acorus gramineus, Miniature sweet flag
  semi-shade, closed or open terrarium
Aglaonema spp., Chinese evergreens,
  semi-shade, shade, closed or open terrarium
Alternanthera bettzickiana, Red calico plant; also
A. amoena, A. bettzickiana, 'Aurea Nana', A. versicolor
  bright light, closed or open terrarium
Aphelandra squarrosa cvs., 'Louisae Compacta', 'Uniflora Beauty',
'Dania' - Zebra plants
  semi-shade, closed or open terrarium
Asparagus setaceus, (A. plumosus), Asparagus fern
  semi-shade, closed or open terrarium
Buxus microphylla var. japonica, Japanese little-leaf boxwood
  bright light, open terrarium
Calathea spp., sometimes called Marantas
  semi-shade, closed or open terrarium
Chamaedorea elegans, 'Bella' - Neanthe bella
  semi-shade, shade, closed or open terrarium
Codiaeum variegatum, 'Punctatum Aureum' - Miniature croton
  bright light, closed or open terrarium
Dionaea muscipula, Venus fly trap
  bright light, closed terrarium
Dizygotheca elegantissima, Spider aralia
  semi-shade, closed or open terrarium
Dracaena godseffiana, Gold-dust dracaena
  semi-shade, closed or open terrarium
Dracaena sanderiana, Ribbon plant
  semi-shade, closed or open terrarium
Euonymus fortunei var. radicans, 'Gracilis' - Creeping euonymus
  bright light, closed or open terrarium
Euonymus japonicus cvs., 'Mediopictus', 'Microphyllus Variegatus'
'Albomarginatus'
  bright light, closed or open terrariums
Euonymus japonicus cvs. 'Argenteovariegatus', 'Aureovariegatus'
  semi-shade, closed or open terrarium
Ficus diversifolia, Mistletoe ficus
  bright light, closed or open terrarium
Ficus pumila (F. repens), Creeping fig
  semi-shade, closed or open terrarium
Fittonia verschaffeltii, Mosaic plant
  semi-shade, closed terrarium
Fittonia verschaffeltii, 'Argyroneura' - Nerve plant
  semi-shade, closed terrarium
Hedera helix, cvs. Ivies
  bright light, semi-shade, shade, closed or open terrarium

Helxine soleirolii, Baby's tears
   semi-shade, closed terrarium
Malpighia coccigera, Miniature holly
   bright light, closed or open terrarium
Maranta leuconeura vars. erythroneura, kerchoveana, Prayer plants
   semi-shade, closed or open terrarium
Maranta leuconeura var. massangeana, Rabbit's foot
   semi-shade, closed terrarium
Pellionia daveauana, Trailing watermelon begonia
   semi-shade, closed terrarium
Pellionia pulchra, Satin pellionia
   semi-shade, closed terrarium
Peperomia spp. some common ones are P. caperata, P. incana,
P. obtusifolia 'Variegata', P. velutina
   semi-shade, shade, closed or open terrarium
Pilea cadierei, 'Minima' - Miniature aluminum plant
   semi-shade, closed or open terrarium
Pilea depressa, Miniature peperomia
   semi-shade, closed or open terrarium
Pilea microphylla (P. muscosa - Artillery plant
   semi-shade, closed terrarium
Podocarpus macrophyllus var. maki - Southern yew
   bright light, semi-shade, closed or open terrarium
Selaginella kraussiana (S. denticulata) - Trailing Irish moss
   shade, closed terrarium
Selaginella kraussiana 'Brownii' - Cushion moss
   shade, closed terrarium
   LARGE GROUPS OF PLANTS
Begonias
   semi-shade, closed or open terrarium
Bromeliads, A large group of epiphytic plants, which will grow in
bright, filtered light; good specimens found within the genera
Aechmea, Cryptanthus, Tillandsia
   bright light, semi-shade, closed or open terrarium
Cacti and Succulents
   bright light, open terrarium
Ferns - Most ferns prefer warm humid conditions, but many are
vigorous growers and are best confined in small pots. Good specimens
within the genera Adiantum, Asplenium, Davallia, Nephrolepsis, Pteris.
   semi-shade, shade, closed or open terrarium
Gesneriads, Most popular genera are Episcia (very vigorous),
Saintpaulia (African violets), Sinningia, Streptocarpus
   bright light, closed or open terrarium

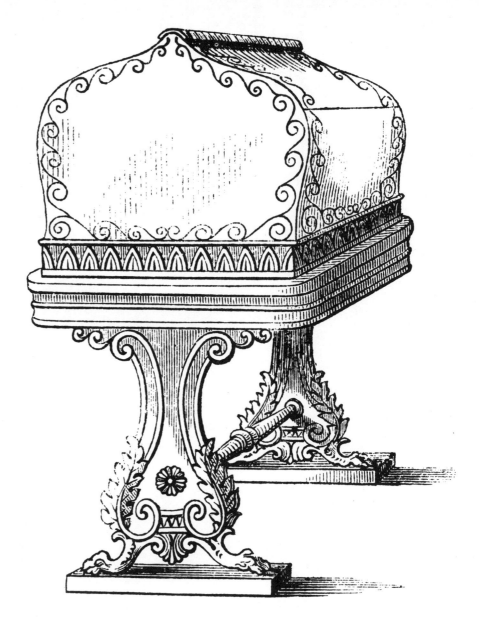

House plants.—American gardeners have taken bonsai concepts and have applied them to house plants. By combining traditional procedures for handling house plants with bonsai concepts of design, growers have created different bonsai styles. The following alphabetical list consists of woody plants (native to the tropics and subtropics of the world) that have been grown as indoor bonsai. These plants can be obtained from either local or specialized nurseries.

BONSAI

ACACIA:
   Acacia baileyana
ARALIA:
   Polyscias balfouriana
   Polyscias fruticosa
   Polyscias guilfoylei
BIRD'S EYE BUSH:
   Ochna multiflora
CAMELLIA:
   Camellia japonica
   Camellia sasanqua
CAPE-JASMINE:
   Gardenia jasminoides radicans
   Gardenia jasminoides
CITRUS:
   Citrus species (calamondin, kumquat, lemon, lime,
      orange, and tangerine)
CHERRY:
   Surinam, Eugenia uniflora
CYPRESS:
   Arizona, Cupressus arizonica
   Monterey, Cupressus macrocarpa
FIG:
   Mistletoe, Ficus diversifolia
HERB:
   Elfin, Cuphea hypssopifolia
HIBISCUS:
   Hibiscus rosa-sinensis Cooperi
HOLLY:
   Miniature, Malpighia coccigera
JACARANDA:
   Jacaranda acutifolia

JADE:
  Crassula species
JASMINE:
  Jasminum parkeri
  Orange, Murraea exotica
  Star, Trachelospermum jasminoides
LAUREL:
  Indian, Ficus retusa
MYRTLE:
  Classic, Myrtus communis
OAK:
  Cork, Quercus suber
  Indoor, Nicodemia diversifolia
  Silk, Grevillea robusta
ORCHID TREE:
  Bauhinia variegata
OLIVE:
  Common, Olea europaea

OXERA PULCHELLA PEPPER TREE:
  California, Schinus molle
PISTACHIO:
  Chinese, Pistacia chinensis
PLUM:
  Natal, Carissa grandiflora
POINCIANA:
  Royal, Delonix regia
POMEGRANATE:
  Dwarf, Punica granatum nana
POPINAC:
  White, Leucaena glauca
POWDERPUFF TREE:
  Calliandra surinamensis
SERISS FOETIDA SHOWER TREE:
  Cassia eremophila
FIR:
  Abies species

ELM:
  American, Ulmus americana
  Chinese, Ulmus parvifolia
  Siberian, Ulmus pumila
FIRETHORN:
  Pyracantha species
GINKGO:
  Ginkgo biloba
GOLDENRAIN:
  Koelreuteria peniculata
GUM:
  Sweet, Liquidambar styraciflua
HAWTHORN:
  English, Crataegus oxyacantha
  Washington, crataegus phaenopyrum
HORNBEAM:
  American, Carpinus caroliniana
  Japanese, Carpinus japonica

HEATHER:
  Calluna vulgaris
HEMLOCK:
  Canadian, Tsuga canadensis and cultivars
IVY:
  Hedera helix and cultivars
JASMINE:
  Winter, Jasminum nudiflorum
JUNIPER:
  Juniperus species and cultivars
LOCUST:
  Black, Robinia pseudoacacia
MAPLE:
  Amur, Acer ginnala
  Hedge, Acer campestre
  Trident, Acer buergerianum
OAK:
  English, Quercus robur

Pin, Quercus palustris
Scarlet, Quercus coccinea
White, Quercus alba
PEACH:
Prunus species
PINE:
Bristlecone, Pinus aristata
Japanese white, Pinus parviflora
Japanese black, Pinus thunbergi
Mugo, Pinus mugo mughus
Swiss stone, Pinus cembra
White, Pinus strobus
PLUM:
Prunus species
POMEGRANATE:
Dwarf, Punica granatum nana

QUINCE:
Japanese, Chaenomeles japonica
SNOWBELL:
Japanese, Styrax japonica
SPRUCE:
Picea species and cultivars
WILLOW:
Weeping, Salix blanda
WISTERIA:
Japanese, Wisteria floribunda
YEW:
Taxus species and cultivars
ZELKOVA:
Graybark elm, Zelkova serrata

BONSAI GUIDE

Trees and shrubs.—The following alphabetical list of plants includes trees and shrubs suitable for traditional bonsai. This is not intended to be a complete list. Specialty nurseries often have a wide selection of dwarf and semi-dwarf varieties of many of these species. Dwarf plants, however, do not always convey the same impression as their full size counterparts because their growth habit is quite different.

APRICOT:
Prunus species
ARBORVITAE:
American, Thuja occidentalis
Oriental, Thuja orientalis
AZALEA:
Hiryu, Rhododendron obtusum
Indica azalea, Rhododendron indicum
Kurume, Rhododendron hybrids
BEECH:
American, Fagus grandifolia
European, Fagus sylvatica

BIRCH:
White, Betula alba
BOX:
Buxus species
BURNINGBUSH:
Euonymus nana
CEDAR:
Atlas, Cedrus atlantica
Deodar, Cedrus deodara
CHERRY:
Prunus species

COTONEASTER:
Cotoneaster species
CRABAPPLE:
Malus species
CRYPTOMERIA
Cryptomeria japonica and cultivars
CYPRESS:
Bald, Taxodium distichum
Dwarf hinoki, Chamaecyparis obtusa
var. compacta

PLANTS ATTRACTIVE TO BIRDS

Autumn-olive—Elaeagnus umbellata Bird use: 15 species Ornamental value: Large, spreading shrub with gray-green foliage, fragrant, small, yellowish blooms; abundant red fruits. Adaptation: Moist to dry soil; sun to light shade; Cardinal variety, winter hardy. In bloom: May-July. In fruit: September-December Height: 8 to 15 ft. Sources: Commercial nurseries, several State nurseries.

Dogwood—Cornus spp. Bird use: 47 species Ornamental value: Variable forms: small to large shrubs, small trees; leaves strongly veined, red to bronze in the fall; whitish to yellowish blooms; fruits bunched or clustered—red, blue, or white. Adaptation: Moist to well-drained soil; sun to shade. Height: shrub, 5 to 8 ft.; tree, 20 to 30 ft. In bloom: April-June. In fruit: August-February Sources: Commercial and State nurseries, wild transplants, cuttings.

Mountain-ash—Sorbus spp. Bird use: 20 species Ornamental value: Medium-size trees with compound leaves; flat, white flower clusters; bright red to orange berry clusters. Adaptation: Moist to dry soil; sun; cool climate. In bloom: May-June. In fruit: August-March Height: 20 to 40 ft. Sources: Commercial nurseries, wild transplants.

Russian-olive—Elaeagnus angustifolia Bird use: 31 species Ornamental value: Large shrub to small tree; introduced species widely established in dry alkaline sites in West; silvery yellow to pink fruits persist nearly all winter; narrow green leaves silvery below. Adaptation: Well-drained to dry soil; sun. In bloom: June-July. In fruit: September-February Height: 15 to 25 ft. Sources: Commercial nurseries and wild transplants.

Firethorn—Pyracantha spp. Bird use: 17 species Ornamental value: Medium to large shrubs; white blooms; showy, orange to red fruits. Adaptation Moist to well-drained soil; sun to partial shade. In bloom: June. In fruit: September-March Height: 6 to 12 ft. Sources: Commerical nurseries.

Sunflower—Helianthus spp. Bird use: 52 species Ornamental value: Tall annual plant; has large yellow flowers. Adaptation: Well-drained soil; sun. In bloom: June-August. Ripe seed: August-September Height: 4 to 8 ft. Sources: Commercial seed stores.

Crabapple—Malus spp. Bird use: 29 species Ornamental value: Small to medium-size trees; showy, white to pink blooms; red, purple, orange, or yellow fruits. Adaptation: Well-drained soil; sun and light shade. In bloom: April-May. In fruit: September-April Height: 10 to 30 ft. Sources: Commercial nurseries, grafting, budding.

Elderberry—Sambucus spp. Bird use: 50 species Ornamental value: Tall shrubs; flat, whitish flower clusters; red to purple-black fruits. Adaptation: Moist to well-drained soil; sun to shade. In bloom: May-July. In fruit: July-October Height: 5 to 8 ft. Sources: Commercial nurseries.

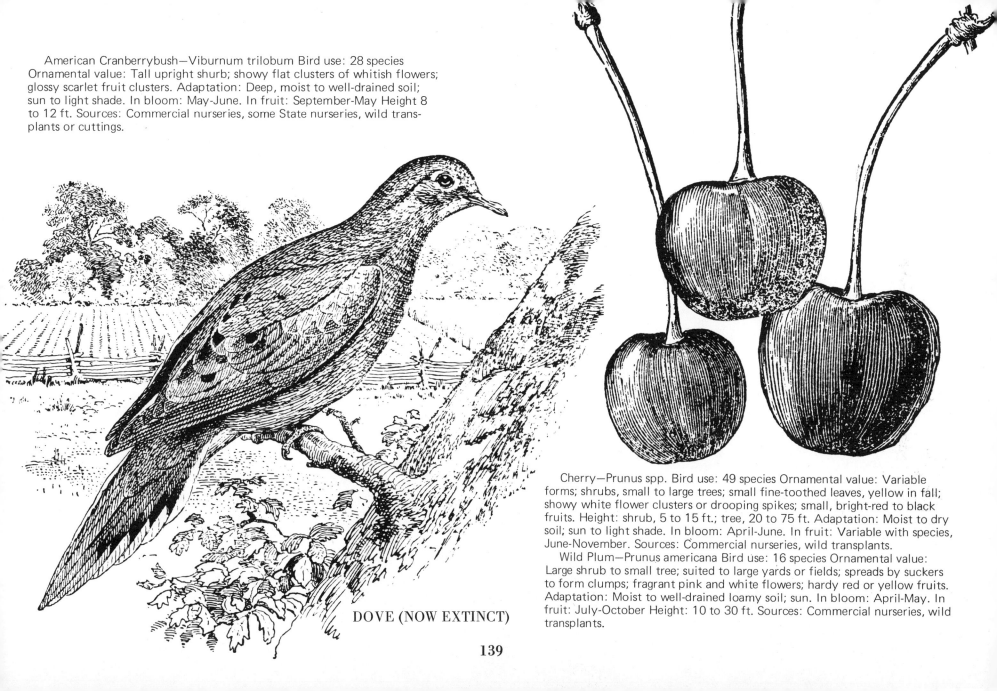

American Cranberrybush—Viburnum trilobum Bird use: 28 species Ornamental value: Tall upright shurb; showy flat clusters of whitish flowers; glossy scarlet fruit clusters. Adaptation: Deep, moist to well-drained soil; sun to light shade. In bloom: May-June. In fruit: September-May Height 8 to 12 ft. Sources: Commercial nurseries, some State nurseries, wild transplants or cuttings.

DOVE (NOW EXTINCT)

Cherry—Prunus spp. Bird use: 49 species Ornamental value: Variable forms; shrubs, small to large trees; small fine-toothed leaves, yellow in fall; showy white flower clusters or drooping spikes; small, bright-red to black fruits. Height: shrub, 5 to 15 ft.; tree, 20 to 75 ft. Adaptation: Moist to dry soil; sun to light shade. In bloom: April-June. In fruit: Variable with species, June-November. Sources: Commercial nurseries, wild transplants.

Wild Plum—Prunus americana Bird use: 16 species Ornamental value: Large shrub to small tree; suited to large yards or fields; spreads by suckers to form clumps; fragrant pink and white flowers; hardy red or yellow fruits. Adaptation: Moist to well-drained loamy soil; sun. In bloom: April-May. In fruit: July-October Height: 10 to 30 ft. Sources: Commercial nurseries, wild transplants.

Cotoneaster—Cotoneaster spp. Bird use: 6 species Ornamental value: Medium size shrub; usually planted as a hedge but also as ground cover; dark-green leaves turning red-gold in fall; small pink or white flowers; showy red, orange, or black fruits. Adaptation: Moist to well-drained soil; sun. In bloom: May-June. In fruit: September-November Height: 2 to 10 ft. Sources: Commercial nurseries.

Tatarian Honeysuckle—Lonicera tatarica Bird use: 18 species Ornamental value: Large shrub; pink to yellow-white blooms; yellow to red fruits. Adaptation: Well-drained to dry soil; sun to light shade. In bloom: May-June. In fruit: July-September Height: 5 to 15 ft. Sources: Commercial nurseries.

Redcedar—Juniperus virginiana Bird use: 25 species Ornamental value: Medium-size coniferous tree (many varieties); dense, green to blue-green needles; small, dusty-blue, berrylike cones. Adaptation: Moist to dry soil; sun to light shade. In bloom: April-May. In fruit: September - May Height 15 to 40 ft. Sources: Commercial nurseries, some State nurseries, and wild transplants.

Bittersweet—Celastrus scandens Bird use: 12 species Ornamental value: Twining vine; pale-green flowers; bright-red berries in yellow or orange husks. Adaptation: Well-drained to dry soil; light shade. In bloom: May-June. In fruit: September-December Height: Climbs to 25 ft. Sources: Commercial nurseries, some State nurseries, cuttings.

Holly—Ilex spp. Bird use: 20 species Ornamental value: Variable forms: upright rounded shrubs, small to medium-size trees; many varieties; dark green foliage, evergreen or deciduous; small whitish blooms, bright-red, black, or yellow fruits (very persistent). Adaptation: Moist to well-drained soil; sun to shade. In bloom: April-June. In fruit: September-May Height: Shrub, 5 to 15 ft.; tree, 30 to 50 ft. Sources: Commercial nurseries, wild transplants, cuttings.

Hawthorn—Crataegus spp. Bird use: 19 species Ornamental value: Small trees; pale-green toothed leaves; abundant, clustered, white flowers; orange to red fruits (very persistent). Adaptation: Deep, moist to dry soil; sun to shade. In bloom: May-June. In fruit: October-March Height: 15 to 30 ft. Sources: Commercial nurseries.

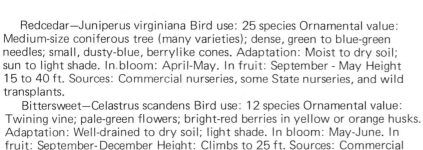

141

SOUTHERN FRUIT TREES

ACEROLA (Malpighia glabra): Florida Sweet, B 17, others Bright red ade drinks and ices of sprightly flavor. Rich in Vitamin C. Zone 10b (10a). Shrub or small tree with glossy dark foliage. CF.

AVOCADO (Persea americana) West Indian and hybrid: Ruehle, Simmonds, Fairchild, others Salads, guacamole spread, sandwiches, puree to add to soup; a rich pie filling, milk shakes. Zone 10b. Medium-sized to large tree. A rich soil is very desirable, and perfect drainage is absolutely essential.

BANANA (Musa spp.): Apple, Cavendish, Orinoco, many others Fresh and in puddings, cakes and custards, and ice cream. Fruit is delicious fried or baked. Patios, large tubs (Cavendish); Zone 10b (10a). Giant herb which gives a tropical "jungle" effect. LDSCP.

BLACK SAPOTE (Diospyros digyna): Seedlings Blend pulp with cream or brandy and spices to substitute for chocolate pudding, mousse or pie filling. Richer in Vitamin C than Citrus. Zone 10b. Handsome medium-sized tree with glossy deep-green leaves and dark-colored bark. LDSCP.

CARAMBOLA (Averrhoa carambola): Golden Star, Robert Newcomb, Mih Tao, Tean Ma, others. Float star-shaped slices on punch or add to salads. Juice is rich in Vitamin C and has a tea-rose scent. Zone 10b (10a). Small or medium tree that bears waxy orange or yellow fruit at least twice a year.

COCONUT (Cocos nucifera): Malay Golden Milk and pulp used in cakes, pies, beverages and puddings. Zone 10B. Malay Golden resists lethal yellows disease. LDSCP.

GRUMICHAMA (Eugenia dombeyi): seedlings Milk and pulp used in cakes, pies, beverages a nd puddings. Eat fresh; similar to northern cherry, black with a single stone. Tub for patios. 10b (10a). Large shrub with glassy leaves and white flowers like pear blossoms. CF. LDSCP.

GUAVA (Psidium guajava): Indian Red, many others Jelly, paste, preserved shells, punch. Rich in Vitamin C. Zone 10. Medium-sized tree with ribbed leaves. CF.

JABOTICABA (Myrciaria cauliflora): Sabara, others, seedlings Used as grapes are: fresh, or for juice, jelly, or wine. Tub for patios. 10b (10a). Large shrub or small tree bearing white flowers and black grape-like fruit on trunk. Grows slowly. CF. LDSCP.

LIMES (Citrus aurantifolia): Key (Mexican), C. latifolia: Tahiti (Bearss) Essential component of many drinks, sherbet, and one of the world's great pies, a gourmet dessert. Zone 10b (10a). Straggly, shrubby trees that need frequent pruning to shape them properly. Thorny.

LONGAN (Dimocarpus longan): Kohala, Shek Kip, Chom Poo, others Eat fresh; peel, pit and can like cherries. Stew for an ice cream topping, quick freeze whole or dry in the traditional way. 10b (10a). Vigorous, excellent shade tree. Bears erratically; in "off" years branches may be girdled to induce fruit. LDSCP.

LYCHEE (Litchi chinensis): Brewster, Mauritius, Sweetcliff, Bengal, others. A superior fruit to eat fresh, canned, frozen, or dried (the traditional method). Fresh fruit resembles a strawberry with a thin, rigid skin and a grapelike flavor. 10b (10a). Umbrella-shaped tree that needs rich acid soil, good drainage and a dependable moisture supply. Brewster and Bengal may crop erratically. LDSCP.

MANGO (Mangifera indica): Florigon, Irwin, Keitt, many others. Popular everywhere. Eat fresh, juiced, and in or on ice cream. Immature fruit an essential ingredient of chutney recipes, makes an excellent pie. 10b (10a). Medium to large tree of graceful habit, it thrives on most soils. Don't plant near air conditioner inlet or bedroom windows because flowers are allergenic. CF (occasional).

PASSIONFRUIT (Passiflora edulis, purple; P. edulis f. flavicarpa, yellow): seedlings of purple and yellow forms Fresh in salads, as a richly aromatic juice in ades and sherbets, or a fine-flavored jelly, also pie and cake fillings. Makes an aromatic wine suggestive of sherry. Zone 10a (purple), 10b (yellow). Vigorous vines that need support and late-winter pruning to remove old wood. Plant more than one yellow seedling for pllination.

PINEAPPLE (Ananas comosus): Abachi, Red Spanish, Cayenne, others Eat fresh, candied, in pies, sherbets and as juice. Fruit ripened on your own plant is superior to shipped. Harvest when it "smells ripe". 10b (10a). Patios, planters. Large leafy perennial, a favorite house plant. Cut-off tops of fruit from stores often root to make healthy plants that may fruit after two years.

SAPODILLA (Manilkara zapota): Prolific, Brown Sugar, others Eat fresh; latex from trunk, chicle, was formerly the chief ingredient of chewing gum. Zone 10b. Medium-sized to large shade tree, resistant to high winds. LDSCP. CF

SEAGRAPE (Coccolobis uvifera): seedlings, selected cuttings. **Large-seeded** fruit makes a mild-flavored jelly. 10b (10a). Highly ornamental tree resists salt. LDSCP.

MODERATELY HARDY FRUITS FOR WARM REGIONS

AVOCADO (Persea americana) Guatemalan and hybrid: Choquette (E), Fuerte (W), Hass (W), Winter Mexican (E), Yon (E)Mexican race: Bacon (E-W), Brogden (E), Duke (E-W), Gainesville (E), Mexicola (E-W), others Fresh in salads, guacamole spread; pureed in soups, as pie filling and in milk shakes. Eaten alone with salt and/or lime juice as a vegetable. Halves of 'Mexicola', unpeeled, make excellent canape containers for shrimp spread and such foods. Guatemalan and hybrid cultivars, Zone 10 (9b); Mexicans, 9b (9a). Attractive spreading or tall trees that prefer rich soil and demand perfect drainage.

CALAMONDIN (Citrus blancoi) Aromatic juice is excellent in drinks. Fruit makes a superb marmalade. Patios, pot culture. Zone 9b (9a). An upright tree which bears colorful mini-oranges. LDSCP. CF.

CARISSA (Carissa grandiflora): Fancy, Alles, Atlas Makes a beautiful jelly resembling red currant jelly; also jam; eat fresh when fully ripe. Zone 9b-10. Patios. Fancy is upright, Alles low and spreading, Atlas moderately upright and nearly thornless. CF. LDSCP. Thorny.

CATTLEY GUAVA (Psidium cattleianum): seedlings of red and yellow-fruited forms. Eat fresh; makes an excellent jelly and a good "butter" or marmalade. Zones 9b-10. Shrub or small tree of outstanding ornamental value with smooth, vari-colored trunk. CF. LDSCP.

FEIJOA (Feijoa sellowiana): Coolidge, Pineapple Gem, others. Eat fresh; juice jells easily because it is high in pectin. Flowers are edible. Zones 8b-10. Attractive shrubs with dark, glaucous foliage. CF. LDSCP.

KUMQUAT (Fortunella japonica): Nagami, Marumi, Meiwa Fresh fruit is unique with sweet peel, tart flesh. Whole spiced preserved kumquats are a gourmet treat, as is kumquat marmalade. Patios, pots. Zones 9-10. Small citrus tree of unsurpassed ornamental value. CF. LDSCP.

LIMEQUAT (Citrus aurantifolia x Fortunella japonica); Eustis, Lakeland Hybrid for same uses as lime: acid juice for drinks; used as condiment and in confectionery. Patios, pots. Zones 9b(a)-10. Hardier than the Key lime which it resembles. LDSCP. Thorny.

LOQUAT (Eriobotrya japonica): Champagne, Thales (Gold Nugget), Wolfe, others Eat fresh; can, preserve; use in pies. Zones 8b-10. Small tree of elegant aspect with ribbed, glaucous green leaves. Fire blight disease can be serious. CF. LDSCP.

MACADAMIA NUT (Macadamia intergrifolia and hybrids): Keauhou, Beaumont, others. Fine quality nut, usually borne in a very hard shell, is roasted and salted or used in confectionery. Zone 9b(9a)-10. Beautiful oak-like tree of moderate size; plant more than one for cross-pollination.

ROSE-APPLE (Syzygium jambos): seedlings Children like the crisp fresh fruit which can be brandied like peaches. Zone 9b-10. Moderately large shade tree with pointed leaves and creamy colored mimosa-like flowers.

SURINAM-CHERRY (Eugenia uniflora) Eat ribbed red or black fruit fresh, drink juice, or use in ices. Zones 9b-10. Compact shrub with glossy green leaves. CF. LDSCP.

TANGELO (Citrus reticulata x C. paradisi) Minneola, others Fresh dessert fruit, easily peeled; juice is comparable to orange juice but brighter colored. Citrus tree, handsome at all seasons. LDSCP.

Cities in Zone 9A: Charleston, Savannah, Jacksonville, Baton Rouge, San Antonio, Corpus Christi and San Bernardino; in Zone 9B: Daytona Beach, Orlando, McAllen, Sacramento; in Zone 10a: Melbourne, Tampa-St. Petersburg, Brownsville, San Diego to Santa Barbara (S. Calif. Coast) San Francisco Bay cities; in Zone 10b: Palm Beach, Ft. Lauderdale, Miami, Naples and Key West. CF: this designates soft fruits prone to infestation by Caribbean fruitfly larvae. LDSCP: indicates trees or shrubs outstandingly attractive and useful for landscape planting.

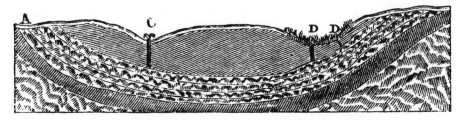

PLANTS FOR SEASIDE GARDENS

VINES

Actinidia arguta	Bower Actinidia
Campsis radicans	Trumpet Vine
Celastrus orbiculatus	Oriental Bittersweet
Celastrus scandens	Amer. Bittersweet
Clematis virginiana	**Virgin's Bower**
Hedera helix	English Ivy
Lonicera sps.	Honeysuckle
Parthenocissus quinquefolia	Virginia Creeper
Parthenocissus tricuspidata	Boston Ivy
Vitis labrusca	Fox Grape
Wisteria sinensis	Chinese Wisteria

GROUND COVERS

Arctostaphylos uva-ursi	Bearberry
Cotoneaster horizontalis	Rock Spray
Hedera helix	English Ivy
Juniperus chinensis sargenti	Sargent's Juniper
Juniperus conferta	Shore Juniper
Juniperus horizontalis	Creeping Juniper
Lonicera japonica halliana	Hall's Honeysuckle
Lonicera sempervirens	Trumpet Honeysuckle
Phlox subulata	Moss Pink
Vinca minor	Periwinkle

DWARF SHRUBS 1' to 3'

Aronia melanocarpa	Black Chokeberry
Calluna vulgaris	Heather
Cotoneaster horizontalis	Rock Spray
Hydrangea arborescens grandiflora	Hills of Snow
Hudsonia tomentosa	Beach Heather
Juniperus communis	Common Juniper
Juniperus conferta	Shore Juniper
Pinus mugo mughus	Mugho Pine
Rhus aromatica	Fragrant Sumac

146

SHRUBS 6' to 10'

Clethra alnifolia	Summersweet
Euonymus alatus	Winged Euonymus
Ilex verticillata	Winter Berry
Juniperus chinensis pfitzeriana	Pfitzer's Juniper
Ligustrum obtusifolium	Border Privet
Lonicera tatarica	Tatarian Honeysuckle
Myrica pensylvanica	Bayberry
Rhododendron catawbiense	Catawba Rhododendron
Rhus sps.	Sumac
Rosa sps. (own root)	Rose
Vaccinium corymbosum	Highbush Blueberry
Viburnum (native sps.)	Viburnum

SMALL SHRUBS 4' to 6'

Aronia arbutifolia	Red Chokeberry
Baccharis halimifolia	Goundsel Bush
Berberis julianae	Wintergreen Barberry
Cotoneaster divaricata	Spreading Cotoneaster
Cytisus scoparius	Scotch Broom
Lonicera fragrantissima	Winter Honeysuckle
Lonicera morrowi	Morrow Honeysuckle
Prunus maritima	Beach Plum
Rhododendron carolinianum	Carolina Rhododendron
Rosa rugosa	Rugosa Rose
Spiraea sps.	Spirea

SHRUBS 10' and over

Alnus sps.	Tamarix sps.	
Amelanchier sps.	Taxus sps.	Rose
Elaeagnus angustifolia	Viburnum (native sps.)	Amer. Elder
Elaegnus umbellata		Tamarisk
Hibiscus syriacus	Alder	Yew
Hippophae rhamnoides	Serviceberry	Viburnum
Ilex crenata	Russian Olive	
Ilex glabra	Autumn Elaeagnus	
Ligustrum amurense	Shrub Althea	
Ligustrum ovalifolium	Sea Buckthorn	
Ligustrum vulgare	Jap. Holly	
Lonicera maacki	Inkberry	
Rhododendron maximum	Amur Privet	
Rosa sps. (own root)	California Privet	
Sambucus canadensis	Common Privet	
	Amur Honeysuckle	
	Rosebay Rhododendron	

Flowers of Portulaca grandiflora.

FLOWERS

Ageratum	Geranium	
Anemones	Gladiolus	Pinks
Candytuft	Globe Amaranth	Portulaca
Chrysanthemums	Iresine	Salvia
Coleus	Iris	Snowdrops
Coreopsis	Larkspur	Straw-flower
Cornflower	Lunaria	Sweet Alyssum
Cosmos	Marigold	Trilliums
Day-lilies	Pansy	Zinnia
Gaillardia	Periwinkle	
	Petunia	
	Phlox	

148

TREES

Acer pseudoplatanus	Sycamore Maple
Aesculus hippocastanum	Horse Chestnut
Ailanthus altissima	Tree-of-Heaven
Fagus sylvatica	European Beech
Fraxinus americana	White Ash
Gleditsia triacanthos	Honey Locust
Ilex opaca	American Holly
Juniperus virginiana	Red Cedar
Malus sps.	Crabapple
Nyssa sylvatica	Tupelo
Picea Polita	Tigertail Spruce
Pinus nigra	Austrian Pine
Pinus sylvestris	Scotch Pine
Pinus thunbergi	Jap. Black Pine
Platanus acerifolia	London Planetree

Populus alba	White Joplar
Prunus serotina	Black Cherry
Quercus alba	White Oak
Robinia pseudoacacia	Black Locust
Salix alba	White Willow
Salix blanda	Weeping Willow
Tilia americana	Amer. Linden
Tilia cordata	Littleleaf Linden
Ulmus pumila	Siberian Elm

Platánus

149

PLANTS FOR

TALL GROWING PLANTS OF NOBLE ASPECT
FOR SPECIMEN PLANTING ABOVE WATER
LEVEL IN WILD GARDENS, ETC.

ACONITUM, in variety
ALTHAEA ROSEA (Hollyhock)
ANCHUSA, and forms
ARUNDO DONAX 'MACROPHYLLUS'
BUPTHALMUM SPECIOSUM
CAMPANULA and cvs.
CENTAUREA MACROCEPHALA
CICERBITA PLUMERI
CIMICFUGA, in variety
CRAMBE CORDIFOLIA
CYNARIA, in variety
ECHINOPS, in variety
EREMURUS, in variety
EUPATORIUM, in variety
FOENICULUM VULGARE
GUNNERA MANICATA
HELIANTHUS, in variety
HERACLEUM MANTEGAZZIANUM
INULA HELENIUM
KNIPHOFIA, in variety
MISCANTHUS SACCHARIFLORUS
OSMUNDA REGALIS
REYNOUTRIA, in variety
RHEUM PALMATUM and cvs.
RUDBECKIA, in variety
THALICTRUM, in variety
VERBASCUM, in variety
    And others

SPECIAL PLACES

PLANTS FOR GROUND COVER BETWEEN
SHRUBS

ACAENA, in variety
AJUGA, in variety
ALCHEMILLA MOLLIS
ASARUM CAUDATUM
BERGENIA, in variety
CAMPANULA POSCHARSKYANA
CERASTIUM TOMENTOSUM
CERATOSTIGMA PLUMBAGINOIDES
CONVALLARIA MAJALIS
CYCLAMEN, in variety
DRYAS OCTOPETALA
EPIMEDIUM, in variety
EUONYMUS FORTUNEI 'KEWENSIS'
EUPHORBIA CYPARISSIAS
FERNS, in variety
GALAX APHYLLA
GERANIUM ENDRESSII, and vars.
HELIANTHEMUM, in variety
HELXINE SOLEIROLII
HOSTA, in variety
HOUTTUYNIA CORDATA
LAMIASTRUM GALEOBDOION
   'VARIEGATUM'
LAMIUM MACULATUM, and cvs.
LUZULA SYLVATICA
OMPHALODES VERNA
PACHYSANDRA, in variety
PRIMULA (Polyanthus)
PULMONARIA, in variety
SPIRAEA PECTINATA
SYMPHYTUM GRANDIFLORUM
TIARELLA CORDIFOLIA
VINCA, in variety

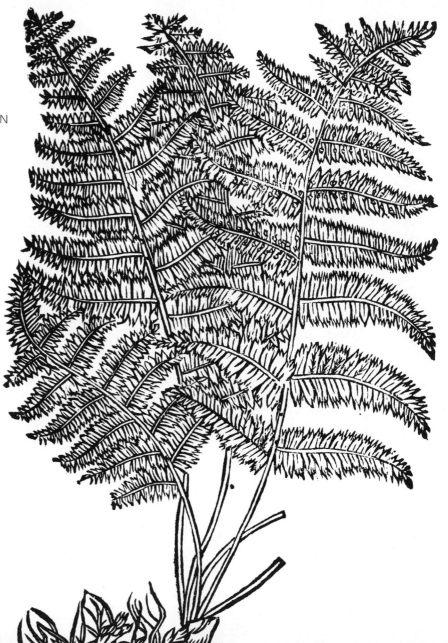

PLANTS FOR SPACES IN PAVED WALKS, STEPS, ETC.

ACAENA, in variety
ACANTHOLIUMUM GLUMACEUM
ACHILLEA, dwarf varieties
ARENARIA, in variety
ARMERIA, in variety
ASPERULA, in variety
AUBRIETA, in variety
BOLAX GLEBARIA
CAMPANULA, dwarf species
CORYDALIS LUTEA OCHROLEUCA
COTULA SQUALIDA
DIANTHUS, in variety
DRYAS, in variety

PLANTS FOR RETAINING WALLS

ACANTHOLIMUM GLUMACEUM
ACHILLEA, dwarf species
AETHIONEMA, in variety
ALYSSUM, in variety
ANDROSACE, in variety
ARABIS, in variety
ARENARIA, in variety
ARMERIA, in variety
ARTEMISIA, dwarf varieties
ASARINA PROCUMBENS
ASPERULA, in variety
AUBRIETA, in variety
CAMPANULA, dwarf species
CARLINA, in variety
CENTRANTHUS RUBER
CORYDALIS LUTEA OCHROLEUCA
CYMBALARIA, in variety
DIANTHUS, in variety
DRYAS, in variety
ERIGERON MUCRONATUS
ERINUS ALPINUS, and cvs.
FERNS, dwarf species
GYPSOPHYLLA, in variety
HABERLEA, in variety
HELIANTHEMUM, in variety

ERIGERON MUCRONATUS
ERINUS ALPINUS, and cvs.
GLOBULARIA, in variety
GYPSOPHILA REPENS, and cvs.
HYPERICUM, dwarf varieties
LEONTOPODIUM ALPINUM
SAXIFRAGA, in variety
SEDUM, in variety
SEMPERVIVUM, in variety
SILENE, in variety
SISYRINCHIUM, dwarf species
THYMUS, in variety
TUNICA SAXIFRAGE, and cvs.
VERONICA, dwarf species
        And others

HELICHRYSUM BELLIDIOIDES
HIPPOCREPIS COMOSA
HYPERICUM, dwarf species
IBERIS, in variety
LEWISIA HYBRIDS
LINARIA PURPUREA, and cvs.
LINUM, in variety
MINUARTIA CAESPITOSA, and cvs.
ONOSMA, in variety
OTHONOPSIS CHEIRIFOLIA
PENSTEMON, in variety
PHLOX, dwarf species
POLYGONUM AFFINE VACCIINIFOLIUM
POTENTILLA, dwarf species
RAMONDA MYCONI
SAPONARIA OCYMOIDES
SAXIFRAGA, encrusted species
SEDUM, in variety
SEMPERVIVUM, in variety
SILENE, in variety
THYMUS, in variety
TUNICA SAXIFRAGA, and cvs.
VERONICA, dwarf species
VINCA, in variety
ZAUSCHNERIA, in variety
        And others

PENTSTEMON

151

PLANTS FOR SHADY OR SEMI-SHADY BORDERS

ACANTHUS, in variety
ACONITUM, in variety
ANEMONE, in variety
ANTHERICUM LILIAGO
AQUILEGIA, in variety
ASTILBE, in variety
BERGENIA, in variety
BRUNNERA MACROPHYLLA
CAMPANULA, in variety
CIMICIFUGA, in variety
DICENTRA, in variety
DIGITALIS, in variety
DORONICUM, in variety
EPIMEDIUM, in variety
FERNS, in variety
GERANIUMS, in variety

GILLENIA TRIFOLIATA
HELLEBORUS, in variety
HEMEROCALLIS, in variety
IRIS FOETIDISSIMA
KIRENGESHOMA PALMATA
LIATRIS, in variety
LIGULARIA, in variety
LILIUMS, in variety
LYSIMACHIA, in variety
LYTHRUM, in variety
MECONOPSIS, in variety
Mertensia, in variety
MONARDA, in variety
MYOSOTIS, in variety

OENOTHERA, in variety
PAEONIA, in variety
PLATYCODON, in variety
POLYGONUM, in variety
PRIMULA, in variety
PULMONARIA, in variety
RODGERSIA, in variety

SANGUISORBA, in variety
SENECIO, in variety
SOLIDAGO, in variety
THALICTRUM, in variety
TRADESCANTIA, in variety
TROLLIUS, in variety
And many others

**PRIMULA SINENSIS
FLORE-PLENO**

152

PLANTS FOR MOIST GROUND

ACONITUM, in variety
ARUNCUS DIOICUS
ASTILBE, in variety
ASTRANTIA, in variety
CIMICIFUGA, in variety
FERNS, in variety
FILIPENDULA, in variety
GENTIANA ASCLEPIADEA LUTEA
GRASSES, in variety
GUNNERA MANICATA
HEMEROCALLIS, in variety
IRIS KAEMPFERI LAEVIGATA
   SIBIRICA, and cvs.

PETASITES JAPONICUS GIGANTEUS
PODOPHYLLUM EMODI
POLYGONUM BISTORTA 'SUPERBUM'
PRIMULA, in variety
RANUNCULUS ACONITIFOLIUS, and cvs.
RHEUM PALMATUM, and cvs.
RODGERSIA, in variety
SANGUISORBA CANADENSIS OBTUSA
SENECIO, in variety
TRADESCANTIA, in variety
TROLLIUS, in variety
    And others

LIGULARIA, in variety
LOBELIA CARDINALIS, and hybrids
LYSICHITON, in variety
LYSIMACHIA, in variety
LYTHRUM, in variety
MONARDA, in variety
PELTIPHYLLUM PELTATUM

THE ROCK GARDEN

ACAENA, in variety
ANEMONE, in variety
ARENARIA BALEARICA
BERGENIA, dwarf species
CAMPANULA, dwarf species
CHRYSOGONUM VIRGINIANUM
CORNUS CANADENSIS
CORYDALIS LUTEA OCHROLEUCA
CYANANTHUS LOBATUS
CYCLAMEN, in variety
DODECATHEON, in variety
EPIMEDIUM, in variety
GALAX APHYLLA
GALEOBDOLON LUTEUM 'VARIEGATUM'
GENTIANA, in variety
HABERLEA FERDINANDI-COBURGI
    RHODOPENSIS
HEPATICA, in variety
IRIS, dwarf species
LAMIASTRUM GALEOBDOLON 'VARIEGATUM'
LITHOSPERMUM, in variety
LYSIMACHIA, dwarf species
MAZUS REPTANS
MYOSOTIS, in variety
OURISEA COCCINEA
POLYGONUM AFFINE, and forms
PRIMULA, in variety
RAMONDA, in variety
ROSCOEA, in variety
ROSULARIA PALLIDA
SANGUINARIA CANADENSIS
SAXIFRAGA, mossy, etc.
SHORTIA UNIFLORA, and forms
SOLDANELLA, in variety
TIARELLA, in variety
VIOLA, in variety
WALDSTEINIA TERNATA
    And many others

PLANTS OF DISTINCT APPEARANCE OR OF ARCHITECTURAL VALUE

ACANTHUS MOLLIS LATIFOLIUS
  SPINOSUS
AGAPANTHUS HEADBOURNE HYBRIDS
ARUNDO DONAX 'MACROPHYLLA'
BERGENIA, in variety
CAREX PENDULA
CARLINA, in variety
CICHORIUM INTYBUS
CIMICIFUGA, in variety
CORTADERIA, in variety
CRAMBE CORDIFOLIA
CYNARA CARDUNCULUS
  SCOLYMUS 'GLAUCA'
DIERAMA PULCHERRIMUM
DRACUNCULUS VULGARIS
EREMURUS, in variety
ERYNGIUM SERRA BROMELIIFOLIUM
EUPHORBIA CHARACIAS LATHYRUS
  WULFENII
GUNNERA MANICATA
HERACLEUM MANTEGAZZIANUM
HOSTA, in variety
KIRENGESHOMA PALMATA
KNIPHOFIA, in variety
LIGULARIA, in variety
MACLEAYA, in variety
MISCANTHUS, in variety
MORINA LONGIFOLIA
ONOPORDUM ACANTHIUM
OSMUDA REGALIS
REYNOUTRIA, in variety
RHEUM PALMATUM, and cvs.
RODGERSIA, in variety
STIPA GIGANTEA

PLANTS WITH GREY, SILVER OR GLAUCOUS FOLIAGE

ACAENA BUCHANANII
ACHILLEA, in variety
ALYSSUM MONTANUM
ANAPHALIS, in variety
ANTHEMIS CUPANIANA
ARTEMISIA, in variety
LAVANDULA, in variety
LAVATERIA OLBIA 'ROSEA'
LEONTOPODIUM ALPINUM
LYCHNIS CORONARIA
ARUNDO DONAX 'MACROPHYLLA'
BALLOTA PSEUDODICTAMNUS
CENTAUREA SIMPLISSICAULIS
CHRYSANTHEMUM ARGENTEUM
    HARADJANII PRAETERITUM
CONVOLVULUS CNEORUM
    TENUISSIMUM
CYNARIA, in variety
DIANTHUS, in variety
ELYMUS ARENARIUS
ERYNGIUM BOURGATII

EUPHORBIA, in variety
HELIANTHEMUM, in variety
HELICHRYSUM, in variety
HIERACEUM, in variety
HOSTA SIEBOLDIANA
KNIPHOFIA CAULESCENS NORTHIAE
MACLEAYA CORDATA
NEPETA X FAASENII
ONOPORDON ACANTHIUM
ONOSMA ALBOROSEUM
OTHONNOPSIS CHEIRIFOLIA
PHLOMIS VISCOSA
ROMNEYA COULTERI
RUTA GRAVEOLENS
SALVIA ARGENTEA
SANTOLINA, in variety
STACHYS LANATA LAVANDULIFOLIA
THALICTRUM FLAVUM GLAUCUM
THYMUS DRUCEI PSEUDOLANUGINOSUS
VERONICA, in variety
ZAUSCHNERIA, in variety

PLANTS FOR FLORAL ARRANGEMENT

ACANTHUS MOLLIS LATIFOLIUS
   SPINOSUS
ACHILLEA, in variety
AGAPANTHUS, in variety
ALCHEMILLA MOLLIS
ASTRANTIA, in variety
CAREX PENDULA
CARLINA, in variety
CORTADERIA, in variety
DIERAMA PULCHERRIMUM
ECHINOPS, in variety
EPIMEDIUM, in variety
EREMURUS, in variety
ERYNGIUM, in variety
EUPHORBIA CHARACIAS
   WULFENII

FERNS, in variety
GRASSES, in variety
HOSTA, in variety
KNIPHOFIA, in variety
LIASTRIS 'KOBOLD' SPICATA
LIBERTIA, in variety
LINARIA PURPUREA
   'CANON J. WENT'
LUZULA NIVEA
LYSIMACHIA CLETHROIDES EPHEMERUM
MACLEAYA, in variety
MISCANTHUS, in variety
MORINA LONGIFOLIA
PELTIPHYLLUM PELTATUM
PHYGELIUS, in variety
PHYSALIS FRANCHETII
POLYGONATUM X HYBRIDUM
POLYGONUM AMPLEXICAULE, and forms
SANGUISORBA, in variety
SCHIZOSTYLIS COCCINEA, and forms
SILPHIUM PERFOLIATUM
SISYRINCHIUM STRIATUM
STACHYS LANATA
STIPA GIGANTEA
THALICTRUM, in variety
VERBENA BONARIENSIS

ACANTHUS

157

AIR

How Much Clean Air Is There?

Air is our most vital resource, and its pollution is our most serious environmental problem. Up-trends are being recorded for all major sources of air pollution. Production and consumption of goods and services increase steadily. Streets and highways are jammed with growing numbers of automobiles and trucks. Power companies burn larger quantities of fossil fuels to meet the need for more electricity. New technology adds complex dimensions to the air pollution problem.

Urban and suburban population is already several times greater than the farm population. Soon, the majority of the world's people will live in an urban environment. In 1976, three-fourths of America's 235 million citizens will be compacted into an area which equals about 10 percent of our total land. And while the users of air burgeon in number, the amount of land available will remain constant. Elimination of polluted air is the only answer. As former President Johnson put it, "Either we stop poisoning our air—or we become a nation in gas masks, groping our way through dying cities and a wilderness of ghost towns."

Plants Are Air Pollution Detectives

"Ordinary" air in most large cities is filled with tons of pollutants: Carbon monoxide from gasoline, diesel, and jet engines; sulfur oxides from factories apartment houses, and power plants; nitrogen oxides and hydrocarbons from the combustion of gasoline and other fossil fuels; and a broad variety of other contaminants.

Plants are taking on the job of air pollution detectives in our smog-ridden communities—much as canaries once were used to detect methane gas in coal mines. Air pollution injury to plants generally becomes evident before visible effects can be noted on animals or materials such as paint, cloth, or metal. Even weeds get into the act as pollution detectors—ragweed and wild blackberry, for example. But plants and field crops do most of the "detective work."

Nature's Air Fresheners

Trees, shrubs and other vegetation supply the oxygen that means requires to live. Enormous amounts of oxygen are released from plants to freshen the air. The oxygen is most abundant relatively close to the earth's surface, thinning out in the upper reaches of the atmosphere. By breathing in carbon dioxide and other combustible gasses and releasing it in the form of oxygen, plants sweeten the air.

"Greenbelts" Fight Smog

Belts of greenery, not just smog control devices on cars, are the solution to smog build-up along the nation's highways. While smog control devices are needed, they can't overcome the smog problem alone. "Greenbelts"—plantings of trees and shrubs a half-mile thick—have been found to be effective smog fighters. Research conducted by the University of California showed that people who live near freeways breathe air containing less than 1,000 parts of fresh air to one part of auto exhaust. For a healthful environment, the proportion should be 2,000 to one. Unpolluted fresh air from forested areas dilutes smog build-up. The green vegetation removes pollutants and restores oxygen to the atmosphere.

Oxygen Generators

Man can live without food or water for quite a while, but not for more than a few minutes without oxygen. During the course of the 23,000 times we each inhale and exhale in the course of a day, we take in 35 pounds of oxygen. Green plants on land, and vegetation in the sea supply man with all of his oxygen—and in the process (called photosynthesis) absorb huge quantities of carbon dioxide from the atmosphere. Scientists have detected a tremendous increase in the size of the "blanket" of carbon dioxide which surrounds the earth. Since it has the tendency of trapping heat, the carbon dioxide layer could raise surface temperature of the earth to a disastrous level, scientists believe. A rise in earth's surface temperature could melt polar ice caps, inundate shorelines and flood coastal cities under many feet of water. Extensive plantings of trees and other green plants help break the heat barrier because of their tremendous capacity for consuming carbon dioxide in photosynthesis. Plantings of trees and shrubs, spread across the nation along arterial highways, make for safe and scenic driving and for fresh, clean air as well.

Plants Are Dust Traps

Twelve million tons of particulate matter—dust, grit, cinders—are released into the atmosphere of the U. S. every year. Motor vehicles contribute 1 million tons; industry 6 million tons; power plants 3 million tons; space heating 1 million tons; and solid waste disposal 1 million tons. Trees, shrubs, vines and flowers act as natural traps for this airborne matter. The hairy leaf surfaces cloutch falling particles and keep a steady rain of dust and dirt from saturating the air with solid pollutant. Trees in Los Angeles are such effective dust catchers they must be washed periodically in a detergent solution to relieve them of their unsightly burden. In another large city, the dust count on the sheltered side of a planted area was 75% lower than a similar count on the windward side.

SOIL

We're Undercutting The Foundation Of All Living Things.

Soil erosion takes an enormous toll. About 180,000,000 acres of crop land lose precious top soil through action of wind or water every year—a $1 billion loss. Through a destructive combination of misuse and pollution, an important balance of nature has been seriously disturbed. Loss of the productive top layer of earth, which sustains both man and nature, occurs because of the lack of proper ground cover. Trees and the top soil they form are vitally important natural resources which must be protected, whatever the cost.

Shrubs And Vines Stop Erosion

On any steeply sloping land, the planting of shrubs and vines prevents erosion and washing away of the top soil. Vegetation alone will not hold steep banks in place during a heavy fall of rain. But foliage plantings break up the raindrops as they fall to earth, softening their impact while holding top soil in place with deep-running roots.

Efficient plantings along roadways help greatly in halting the drift of soils and the dust storms which loose dirt can cause. A 40-mile per hour wind has about four times as much power to pick up soil as a 20-mile per hour wind. When its velocity is reduced by half, the dust-carrying capacity of a 40-mile wind is reduced 75 percent. Trees and shrubs planted to utilize this simple relationship effectively help prevent a common form of soil erosion.

Streambank erosion is a major problem along many miles of the nation's rivers and streams. About 300,000 miles of streambanks in the United States are subject to erosion which produces 500 million tons of sediment annually. Removal of sediment from stream channels, harbors, and reservoirs costs approximately $250 million a year. About $11 million worth of land adjacent to stream channels is lost through erosion every year. By planting vegetation and using mechanical means, it is estimated that streambank erosion can be reduced 75 percent.

WATER

It's Time For A Showdown.

The water quality crisis in America has been building for decades. It is now full-blown in many localities throughout the country. Many lakes, both great and small, are poison-filled. Lake Erie, so badly contaminated has an oxygen content approaching zero. Rivers have been turned into open sewers for municipal , industrial, and agricultural wastes. Beaches have been closed and fishing prohibited. Many underground water resources are in jeopardy, and finding a year-round supply of clean water is a major problem for many municipalities. As the pollution problem grows, so does population. The result: Steadily increasing demand for clean water and a critically short supply, overall. Generation after generation, pollution has choken off the supply of clean, usable water from lakes, streams, bays, and estuaries. The trend can be reversed, but it will require the combined effort of the nation's populace to return the water-quality level to its former pure and plentiful condition.

Streamflow

At the time each year when cities most need it, water is often in desperately short supply. In late summer when demands for electric power are greatest, recreational use is at peak level, and individual consumption reflects the mass effort to slake a burning thirst, streamflow is often weakest. Impoundment of more water is one of the major solutions to water-shorage problems. Since most of the water comes from forest land, trees play an important role in helping to increase water supply. Species selected for their low rate of transpiration make more water available for runoff.

Purification

Work is being done to find plants tolerant to acid conditions in the soil— as in the vicinity of strip mining operations, for example. Soil acidity in such areas increased to a point which plants find almost intolerable. When vegetation is found which ties down the soil, streams flowing from the strip mines will be of better quality than they are now; and the barren waste of the mined-out land will be relieved by the presence of green and growing plant life.

Cleveland is now experimenting with irrigation of coal strip-mine spoilbanks with effluent and sludge containing 4 to 5 percent solids. Water, percolating through the spoilbanks, is cleared of disease organisms and reappears as a safe addition to streamflow.

Pennsylvania State University has completed five years of successful operation of a system of spray irrigation for disposal of sewage treatment plant effluents on both cropland and woodland. Detergents not removed by ordinary sewage treatment are broken down for their phosphate content by the soil organisms. The phosphate is almost entirely removed—and much of the nitrate, too—as the effluent filters down through the top 8 inches of soil.

Engineers are testing a new way to keep lagoon runoff from polluting water supplies. A series of basins have been constructed downhill from a manure lagoon on a Maryland dairy farm. The basins are planted to grass. The grass grows hydroponically in the basins, nourished by the nutrients in the runoff. In addition, the grass strains out suspended solid wastes from the runoff water. The system of covered basins, therefore, forms a mechanical and chemical filter for purifying runoff water before it reaches a stream or lake.

Pulp and papermill companies in several states are disposing of their waste effluents by spray irrigation on woodland and pasture to avoid stream pollution.

For 30 years, a vegetable-processing plant in New Jersey has used spray irrigation for disposal of waste water and has put about 400 inches a year on the forest acreage set aside to receive the spray. Organic materials are taken up by the luxuriant growth on the treated area. Ground water is amply and safely recharged. Similar disposal operations are being carried on successfully by other vegetable-processing factories in Ohio and Michigan.

Water re-use is a coming imperative in our society. Finding ways to re-cycle all of our wastes will remove much of the pressure from sources of water supply. Toward that end, plant material plays a role of increasing importance in view of conclusive evidence that plants modify chemical substances in their presence.

NOISE

Intensity Makes The Difference.

Modern man lives in an environment polluted by excessive noise. Health and well-being of urban dwellers is threatened constantly by the cacophony generated by a bustling, mobile society. Transportation, construction, increasing population density, industry, more use of mechanical equipment by the homeowner—all of these contribute to the steadiy rising din. Tempers fray, sleep eludes the weary, concentration and relaxation become harder to achieve. Over the years, noise levels have increased to the point where they are producing both psychological and physiological problems. Hearing loss results from exposure to excessive noise in a number of industries. An estimated seven million industrial workers are exposed to noise levels on the job that could damage their hearing. Plant material can be used to deflect, absorb, break up, and muffle many of the sounds which make community living miserable.

Trees And Shrubs Reduce Traffic Noise.

Highway planners are increasingly conscious of the need for heavy plantings to provide a sound barrier for adjacent property owners. Plant parts break up sound waves, change their direction, and reduce their intensity. Various types of buffer plantings are used: Hedges, trees; shrubs; vines; and combinations of structural barriers and buffer plantings. The noise level above wide expanses of concrete can be reduced as much as threefold if the concrete surface is interspersed with plantings of trees, shrubs and grass. Planting not only decreases noise, it also screens moving vehicles from sight, giving a sense of privacy which makes traffic sounds less objectionable. Heavy street taffic registers a noise level of 70 decibels. Proper landscaping can reduce the noise about 60 percent. Through judicious use of plant material, the sounds of a heavily-traveled highway can be reduced to the level of a suburban street in the quiet of evening.

Habitat Of "Megalopolis Man"

Destruction of natural beauty is a disastrous by-product of material growth and progress. Modern cities are all too often asphalt jungles, cheerless canyons of concrete which aggravate the tensions of urban life and depress the mind of the city dweller.

It is clear that city life produces psychological damage—sometimes irreparable. In fact, one aspect of environmental pollution must be recognized as purely mental. Man, who appears to be genetically programmed to natural surroundings—fresh, clean air, and a green landscape—is plainly out of place in the concrete and asphalt jungle which characterizes the modern metropolis. Filthy air and cold, stark, angular outlines devoid of greenery contrast strikingly with the idealized landscape man contemplates deep within his subconsciousness. The resultant "mental pollution" (depression, tension, spiritual barrenness) acts on man to stir a sublimated urge as old as human history. Millions of passing years have failed to quench man's longing for the type of surroundings in which he lived at the dawn of human history. According to Iltis, Loucks and Lawrence, man is by nature a nomadic creature, a hunter, who is best adapted to small family groups and to whom congested masses of humanity are anathema.

Plants Aid In Urban Renewal

Steady progress is being made toward more abundant and graceful use of plant material, and toward providing more open space in the "Center Cities" of America. Hundreds of communities are planting flowering shrubs and trees along their avenues, especially in downtown shopping areas. Permanently-planted malls heighten enjoyment of the shopper on Washington's busy "F" Street and on Miami's Lincoln Road—a mile-long promenade of gardens and fountains. Large planters, sprouting with flowers of the season, are appearing on usually dreary downtown streets, nationwide. Merchants are often leaders in the campaign to bring order and beauty to the urbanized chaos which the heart of metropolitan areas too often represent.

Highway Planting For Beauty and Safety

Few people drive for pleasure along the cluttered, slum-like highways which exist in many areas today. Polls show that two out of three Americans want their highways to be scenic and beautiful. The nursery industry is providing ever-increasing quantities of plant material for the purpose of highway landscaping. Highway plantings supplement the primary function of the road while preserving natural features and enhancing appearance. They improve adjacent land by creating a "greenbelt," screening nearby residences and creating a parklike atmosphere which increases property value. Mature trees are needed for highway plantings and nursery-grown trees are generally used because they develop faster and are hardier than the collected trees. Maintenance problems are a key consideration in the designer's plans. Functional planting facilitates mowing operations and creates scenic views which help counter the monotony of highway driving. Center strip and directional plantings prevent many head-on, and off-the-road crashes, thus helping to minimize highway accidents and loss of life.

Homeowners Lead The Fight On Visual Pollution.

The plain fact is, people don't like ugliness in their surroundings, and their pride makes them want to do something about it. The effort to stamp out "uglification" of the landscape has its roots deep in the psyche of civilized man. Trees, grass, shrubs, and flowers provide solace for the spirit. We plant and tend green things to satisfy a desire to live our lives in beautiful surroundings, and to express our individuality.

Big highway planting projects and costly urban renewal programs are an extension of the individual's continuing effort to brighten his own small corner of the world. The homeowner who plants a grassy front lawn and dots it with trees, shrubs and flowers may think he's just making war on ugliness. In fact, however, he's also being an activist in the campaign to stamp out a major part of environmental pollution—dreary, depressing urban landscapes.

The easiest way to strike a telling blow for beauty in our land is for people to keep their homes and neighborhoods from sinking to slum-level appearance. Decline begins with exteriors. Rundown lawns, broken hedges, scraggly trees, withered flowers produce a ghetto atmosphere which destroys morale and property value alike. The simple acts of planting and maintaining greenery and flowers create natural beauty and charm. Landscaping reflects the innate love of beautiful surroundings, the intimate connection which exists between man and nature.

The battle again visual pollution really begins at the doorstep of the home. In effect, you step forth into whatever kind of environment you help form and permit to exist.

"There is nothing more practical in the end," said President Theodore Roosevelt, "than the preservation of beauty, than the preservation of anything that appeals to the higher emotions of man." If he had witnesses the pollution of latter-day America, the great conservationist might have added the fact that we can no longer afford not to choose to preserve the sources of our natural beauty. Time is fast running out on the opportunity to pay our debt to the past and provide a legacy for the future by restoring our national environment to the point where it once again justifies the description, "America the Beautiful."

A Legacy of Beauty For Generations To Come

Scientists say that mankind's genetic endowment has been shaped by evolution to require "natural" surroundings for optimum mental health. For centuries we have tried to recreate in our homes the primordial setting— green plants, warm humid air; conditions symbolic of the tropical environment to which we appear best adapted. Today's life-style in America emphasizes communion with air, water, sun. Houses are designed for "outdoor living." We build swimming pools in our backyards, or buy week-end places in the forested acres of exurbia. The response to green, growing things is pronounced in the minds of the millions of campers who seek the refreshing shelter of tree-shaded parks and recreation areas. It is clearly evident that natural beauty in our daily life is a genuine biological need.

But opposed to this native longing is the artificial, urbanized world which man himself has constructed. He lives in his steel and concrete cell with a growing sense of frustration; and urban tensions grow.

2300 years ago, Aristole said that people gather in cities "in order to live the good life." But city dwelling is increasingly barren of the qualities which make for "the good life", and degradation of the environment is a major cause of the growing discontent which plagues the urban dweller. More than ever, we realize that natural beauty has a unique capacity to lift man's spirit, to brighten his outlook. And we realize that it is visual pollution which gives rise to much of the frustration which tortures our minds. But man, the great polluter, can change the drab and ugly scene. The horticulturist, in particular, can help bring to teeming millions the changed outlook which cure of visual pollution can produce.

Public awareness of the importance of ecology was tragically slow in coming. But Americans are now alert and alarmed, and filled with a compelling sense that it's literally "now or never." We can wait no longer to repair the damage already done. And we must establish quality guidelines to avoid future crises related to our environment. We're no longer a handful of people living a comparatively simple life. There are more than 200 million of us now, and millions more to come. We cannot postpone action until tomorrow, or another year, or another decade.

From this point in time, much of the horticulturist's effort will be aimed directly toward developing plant material to help solve environmental problems. Plant explorers, plant breeders, plant physiologists, plant pathologists, entomologists—all will apply their green magic to erase visual pollution and put back into the American scene an abundance of the green, growing things which make for healthy, zestful living in the midst of natural beauty.

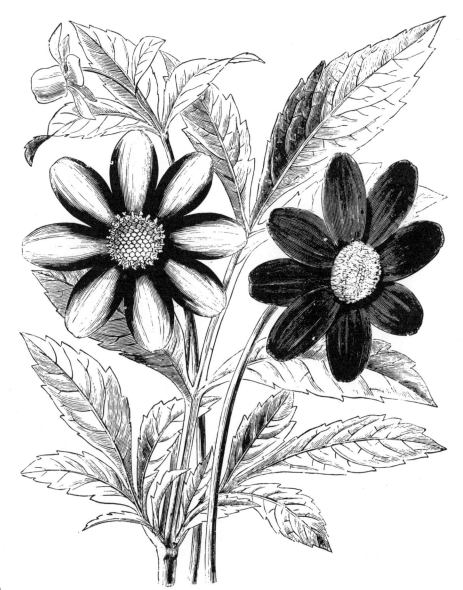

163

AIR POLLUTION PROBLEMS
FOR TREES, SHRUBS & FLOWERS

Air pollution comes from many sources and most of these sources are concentrated in urban areas. Automobile engines produce such gases as carbon monoxide, hydrocarbons, nitrogen dioxide, and lead compounds. Electric generators and industrial plants contribute sulphur dioxide, hydrogen fluoride, and hydrocarbons. Refuse burning, heating plants, and forest fires emit tons of smoke into the air. All of the pollutants in the air are known collectively as smog.

The two pollutants that cause the most damage to growing plants are produced by the chemical action of sunlight on smog. These pollutants are ozone and peroxyacetyl nitrate, better known as PAN. Ozone and PAN are known as photochemical pollutants.

Some of the most common pollutants and the damage they cause to plants are as follows:

Ozone and PAN.—Spotted, streaked, and bleached foliage; retarded plant growth; leaves drop early.

Nitrogen dioxide.—Tan or white, irregular lesions near leaf margins.

Sulphur dioxide.—Bleached spots between leaf veins; retarded plant growth.

Hydrogen fluoride.—Bleached leaf tips and margins; dwarfed plant growth.

Ethylene.—Withered and twisted leaves; flowers drop early.

You may have difficulty identifying some of the particular kinds of air pollution damage that you see in your garden. A color guide showing damage to plants is available from the Superintendent of Documents, U. S. Government Printing Office, Washington, D. C. 20402, at $1.25 a copy. Ask for National Air Pollution Control Administration Publication No. AP-71, in color. Include your ZIP Code in your return address.

Pollution damage comes and goes, but more damage occurs in spring and fall than in other seasons. In spring and fall, stationary layers of warm and cold air create barriers to the movement of gases in the atmosphere. When this happens, smog collects beneath these barriers and damages plants.

Some plants can tolerate smog better than others, particularly photochemical smog. Plants that are especially resistant to photochemical smog are in the first of the following two lists; plants that are acutely sensitive to photochemical smog are in the second of the two lists.

Within a given species of plant, some forms will be more resistant or sensitive than others. For example, common white petunias are extremely sensitive to smog but purple, blue, and red ones are more resistant. Besides color, size is a factor. Small-flowered petunias, called multiflora, are generally more resistant than large-flowered ones, called grandiflora. And small-leaved types of plants are more resistant than large-leaved types.

The stage of plant development is very critical to air pollution damage. Young leaves and old leaves usually are more resistant to pollutants than recently matured leaves. Slow growing plants are more resistant than soft, rapidly growing plants. Before you select plants for your garden, visit other gardens in the area and see what kinds of plants are growing best.

If your plants show signs of pollution damage, reduce the amount of nitrogen fertilizer and the frequency of watering. High levels of nitrogen and water stimulate plant growth and increase sensitivity to air pollution. Moderate fertilizer and watering will slow growth and help plants survive. There are no practical chemical treatments available that can be used on plants to increase their tolerance of the polluted environment.

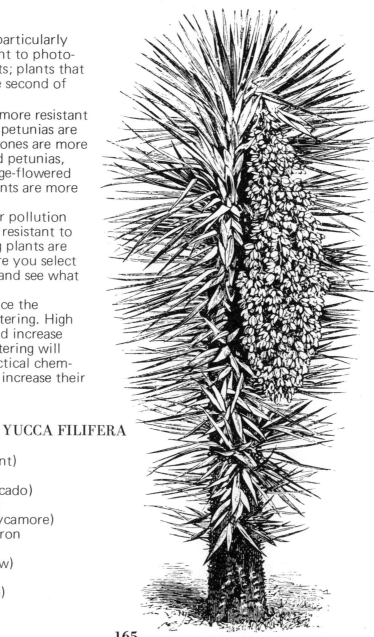

YUCCA FILIFERA

PLANTS SENSITIVE TO PHOTOCHEMICAL SMOG

SHRUBS AND TREES
Acer (Maple)
Alnus (Alder)
Calycanthus (Carolina Allspice)
Ficus (Fig)
Gleditsia (Locust)
Hibiscus
Juglans (Walnut)
Mentha (Mint)
Petunia
Persea (Avacado)
Pinus (Pine)
Platanus (Sycamore)
Rhododendron
Robinia
Salix (Willow)
Salvia
Ulmus (Elm)

PLANTS RESISTANT TO PHOTOCHEMICAL SMOG

SHRUBS AND TREES
Acacia
Aralia
Arbutus
Buxus (Boxwood)
Camellia
Cedrus
Cistus
Cotoneaster
Cupressus (Cypress)
Fraxinus (Ash)
Ginkgo (Maidenhairtree)
Prunus
Pittosporum
Pyracantha (Firethorn)
Quercus (Oak)
Spiraea (Bridal Wreath)
Syringa (lilac)
Viburnum
Yucca

HOUSE PLANTS
Dieffenbachia
Dracacaena
Fatsia
Phiodendron
Pittosporum

GRASSES AND GROUND COVER PLANTS

You don't have to be an expert to grow a good lawn. But you do have to adhere to sound establishment and maintenance practices.

You have to consider: (1) Construction of the lawn—how it is graded and drained, and how the seedbed is prepared; (2) selection of grasses, and how and when they are planted; and (3) maintenance, which includes fertilizing, mowing, watering, and controlling weeds, diseases, and insects.

Following are descriptions of common lawn grasses and ground cover plants, including statements on how they grow, where they grow best, their requirements, and how to establish them.

GRASSES

ANNUAL BLUEGRASS

Annual bluegrass (Poa annua) has little value as permanent turf because it dies suddenly when high temperatures occur in June, July, or August. It is used chiefly to overseed warm-season turf grasses during the winter months. Only small amounts of seed are available. It normally begins growth in late summer or early fall from seed produced earlier in the same year. It will often grow throughout the winter.

Annual bluegrass requires a cool, moist soil and good fertility. It will survive under close mowing and shade. It produces large quantities of seed heads even when mowing as low as ¼ inch. It is a pest in many highly specialized turf areas, particularly golf courses.

BAHIAGRASS

Bahiagrass (Paspalum notatum) is a low-growing perennial that spreads by short, heavy runners. It grows best in the southern Coastal Plains region. It is established by seeding.

Common bahia, which has extremely coarse-textured leaves, is recommended for forage only. Paraguay and Pensacola, strains having finer-textured leaves than common bahia, are useful on

large areas such as airfields, where good cover is more important than turf quality. These strains produce a dense, rather coarse and uneven turf, and are difficult to mow with an ordinary reel-type mower.

167

BERMUDAGRASS

Many varieties or strains of bermudagrass (Cynodon dactylon) are sold. Each variety generally has a specialized use. Common bermuda, a coarse-textured grass, is the only variety for which seed is available. Other varieties are established vegetatively.

Bermudagrass is commonly grown in the southern part of the United States. Common seeded bermudagrass is not suited to the northern part of the United States, but vegetative plantings of cold-tolerant sections have survived as far north as Chicago and New York.

Varieties of bermudagrass used in lawns in the southern part of the United States include Tiflawn, Everglades No. 1, Ormond, Sunturf, Texturf 10, and Texturf 1F. Tiflawn is finer in texture than common bermudagrass, and it is deep green. It has outstanding disease-resistant qualities. Tiflawn is a vigorous grower and will form a heavy mat unless it is mowed closely and often. The texture of Everglades No. 1 is finer than that of Tiflawn, and the green is darker. This grass tends to grow prostrate. Ormond is coarser in texture and grows more upright than Everglades No. 1. Of the three varieties, Everglades No. 1 requires the least maintenance.

Varieties of bermudagrass that are used in high-quality lawns receiving maximum maintenance, and in golf course putting greens and fairways, include Tifgreen, Tiffine, Tifway, Bayshore, and Tifdwarf. These varieties are medium green. They are fine in texture.

A variety of bermudagrass called U-3 has been grown successfully in the vicinity of Philadelphia, Pa., Norfolk, Nebr., Cleveland, Ohio, and St. Louis, Mo. It is most widely used in the so-called "crabgrass belt," a roughly triangular region cornered on Philadelphia, St. Louis, and Richmond, Va. U-3 has finer blades than common bermudagrass. It resists disease and insect damage, and holds its color late into the fall when properly fertilized. It grows well in hot, humid weather. Tufcote is also grown in this area.

Bermudagrass grows vigorously, spreading by aboveground runners and underground rootstalks. It often becomes a serious pest in flower beds and other cultivated areas. Once established in those places it is difficult to eradicate.

BERMUDA GRASS—WIRE GRASS
(Cynodon Dactylon)

Bermudagrass will not thrive under conditions of shade, poor drainage, high acidity, or low fertility. It requires frequent heavy applications of nitrogen in readily available form. Although drought resistant, it requires moderate amounts of water during the dry periods. It must be clipped closely in order to form a dense turf.

BLUE GRAMAGRASS

Blue gramagrass (Bouteloua gracilis) is a low-growing, parennial grass that is adapted to a wide range of soil conditions throughout the Great Plains region. It is highly drought resistant. Its use as a turf grass is limited to cool, dry places where little or no irrigation water is available.

Blue gramagrass is a bunch-type grass that can be established easily from seed. Unless watered, it becomes semidormant and turns brown during severe drought periods. Seed produced in a given area should be used for plantings in that area only.

BUFFALOGRASS

Buffalograss (Buchloe dactyloides) is a stoloniferous perennial grass that is used commonly in sunny lawns of prairie homes in the Great Plains region. It is highly drought resistant. The grass is fine leaved and dense during the growing season. It turns from grayish green to the color of straw when growth stops in the fall. It grows best in well-drained, fairly heavy soils. Buffalograss can be established by sodding or seeding.

CANADA BLUEGRASS

Canada bluegrass (Poa compressa) forms a thin, poor-quality, open turf. It can be used in seed mixtures on playgrounds, athletic fields, or similar areas.

Canada bluegrass will grow in sandy or gravelly soils of low fertility. It will not grow well in soils having high acidity or poor drainage. It will not withstand clipping below 1½ inches. It is extremely tough and resists wear.

CARPETGRASS

Carpetgrass (Axonopus compressus) is a rapidly spreading stoloniferous perennial grass that produces a dense, compact turf under mowing, but is quite coarse textured. It can be established quickly by seeding or by sprigging or sodding. Seeding is the cheapest method.

Carpetgrass grows best in moist, sandy-loam soils or those that have a relatively high-moisture content throughout the year. It does not grow well in dry soils or in regions that remain dry during part of the growing season. It will thrive under limited fertilization in poor soils, but is extremely sensitive to lack of iron. It resists disease and insect damage, but does not tolerate water spray. It will withstand trampling and heavy wear.

Carpetgrass produces tall seed heads that are difficult to mow and make the lawn look rough or rugged. Mowing frequently with a rotary mower to a height of 1 inch is recommended.

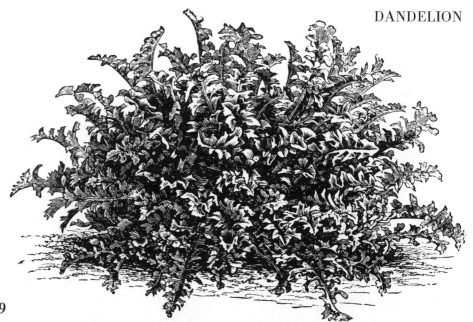

DANDELION

169

CENTIPEDEGRASS

Centipedegrass (Eremochloa ephiruroides) spreads rapidly by short creeping stems that form new plants at each node. It forms a dense, vigorous turf that is highly resistant to weed invasion. It is usually established vegetatively; some seed is available.

Centipedegrass is considered the best low-maintenance lawn grass in the southern part of the United States. It requires less mowing, less watering, and less fertilizing than other southern lawn grasses. It is seldom damaged by disease or insects, but may be severely damaged by salt water spray. It is sensitive to the lack of iron. An annual application of a complete fertilizer will improve the quality of centipedegrass lawns. Although it is drought resistant, centipedegrass should be watered during dry periods.

Centipedegrass should not be planted in farm lawns; it may escape into pastures and destroy their grazing value.

COLONIAL BENTGRASS

Colonial bentgrass (Agrostis tenuis) is a fine-textured, tufted-type grass with few creeping stems and rhizomes. It forms a dense turf when heavily seeded and closely mowed.

Colonial bentgrass is used chiefly in high-quality lawns and putting greens. It is more expensive to maintain than ordinary lawn grasses. It is popular in the New England States, Washington, and Oregon.

Colonial bentgrass requires fertile soil and frequent fertilizer applications. It must be watered during dry periods. It is susceptible to a wide variety of diseases. It must be mowed closely; when cut about 3/4 inch it becomes fluffy and forms an undesirable spongy mat.

Several strains of colonial bentgrass are sold. Highland is the hardiest variety. It is bluish green. It grows moderately fast. Another variety, Astoria, is bright green. It is not as drought resistant or as aggressive as Highland. Although Astoria requires more care than Highland, it produces a better-quality lawn if properly managed. Other colonial bentgrass suitable for lawns include New Zealand browntop and some strains of German bentgrass.

SOUTHERN BENT

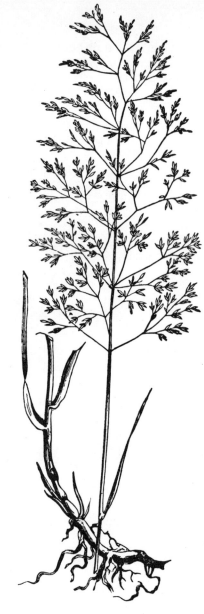

REDTOP

CREEPING BENTGRASS

Creeping bentrgass (Agrostis palustris) is not often used in home lawns, but it is used extensively in golf course putting greens throughout the United States. It has profuse creeping stems that produce roots and stems at every node, and it develops a dense sod. It must be mowed closely (3/16 to 3/8 inch), brushed regularly, and topdressed periodically to prevent formation of an undesirable mat or thatch.

Creeping bentgrass requires soils having high fertility, low acidity, good drainage, and high water-holding capacity. A regular program of fertilization, watering, and disease control must be followed to maintain good-quality turf.

Varieties available include Seaside, which is established by seeding and is used in golf greens along the west coast; Penncross, a seeded type that is available for specialized turf areas; and several strains that have been selected from established greens and are established vegetatively—Arlington, Collins, Cohansey, Washington, Congressional, Pennpar, Pennlu, and Old Orchard.

CRESTED WHEATGRASS

Crested wheatgrass (Agropyron cristatum) is a perennial bunchgrass. It thrives in most soils in the central and northern Great Plains and Intermountain regions. It is recommended in dry, cool areas of those regions where irrigation water is not available. It is established by seeding.

Crested wheatgrass will withstand long, dry periods and heavy wear if not cut too closely. It makes most of its growth in the spring and fall; it becomes semi-dormant and turns brown in the hot summer months.

TALL RED TOP
(Tricuspis sesleroides)

Little blue stem
(Andropogon scoparius)

JAPANESE LAWNGRASS

Japanese lawngrass (Zoysia japonica) is a low-growing perennial that spreads by above-ground runners and shallow rootstocks. It forms a dense turf that resists weed invasion and disease and insect damage.

Japanese lawngrass grows best in the region south of a line drawn from Philadelphia, Pa., westward to San Francisco, Calif. It will survive in the region north of that line but its use there, except in some localities, is impracticable because of the short summer growing season. The grass turns the color of straw when the first killing frost occurs in the fall and it remains off-color until warm spring weather.

Common Japanese lawngrass is coarse in texture. It is somewhat undesirable for home lawn use but is excellent for large areas such as airfields and playgrounds. Meyer zoysia, a selection of common Japanese lawngrass, is more desirable than Japanese lawngrass for home lawns. It is more vigorous, retains its color later in the fall, and regains it earlier in the spring. Meyer zoysia sod is available from a number of nurseries. There is no seed.

Although Japanese lawngrass will survive in soils of low fertility, it makes best growth when given liberal applications of complete fertilizers having a high nitrogen content. It is relatively drought tolerant in the humid regions. It is highly resistant to wear and will withstand close clipping.

Japanese lawngrass may be established by sprig planting the stems, by spot sodding, or by seeding. Three to four growing seasons are generally required to get complete coverage.

Emerald zoysia is a hybrid between Japanese lawngrass and mascarene grass that has proven superior to Meyer zoysia in the southern part of the United States. The grass is fine leafed, dense growing and dark green in color.

KENTUCKY BLUEGRASS

Kentucky bluegrass (Poa pratensis) is a hardy, long-lived, sod-forming grass that spreads by underground rootstocks. It is one of the most widely used lawn grasses in the United States. It is the

172

basic lawn grass in cool, humid regions and in cool, dry regions where adequate irrigation water is available.

Common Kentucky bluegrass will not withstand poor drainage or high acidity. It grows best in heavy, well-drained soils of good fertility that are neutral or nearly neutral in reaction. In soils of low fertility, liberal applications of nitrogen, phosphorus, and potash are needed. Bluegrass is highly drought resistant; it has the ability to go into a semidormant condition during hot summer months.

Common Kentucky bluegrass may be injured if mowed shorter than 1½ inches. It will not tolerate heavy shade. Because it becomes established slowly, common Kentucky bluegrass is often planted with faster-growing grasses that provide cover and prevent weed invasion while the bluegrass is becoming established.

KIKUYUGRASS

Kikuyugrass (Pennisetum clandestinum) is a perennial grass that spreads by coarse underground rootstocks. It produces a coarse-textured spongy or matted turf that is 3 to 5 inches thick and difficult to mow at lawn height. Its use has been confined to locations in coastal California, where it is now considered a pest and is being eradicated. It is not recommended for lawn use.

MERION

Merion Kentucky bluegrass has proved superior to common Kentucky bluegrass in many regions of the United States. It can be clipped more closely, and is less susceptible to leafspot disease than common Kentucky bluegrass, although it is susceptible to rust and stripe smut. Merion Kentucky bluegrass also appears to be more heat and drought tolerant, more vigorous, and more resistant to weed invasion than common Kentucky bluegrass. For best growth, it requires greater fertility and more maintenance than common Kentucky bluegrass. It responds well to high applications of nitrogen.

Among other varieties of Kentucky bluegrass found commercially are: Newport, Park, Nugget, Pennstar, Windsor, Baron, and Fylking.

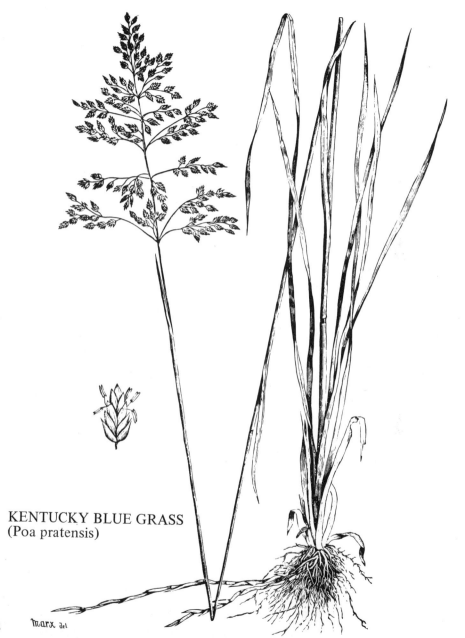

KENTUCKY BLUE GRASS
(Poa pratensis)

Marx del

173

MANILAGRASS

Manilagrass (Zoysia matrella) is closely related to Japanese lawn-grass and has many similar characteristics. It is stoloniferous, and forms a dense carpetlike turf that resists weeds, wear, disease, and insect damage. Manilagrass is adapted to the southern part of the United States.

Manilagrass is sensitive to highly acid soils. It responds well to liberal applications of nitrogenous fertilizer. It turns brown when the first killing frost occurs and remains dormant until spring. It is established by sprigging or spot sodding.

MASCARENEGRASS

Mascaranegrass (Zoysia tenuifolia) is a low-growing stoloniferous grass that is adapted to very few locations in the United States. Its growth requirements with respect to moisture, nutrients, and soil are about the same as those for manilagrass, but it is not as winter hardy as manilagrass or Japanese lawngrass. It becomes sodbound and humps up as it grows older, which encourages weed invasion. Limited amounts of mascarenegrass sod are available in Florida and California.

MEADOW FESCUE

Meadow fescue (Festuca elatior) is a hardy, short-lived perennial that is used primarily for pasture and hay. It does not form a solid sod. It grows best in heavy, moist soils, and will withstand extreme-ly wet soils. An excellent seed producer, it is often found in poor-quality lawn seed mixtures.

ORCHARDGRASS

Orchardgrass (Dactylis glomerata) is a tall-growing, perennial bunch grass that forms coarse-textured tufts but never a solid turf. It does not grow well in soils having high acidity or poor drainage, but it resists drought and tolerates shade. It can withstand low fer-tility. Seed is abundant, and it is sometimes used in poor-quality lawn seed mixtures.

ORCHARD GRASS

RED FESCUE AND CHEWINGS FESCUE

Red fescue (Festuca rubra) and Chewings fescue (F. rubra var. commutata) rate next to Kentucky bluegrass as the most popular lawn grasses in the cool humid regions of the United States. Red fescue spreads slowly by underground rootstocks. Chewings fescue is a bunch-type grower. Both are established by seeding.

Both fescues are used extensively in lawn seed mixtures. They grow well in shaded areas, and they tolerate high acidity. They require good drainage but will grow in poor, droughty soils.

Red fescue and Chewings fescue are fine textured. They have bristlelike leaves that stand upright. When seeded heavily they form a dense sod that resists wear. They heal slowly when injured by insects, disease, or other means. Mowing consistently below 1½ inches can cause severe damage. The grasses grow slowly.

Improved strains of red fescue on the market include Pennlawn, Illahee, and Rainier. No improved strains of Chewings fescue are on the market.

REDTOP

Under lawn conditions, redtop (Agrostis alba) is a short-lived perennial. It seldom lives more than two seasons when closely mowed. It is commonly used in lawn seed mixtures in the northern temperate regions of the United States to provide quick cover while more permanent grasses are developing. It is often seeded alone in temporary lawns. In the southern part of the United States it is used for winter overseeding of bermudagrass to provide year-round green color.

Heavy seeding helps overcome redtop's tendency to develop a coarse open-type turf. Redtop tolerates a wide range of soil and climatic conditions, including temperature extremes. It grows in soils that are highly acid and poorly drained. It resists drought and has a low fertility requirement.

MOUNTAIN RED TOP
NORTHERN RED TOP
(Agrostis exarata)

RESCUEGRASS

Rescuegrass (Bromus catharticus) is a short-lived perennial bunch grass that grows best in fertile soils in humid regions where the winters are mild. It is sometimes used in the southern part of the United States as a winter grass in large bermudagrass plantings, such as golf course fairways.

ROUGH BLUEGRASS

Rough bluegrass (Poa trivialis), also known as roughstalk bluegrass, is a shade-tolerant perennial that is useful in lawns only in the extreme northern part of the United States. It is established by seeding. It is seriously injured by hot, dry weather. It has leaves of the same texture as Kentucky bluegrass. The stems and leaves lie flat, giving the turf a glassy appearance. Roughstalk meadowgrass is lighter green than Kentucky bluegrass. It spreads by short aboveground runners.

Roughstalk meadowgrass has a shallow root system, and will not withstand heavy wear. It should be used in shady areas where the traffic is not heavy.

RYEGRASS

Italian or annual ryegrass (Lolium multiflorum) and perennial ryegrass (Lolium perenne) are propagated entirely by seed that is produced in the Pacific Northwest, or imported. Much of the ryegrass used for lawns in the United States is a mixture of annual, perennial, and intermediate types.

Many commercial lawn seed mixtures contain too much ryegrass; the ryegrass competes with the permanent grass seedlings for moisture and nutrients. On sloping areas, it is sometimes advisable to include a small amount of ryegrass in the lawn seed mixture to help prevent soil erosion. The use of perennial ryegrass in lawn seed mixtures often results in ragged-appearing lawns that are difficult to mow. Coarse clumps of ryegrass may persist in the lawn for several years.

In the southern part of the United States annual or common ryegrass is used for winter overseeding of bermudagrass in lawns, and on golf greens and tees. Among fine-textured ryegrass varieties are Pennfine, Manhattan, Norlea, Pelo, and NK101.

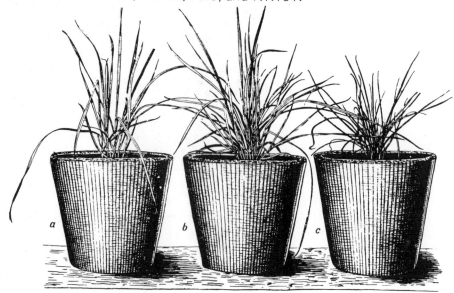

VELVET BENTGRASS

Velvet bentgrass (Agrostis canina), the finest textured of the bentgrasses, is used mainly in high-quality lawns and putting greens in the New England States and the Pacific Northwest. It forms an extremely dense turf from creeping stems. It can be established by seeding or by vegetative planting.

Velvet bentgrass is adapted to a wide range of soil conditions but makes its best growth on well-drained, fertile soils having low acidity. It is not as aggressive as creeping bentgrass and is slow to recover from all types of injury. It requires close mowing, regular brushing, and periodic topdressing. A regular program of fertilizing, watering, and disease control is necessary to maintain high-quality turf. Only one variety of velvet bentgrass is available in the United States: the Kingstown variety.

TIMOTHY

ST. AUGUSTINEGRASS

St. Augustinegrass (Stenotaphrum secundatum) is the No. 1 shade grass of the southernmost States. It is a creeping perennial; it spreads by long runners that produce short, leafy branches. It can be grown successfully south of Augusta, Ga., and Birmingham, Ala., and westward to the coastal regions of Texas. It is established vegetatively. Seed is not available.

St. Augustinegrass will withstand salt water spray. It grows best in moist soils of good fertility. It produces good turf in the muck soils of Florida. Liberal applications of high-nitrogen fertilizers are necessary, especially in sandy soils.

St. Augustinegrass can be seriously damaged by chinch bugs, and it is susceptible to armyworm damage and several turf diseases.

TALL FESCUE

Tall fescue (Festuca arundinacea) is a tall-growing perennial bunch grass that has coarse, dense basal leaves and a strong, fibrous root system. It is also used for pasture. It is established by seeding.

Because of their wear-resistant qualities, two improved strains of tall fescue, Kentucky 31 fescue and Alta fescue, are used often on play areas, athletic fields, airfields, service yards, and other areas where a heavy, tough turf is needed rather than a fine-textured turf.

Tall fescue will grow in west or dry, acid or alkaline soils, but it grows best in well-drained, fertile soils. It will withstand a moderate amount of shade.

TIMOTHY

Timothy (Phleum pratense) is a coarse perennial bunch grass that grows best in the northern humid regions of the United States where its main use is hay for livestock. It has no use as a lawn grass, but is often found in poor-quality lawn seed mixtures. It is sometimes suitable in nonuse areas to provide cover.

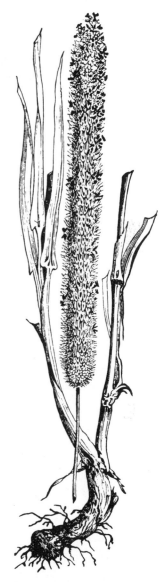

SHEEP'S FESCUE

177

CRAB GRASS

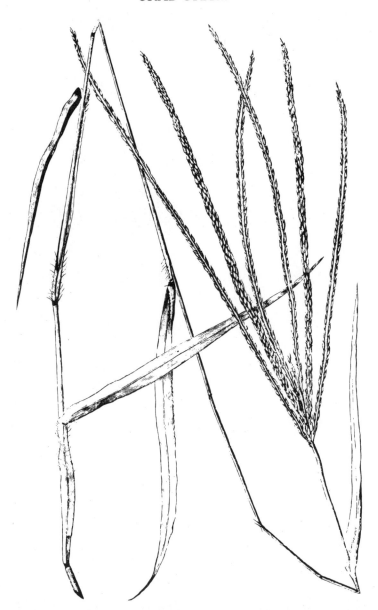

WHAT SHOULD YOU KNOW ABOUT MOWING YOUR LAWN?

ARE YOU MOWING TOO CLOSE?

Mowing at the wrong height could be weakening the turf, making it prone to disease and other problems. Bluegrass and fescue should be mowed at 2" and bermudagrass, St. Augustine and zoysia grass at 1".

To adjust your mower, place it on a flat surface. For most reel mowers, raise or lower the roller until the bedknife is 2" off the ground if your lawn is bluegrass or fescue and 1" if it is bermudagrass, St. Augustine or zoysia grass. A few models have a lever that raises or lowers the entire cutting mechanism without affecting the roller. On most rotary mowers you raise or lower all four wheels until the revolving blade is the right distance off the ground for your particular grass.

Check the service manual for exact details.

IS YOUR MOWER DULL?

Grass dulls the finest steel in a surprisingly short time. Reel mowers need an annual overhaul with several tune-up adjustments during the mowing season. Rotary mowers need sharpening at least monthly; a quick filing of the tip ½" of the blade is all that is needed, as only the tip does any cutting on a rotary.

Dull mowers cause an uneven cut or a whitish appearance to the leaftips a day or so after the lawn is mowed.

MOWING GRASSES IN SHADY AREAS

Since the amount of light reaching the grass under shady conditions is reduced, food manufactured by the grass plants is reduced. This results in thinner, weaker turf. To help compensate for this, mow higher and less frequently. When the shade comes from a building, fertilize and mow less; but if trees cause the shade, fertilize and irrigate more often to help meet the competition for nutrients and water. Thinning out the top portion of the tree and remaining branches for first 6 feet often greatly improves the turf under trees.

DO YOU HAVE UNSAFE MOWING HABITS?

Mowers can and do slice off fingers and toes, hurl rocks with tremendous velocity, or decapitate favored plants. Rotary mowers are by far the most dangerous. The blade is travelling at 90 miles an hour or more and easily slashes through gloves, shoes, and bones of people who should know better.

Always disconnect the sparkplug wire on a power mower before making ANY adjustments. When removing the grass catcher, be sure the blades are in neutral. For rotary mowers it would be safer to shut the engine off, as this is the time when hands and feet are closest, etc.

GROUND COVER PLANTS

Vines and other low-growing plants can often be planted on areas where it is difficult to establish or maintain satisfactory grass cover. Such areas include heavily shaded places, steep banks, rough and rocky areas, terraces, and drainage ditches.

DICHONDRA

Dichondra (Dichondra repens, D. Carolinensis) is a perennial that forms a low, dense mat under favorable conditions. It can be established by seeding or by vegetative planting. Dichondra is native to the Coastal Plain States from Virginia to Texas, but it is not considered a desirable lawn plant escept in central and southern California.

Dichondra is closely related to the milkweed and the morning-glory. Its leaves are pale green, and kidney shaped. It grows best in heavy soils. The plant does not require a high fertility level, but it requires large amounts of water. It will grow in partial shade, but is stemmy and undesirable and will crowd out all other vegetation, including bermudagrass.

ENGLISH IVY

English ivy (Hedera lelix) is a hardy trailing evergreen vine that thrives in shaded areas but will grow in direct sunlight. It develops a very dense mat that should be pruned occasionally. English ivy is particularly useful on steep banks or around the base of trees.

Cymbalaria

PERIWINKLE COMMON

Common periwinkle (Vinca minor) or myrtle, is a hardy low-growing evergreen that spreads by creeping stems. It has small, dark-green, glossy leaves. It develops violet blue flowers.

Common periwinkle will form a dense mat that shades out weeds and grasses. It grows best in moist soils that are high in organic matter. It is partial to dense shade, but it will grow satisfactorily under dry conditions in direct sunlight. Periwinkle is established by cuttings and can be planted any time when the soil is not frozen.

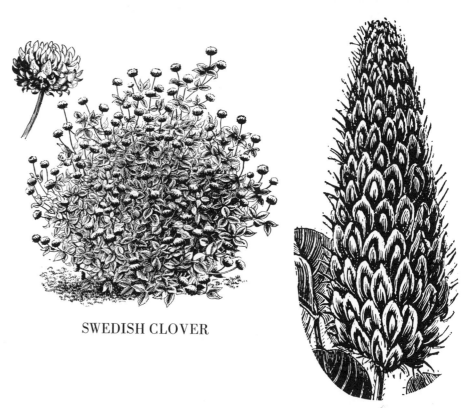

SWEDISH CLOVER

HEAD OF CRIMSON CLOVER

WHITE CLOVER

White clover (Trifolium repens) is regarded by some as a desirable ground cover plant in lawns. It is regarded by others as a pest.

Grass growing in proximity to white clover may be benefited by the nitrogen-fixing ability of the nodules on the clover roots. The plant often grows in patches of varying size, giving the lawn an uneven appearance. Some persons object to the white flower the plants form, and to the fact that it attracts bees. Another disadvantage is that white clover disappears during hot, dry weather. Contrary to claims made, white clover will not compete successfully with crabgrass.

181

AUBRETIAS IN THE ROCK GARDEN.

LIPPIA

Lippia (Lippia canescens) is used as a substitute for grass through-out the Southwest, particularly in Arizona. Lippia leaves are dark green. They are oblong, and seldom more than 1 inch long. Lippia will not survive temperatures below freezing, and may be injured by temperatures somewhat higher than freezing. It is also susceptible to nematode damage. Lippia has been known to crowd out bermudagrass when mowed regularly. It is established by vegetative planting.

PARTRIDGE BERRY

Partridge berry (Mitchella repens) is a low-growing creeping ever-green that is native to the Southeastern United States. It grows well in shaded areas having moist, fertile soils. Its leaves are small, glossy and round. It produces pinkish-white flowers in the spring; these are followed by scarlet fruit in the fall and winter.

Partridge berry is established by cuttings from vegetative material that can be found along streambanks and in wooded areas in the southeastern part of the country.

JAPANESE SNAKEBEARD (MONDO)

Japanese snakebeard (Ophiopogon japonica), or Lilyturf, is a bunch-growing member of the lily family. It grows 8 to 12 inches high, and bears purple to white flowers. It is used in the southern part of the United States under trees in poor soils. It is propagated vegetatively, and should be set close together because it spreads slowly.

JAPANESE SPURGE

Japanese spurge (Pachysandra terminalis), or Pachysandra, is a low-growing evergreen plant that spreads by suckers. The plants are about 8 inches high. They have dense wedge-shaped leaves and bear inconspicuous greenish-white flowers. They are established by divi-sion or by cuttings. Plants should be set 1 foot apart.

Japanese spurge is used in the Eastern United States from New England to Georgia. It is particularly recommended in Virginia, North Carolina, South Carolina, Kentucky, and Tennessee.

182

Climatic regions of the U.S. in which the following grasses are suitable for lawns:

Climatic regions of the U.S. in which the following grasses are suitable for lawns: Region 1. Common Kentucky bluegrass, Merion Kentucky bluegrass, red fescue, and Colonial bentgrass. Tall fescue, bermudagrass, and zoysiagrass in southern portion of the region. Region 2. Bermudagrass and zoysiagrass. Centipedegrass, carpetgrass, and St. Augustinegrass in southern portion of the region with tall fescue and Kentucky bluegrass in some northern areas. Region 3. St. Augustinegrass, bermudagrass, zoysiagrass, carpetgrass, and bahiagrass. Region 4. Nonirrigated areas: Crested wheatgrass, buffalograss, and blue gramagrass. Irrigated areas: Kentucky bluegrass and red fescue. Region 5. Nonirrigated areas: Crested wheatgrass. Irrigated areas: Kentucky bluegrass and red fescue. Region 6. Colonial bentgrass and Kentucky bluegrass.

REGIONS OF GRASS ADAPTATIONS

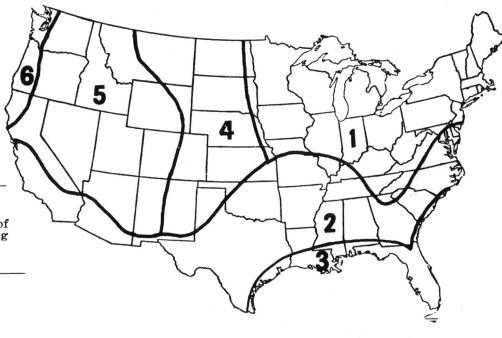

Grass	Pounds of seed per 1,000 square feet	Time of seeding
Bahiagrass	2-3	Spring.
Bermudagrass	2-3	Spring.
Blue gramagrass (unhulled)	1-1½	Spring.
Buffalograss (treated)	½-1	Spring.
Canada bluegrass	2-3	Fall.
Carpetgrass	3-4	Spring.
Centipedegrass	2-3	Spring.
Chewings fescue	3-5	Fall.
Colonial bentgrass (Highland, Astoria)	1-2	Fall.
Creeping bentgrass (Penncross, Seaside)	1-2	Fall.
Crested wheatgrass	1-2	Fall.
Japanese lawngrass (hulled)	1-2	Spring.
Kentucky bluegrass, common	2-3	Fall.
Kentucky bluegrass, Merion	1-2	Fall.
Red fescue	3-5	Fall.
Redtop	1-2	Fall.
Rough bluegrass	3-5	Fall.
Ryegrass (domestic and perennial)	4-6	Spring-fall.
Tall fescue (Alta, Ky. 31)	4-6	Fall.
Velvet bentgrass	1-2	Fall.
Mixture for sunny areas: 75% bluegrass, 25% red fescue	2-4	Fall.
Mixture for shady areas: 25% bluegrass, 75% red fescue	2-4	Fall.

—Vegetative grasses—rate and time of planting

Grass	Amount of planting material per 1,000 square feet	Time of planting
Bermudagrass	10 square feet of nursery sod or 1 bushel of stolons.	Spring-summer.
Buffalograss	25-50 square feet of sod	Spring.
Carpetgrass	8-10 square feet of sod	Spring-summer.
Centipedegrass	8-10 square feet of sod	Spring-summer.
Creeping bentgrass	80-100 square feet of nursery sod or 10 bushels of stolons.	Fall.
Velvet bentgrass	80-100 square feet of nursery sod or 10 bushels of stolons.	Fall.
Zoysia	30 square feet of sod when plugging; 6 square feet of sod when sprigging.	Spring-summer.

SOIL & NUTRIENT PLANT GUIDE

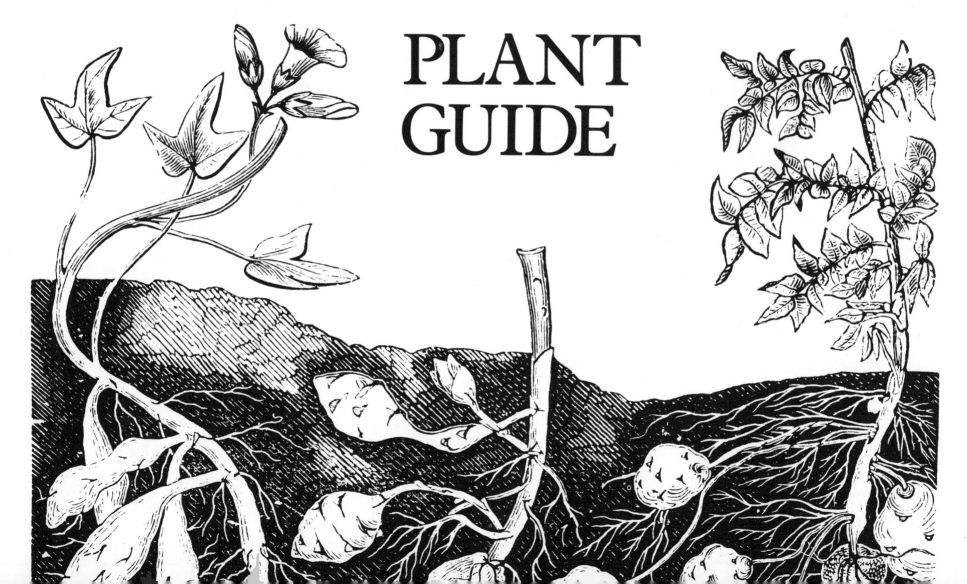

CHEMICAL ELEMENTS REQUIRED BY PLANTS

Some twenty or more chemical elements have been found to be essential to the successful growth of higher plants. Since a plan will require some of these elements in macroquantities (large amounts) and in microquantities (trace amounts) we may classify them as major, and minor trace plant foods on the basis of the amounts required. But this distinction does not alter the essential nature of any single one of the elements, nor does it eliminate the possibility that other elements may be required in smaller amounts than their presence as incidental impurities in raw material encountered in present day scientific studies.

Elements required by plants in Macroquantities

Carbon
Nitrogen
Calcium
Hydrogen
Phosphorus
Magnesium
Oxygen
Potassium
Sulfur

Elements required by plants in Microquantities

Iron
Copper
Chlorine
Vanadium
Manganese
Zinc
Cobalt
Boron
Molybdenum
Sodium

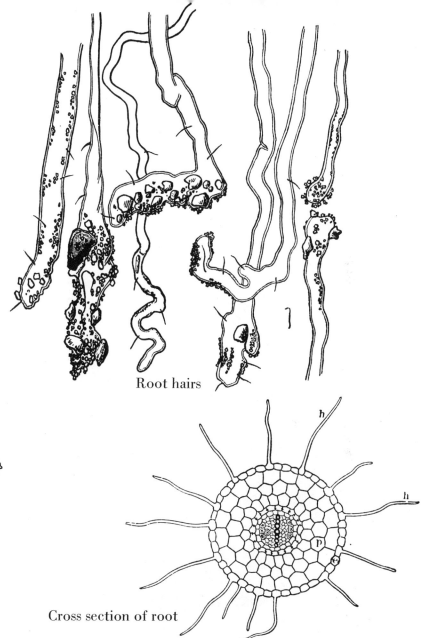

Root hairs

Cross section of root

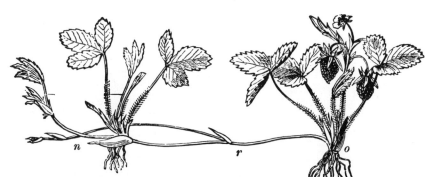

A Strawberry plant sending out a runner

SOIL REACTION PREFERENCES OF VARIOUS PLANTS

To simplify the classification of plants according to their soil reaction preferences, they have been divided into three main groups in these lists. Those plants preferring soils whose reaction is within the neutral zone, 6.0 to 8.0, are placed in Group A. Plants preferring slightly acid soil are placed in Group B, while those acid loving plants which thrive in strongly acid soils are in Group C.

Dr. Edgar T. Wherry, one of the foremost authorities on the subject of soil reaction preferences of plants, has published many excellent articles in scientific journals and it was through his cooperation that the lists given below were made possible.

BLACK PEKIN EGG PLANT

LIST NO. 1—COMMON FARM PLANTS

GROUP A

	pH
Alfalfa	6.0-7.0
Asparagus	6.0-7.0
Barley	6.0-7.0
Beets	5.8-7.0
Bluegrass	6.0-8.0
Broccoli	6.0-7.0
Cabbage	6.0-7.0
Cauliflower	6.0-7.0
Celery	6.0-6.5
Clover	6.0-7.0
Corn	6.0-7.0
Cucumber	6.0-8.0
Eggplant	6.0-7.0
Lettuce	6.0-7.0
Muskmellon	6.0-7.0
Oats	6.0-7.0
Onion	6.0-7.0
Parsnip	6.0-8.0
Pea, common	6.0-8.0
Pepper	6.0-6.5
Radish	6.0-8.0
Redtop	6.0-7.0
Rye	6.0-7.0
Soybean	6.0-7.0
Spinach	6.5-7.0
Squash	6.0-8.0
Timothy	6.0-7.0
Tomato	6.0-7.0
Turnip	6.0-8.0
Wheat	6.0-7.0

GROUP B

	pH
Beans, lima	5.5-6.5
Bentgrass	5.5-6.5
Carrot	5.5-6.5
Fescue	5.0-6.0
Potato	4.8-6.5
Strawberries	5.0-6.0

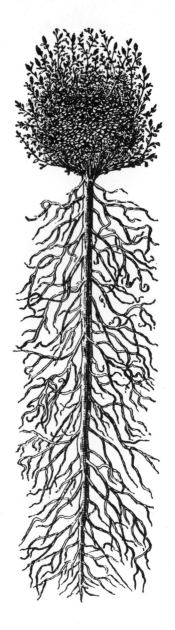

Abelia	Abelia species	A	6.0-8.0
Acacia	Acacia species	A	6.0-8.0
Acanthus, Soft	Acanthus mollis	A	6.0-7.0
Adderstongue, Common	Ophioglossum vulgatum	A	6.0-7.0
Ageratum, White	Eupatorium aromaticum	A	6.0-7.0
Ailanthus	Ailanthus glandulosa	A	6.0-8.0
Alder	Alnus, species	B	5.5-6.5
Alfalfa	Medicago sativa	A	6.0-7.0
Almond	Amygdalus, named varietes	A	6.0-8.0
Alpine-azalea	Loiseleuria procumbens	C	4.0-5.0
Alsike Clover		A	6.0-7.0
Alumroot, Hairy	Heuchera villosa	B	5.0-6.0
Alyssum	Alyssum species	A	6.0-8.0
Amaranth	Amaranthus species	A	6.0-8.0
Amaryllis		B	5.0-6.0
American Hophornbeam	Ostrya virginiana	A	6.0-7.0
American Plum	Prunus americana	A	6.0-8.0
Ampelopsis	Ampelopsis species	A	6.0-8.0
Anemone	Anemone species	A	6.0-8.0
Apple	Malus, species	B	5.5-6.5
Aralia	Aralia, many species	A	6.0-8.0
Aralia, Bristly	Aralia hispida	A	6.0-7.0
Arborvitae	Thuja, many species	A	6.0-8.0
Arbutus, Trailing	Arbutus unedo	C	4.0-5.0
Arbutus, Tree	Epigala repens	B	5.0-6.0
Arethusa	Arethusa bulbosa	C	4.0-5.0
Arnica	Arnica	B	5.0-6.5
Arrow Bamboo	Arundinaria japonica	A	6.0-8.0
Ash	Fraxinus, many species	A	6.0-8.0
Asparagus	Asparagus species	A	6.0-7.0
Aster	Aster, many species	A	6.0-8.0
Aster, Bigleaf	Aster macrophyllus	B	5.0-6.0
Aster, Seaside	Aster spectabilis	B	5.0-6.0
Aster, Sky-drop	Aster patens	B	5.0-6.0
Aster, Stiff	Aster linarifolius	B	5.0-6.0
Aster, Wave	Aster undulatus	A	6.0-7.0
Astilbe	Astilbe, many species	A	6.0-8.0
Atamasco-lily	Zephyranthes atamasco	B	5.0-6.0
Avocado	Persea americana	A	6.0-8.0
Azalea	Azalea	B	5.0-6.0
Baldcypress, Common	Taxodium distichum	A	6.0-8.0
Banana	Musa sapientum	A	7.0
Baneberry	Actaea species	A	6.0-8.0
Barberry	Berberis species	A	6.0-8.0
Barley	Hordeum vulgare	A	6.0-7.0
Bayberry	Myrica	B	5.0-6.0
Beach Plum	Prunus maritima	A	6.0-8.0
Bean	Phaseolus, many species	A	6.0-7.5
Bean, Lima	Phaseolus lunatus macrocarpus	B	5.5-6.5
Beautyberry	Callicarpa, many species	A	6.0-7.0
Bedstraw, Northern	Galium boreale	B	5.0-6.0
Beech	Fagus, named species and varieties	A	6.0-7.0
Beebalm, Oswego	Monarda didyma	A	6.0-7.0

187

Beet	Beta vulgaris	A	5.8-7.0
Beet, Sugar	Beta vulgaris, variety	A	6.0-8.0
Begonia	Begonia species	A	6.0-8.0
Bellflower	Campanula, many species	A	6.0-8.0
Bentgrass, Carpet	Argrostis stolonifera	B	5.5-6.5
Bentgrass, Rhode Island	Argrostis capillaris	B	5.5-6.5
Birch, Sweet	Betula lenta	B	5.0-6.0
Bishopscap, Lace	Mitella nuda	B	5.0-6.0
Bitter Nightshade	Solanum dulcamara	A	6.0-8.0
Bittersweet	Celastrus species	B	5.5-6.5
Blackberry	Rubus, named species and varieties (some in)	B	5.0-6.0
Blackcap, Common	Rubus occidentalis	A	6.0-7.0
Bladdernut	Staphylea, named species and varieties	A	6.0-8.0
Bleedingheart, Fringed	Dicentra eximia	B	5.0-6.0
Bloodroot	Sanguinaria canadensis	B	5.5-6.5
Bluebead	Clintonia borealis	C	4.0-5.0
Bluebell, Feather	Campanula divaricata	B	5.0-6.0
Bluebells, Virginia	Mertensia virginica	A	6.0-8.0
Blueberry	Vaccinium	B	5.0-6.0
Bluegrass, Kentucky	Poa pratensis	A	6.0-8.0
Bluets	Houstonia coerulea	A	6.0-7.0
Bluets, Creeping	Houstonia serpyllifolia	B	5.0-6.0
Bogbean, Common	Menvanthes trifoliata	B	5.0-6.0
Bog-rosemary	Andromeda	C	4.0-5.0
Bowmansroot	Gillenia trifoliata	A	6.0-7.0
Box, Common	Buxus sempervirens	A	6.0-8.0
Bracken	Pteridium aquilinum (latiusculum)	B	5.0-6.0
Brake	Pteris species	A	6.0-8.0
Broccoli	Brassica oleracea botrytis	A	6.0-7.0
Broomgrass	Bromus species	A	6.0-8.0
Broom-crowberry	Corema conradi	C	4.0-5.0
Broom, Scotch	Cytisus scoparius	B	5.0-6.0
Buckeye	Aesculus species	A	6.0-8.0
Buckeye, Red	Aesculus pavia	A	6.0-7.0
Buckthorn	Rhamnus species	A	6.0-8.0
Bugbane, American	Cimicifuga americana	B	5.0-6.0
Bunchberry	Cornus canadensis	C	4.0-5.0
Bunchflower	Melanthium virginicum	B	5.0-6.0
Bushclover	Lespedeza, many species	A	6.0-8.0
Buttercup	Ranunculus, many species	A	6.0-8.0
Butterflybush	Buddleia species	A	6.0-8.0
Butterflyflower	Schizanthus species	A	6.0-8.0
Butterfly-pea, Porcelain	Clitoria mariana	B	5.0-6.0
Buttonbush	Cephalanthus occidentalis	A	6.0-8.0
Button-snakeroot	Eryngium aquaticum	B	5.0-6.0
Cabbage	Brassica oleracea	A	6.0-7.0
Calendula	Calendula officinalis	A	6.0-8.0
Calla, Wild	Calla palustris	C	4.0-5.0
Calypso	Calypso bulbosa	A	6.0-7.0
Camas	Camassia species	A	6.0-8.0
Camellia	Many species	C	4.0-5.5
Campion	Lychnis, many species	A	6.0-8.0

Bluets.
Housatonia caerulea.

Candytuft, Evergreen	Iberis semipervirens	A	6.0-7.0
Canna	Canna species	A	6.0-8.0
Cantaloupe	Cucumis melo	A	6.0-8.0
Cape-jasmine	Gardenia species	A	6.0-8.0
Carnation	Dianthus caryophyllus	A	6.0-8.0
Carolina-jessamine	Gelsemium sempervirens	B	5.0-6.0
Carolina-vanilla	Trilisa odoratissima	B	5.0-6.0
Carrot, Common	Daucus carota	B	5.5-6.5
Catalpa	Catalpa, many species	A	6.0-8.0
Catchfly, Oriental	Silene orientalis	A	6.0-7.0
Cauliflower	Brassica oleracea botrytis	A	6.0-7.0
Celery	Apium graveolens	A	6.0-6.5
Centaurea	Centaurea species	A	6.0-8.0
Cerastium, Starry	Cerastium arvense	A	6.0-7.0
Chainfern	Woodwardia areolata	C	4.0-5.0
Chaste Tree	Vitex agnus-castus	A	6.0-7.0
Cherry	Prunus species	A	6.0-8.0
Cherry, Pin	Prunis pennsylvanica	B	5.0-6.0
Chestnut, American	Castanea dentata	B	5.0-6.0
Chestnut Oak	Quercus prinus	B	5.5-6.5
Chicory	Cichorium intybus	B	5.5-6.5
China-aster	Callistephus chinensis	A	6.0-8.0
Chinese Scholar-tree	Sophora japonica	A	6.0-7.0
Chinquapin	Castanea pumila	B	5.0-6.0
Chive	Allium schoenoprasum	A	6.0-7.0
Chokeberry	Aronia	B	5.0-6.0
Chokecherry	Prunus virginiana	A	6.0-8.0
Chrysanthemum	Chrysanthemum species	A	6.0-8.0
Cinquefoil	Potentilla, many species	A	6.0-8.0
Cinquefoil, Wineleaf	Potentilla tridenta	C	4.0-5.0
Clarkia		A	6.0-6.5
Clematis	Clematis, many species	A	6.0-8.0
Clematis, Curly	Clematis crispa	B	5.0-6.0
Clethra	Clethra	B	5.0-6.0
Clintonia, Speckled	Clintonia umbellulata	B	5.0-6.0
Clover	Trifolium, many species	A	6.0-7.0
Clubmoss, Shining	Lycopodium lucidulum	B	5.0-6.0
Coffee		B	5.0-6.0
Coleus, Common	Coleus blumei	A	6.0-8.0
Colorado Spruce	Picea pungens and varieties	A	6.0-7.0
Coltsfoot, Common	Tussilago farfara	A	6.0-8.0
Columbine	Aquilegia, many species	A	6.0-8.0
Columbine, Colorado	Aquilegia caerulea	A	6.0-7.0
Columbine, Golden	Aquilegia chrysantha	A	6.0-7.0
Columbine, Hybrid Colorado	Aquilegia caerulea hybrida	A	6.0-7.0
Coneflower	Rudbeckia, many species	A	6.0-8.0

CANNA

Convolvulus	Convolvulus species	A	6.0-8.0
Coreopsis	Coreopsis, many species	B	5.5-6.5
Coreopsis, Hairy	Coreopsis pubescens	B	5.0-6.0
Coreopsis, Rose	Coreopsis rosea	B	5.0-6.0
Coreopsis, Threadleaf	Coreopsis verticillata	B	5.0-6.0
Coreopsis, Trefoil	Coreopsis major	B	5.0-6.0
Corn, Indian	Zea mays	A	6.0-7.0
Cosmos, Common	Cosmos bipinnatus	A	6.0-8.0
Cotoneaster	Cotoneaster species	A	6.0-8.0
Cotton, Upland	Gossypium hirsutum	B	5.5-6.5
Cowpea, Common	Vigna sinensis, some varieties	B	5.5-6.5
Cranberry, Mountain	Vaccinium vitisidaea minor	B	5.0-6.0
Cranesbill	Geranium, many species	A	6.0-8.0
Crinkleroot	Dentaria diphylla	B	5.0-6.0
Crocus	Crocus species	A	6.0-8.0
Crowberry	Empetrum nigrum	C	4.0-5.0
Cuckooflower	Cardamine pratensis	A	6.0-7.0
Cucumber	Cucumis sativus	A	6.0-8.0
Cucumber-root	Medeola virginica	B	5.0-6.0
Currant	Ribes, many species	A	6.0-8.0
Cyclamen	c. persicum	A	6.0-8.0
Cypress	Chamaecyparis, named species and varieties	B	5.0-6.0
Daffodil		A	6.0-6.5
Dahlia	Dahlia species	A	6.0-8.0
Dahoon	Ilex cassine	B	5.0-6.0
Dalibarda	Dalibarda repens	B	5.0-6.0
Dandelion	Taraxacum officinale	A	6.0-8.0
Daphne, Winter	D. Odora	B	5.0-6.0
Daphne, Feb.	D. Mezereum	A	7.0-8.0
Daylily	Hemerocallis species	A	6.0-8.0
Deutzia	Deutzia species	A	6.0-8.0
Deviles-walkingstick	Aralia spinosa	A	6.0-7.0
Dewberry, Swamp	Rubus hispidus	B	5.0-6.0
Dogbane, Spreading	Spocynum androsaemifolium	A	6.0-7.0
Dogwood	Cornus, many species	A	6.0-8.0
Dogwood, Flowering	Cornus florida	A	6.0-7.0
Douglas-fir	Pseudotsuga douglasi	A	6.0-7.0
Dropwort	Filipendula hexapetala	A	6.0-7.0
Dutchmans pipe	Aristolochia sipho	A	6.0-8.0
Easterbells	Stellaria holostea	B	5.0-6.0
Egg Plant, Common	Salanum melongena	A	6.0-7.0
Elaeagnus	Elaeagnus, many species	A	6.0-8.0
Elder	Sambucus, many species	A	6.0-8.0
Elm	Ulmus species	A	6.0-8.0
English Ivy	Hedera helix	A	6.0-8.0
English Oak	Quercus robur and varieties	A	6.0-8.0
Eucalyptus	Eucalyptus species	A	6.0-8.0
Eulalia	Miscanthus sinensis	A	6.0-7.0

Euonymus	Euonymus species	A	6.0-8.0
European Mountain-ash	Sorbus aucuparia	A	6.0-8.0
European Turkey Oak	Quercus cerris	A	6.0-8.0
Evening-primrose	Oenothera, many species	A	6.0-8.0
Everlasting, Pearl	Anaphalis margaritacea	B	5.0-6.0
Fairybells	Disporum lanuginosum	B	5.0-6.0
False Indigo	Amorpha, many species	A	6.0-8.0
False Spirea	Sorbaria, named species and varieties	A	6.0-8.0
Fairywand	Chamaelirium luteum	B	5.0-6.0
Featherfleece	Stenanthium robustum	C	4.0-5.0
Fern, Asparagus		A	6.0-8.0
Fern, Bladder	Cystopteris species	A	6.0-8.0
Fern, Braun's Holly	Polystichum brauni	A	6.0-8.0
Fern, Crested	Dryopteris cristata	A	6.0-7.0
Fern, Xmas	Poylstichum acrostichoides	A	6.0-8.0
Fern, Evergreen Wood	Dryopteris species	A	6.0-7.0
Fern, Goldie's	Dryopteris goldiana	A	6.0-8.0
Fern, Hartford	Lygodium palmatum	C	4.0-5.0
Fern, Hay-scented	Dennstedtia punctilobula	B	5.0-6.0
Fern, Maidenhair	Adiantum species	A	6.0-8.0
Fern, Male	Dryopteris filixmas	A	6.0-8.0
Fern, Marsh	Dryopteris thelypteris	A	6.0-7.0
Fern, Massachusetts	Dryopteris simulata	C	4.0-5.0
Fern, Narrow-leaved Chain	Woodwardia aveolata	C	4.0-5.0
Fern, New York	Dryopteris noveboracensis	A	6.0-7.0
Fern, Sword		A	6.0-8.0
Fern, Upland Lady	Athyrium filixfemina (anugstum)	B	5.0-6.0
Fern, Walking	Camptosorus rhizophyllus	A	6.0-8.0
Fescue, Sheep	Festuca ovina	B	5.0-6.0
Fir	Abies, named species and varieties	B	5.0-6.0
Firethorn	Pyracantha species	A	6.0-8.0
Flax	Linum usitatissimum	A	6.0-7.0
Fleeceflower	Polygonum, many species	A	6.0-8.0
Flowering Quince	Cydonia japonica and varieties	A	6.0-8.0
Flytrap, Venus	Dionaea muscipula	C	4.0-5.0
Forget-me-not	Myosoti s, many species	A	6.0-8.0
Forsythia	Forsythia species	A	6.0-8.0
Fothergilla, Dwarf	Fothergilla gardeni	B	5.0-6.0
Foxglove	Digitalis species	A	6.0-8.0
Foxtail, Meadow	Alopecurus pratensis	A	6.0-8.0
Franklinia	Franklinia alatamaha	B	5.0-6.0
Fringe-orchid, Green	Habenaria lacera	B	5.0-6.0
Fringe-orchid, Large Purple	Habenaria fimbriata	B	5.0-6.0
Fringe-orchid, Lesser Orange	Habenaria cristata	C	4.0-5.0
Fringe-orchid, White	Habenaria blephariglottis	C	4.0-5.0
Fringe-orchid, Yellow	Habenaria ciliaris	B	5.0-6.0
Fringetree, White	Chionanthus virginica	B	5.0-6.0
Fumitory, Rock	Corydalis sempervirens	B	5.0-6.0
Fumitory, Climbing	Adlumia Fungosa	A	6.0-7.0

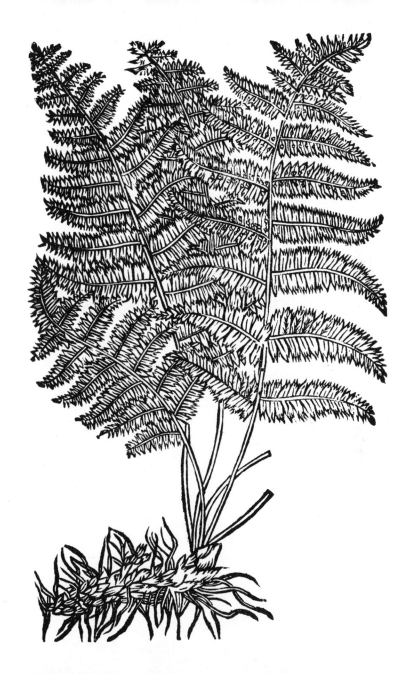

191

Gaillardia	Gaillardia species	A	6.0-8.0
Galax	Galax aphylla	C	4.0-5.0
Garbera		A	6.0-7.0
Gardenia		B	5.5-6.5
Gayfeather, Bristly	Liatris squarrosa	B	5.0-6.0
Gayfeather, Grassleaf	Liatris graminifolia	B	5.0-6.0
Gentian	Gentiana, many species	A	6.0-8.0
Geranium	Pelargonium species	A	6.0-8.0
Gilia	Gilia, many species	A	6.0-8.0
Ginseng, American	Panax quinquefolium	A	6.0-8.0
Gladiolus	Gladiolus species	A	6.0-8.0
Globeflower	Trollius, many species	A	6.0-8.0
Goatsrue, Common	Galega officinalis	A	6.0-8.0
Golden-aster, Maryland	Chrysopsis mariana	A	6.0-7.0
Goldenrod	Solidago, many species	A	6.0-8.0
Goldenrod, Fragrant	Colidago odora (suaveolens)	B	5.0-6.0
Goldenrod, White	Solidago bicolor	B	5.0-6.0
Goldenstar	Chrysogonum virginianum	A	6.0-7.0
Goldeye-grass	Hypoxis hirsuta	B	5.0-6.0
Goldthread	Coptis trifolia	C	4.0-5.0
Gorse, Common	Ulex europaeus	B	5.0-6.0
Grape	Vitis, some species	A	6.0-8.0
Grapefern, Broadleaf	Botrychium matricariae	B	5.0-6.0
Grapefern, Cutleaf	Botrychium dissectum	B	5.0-6.0
Grapefern, Triangle	Botrychium obliquum	B	5.0-6.0
Grapefruit*	Citrus grandis	B	5.0-7.0
Grass, Orchard	Dactylis glomerata	A	6.0-8.0
Grass, Carpet		A	6.0-7.0
Grass, Bermuda		A	6.0-7.0
Grass, Centipede		A	6.0-7.0
Grass, Velvet	Notholcus lanatus	A	6.0-8.0
Greenbrier, Coral	Smilax walteri	B	5.0-6.0
Greenbrier, Laurel	Smilax laurifolia	B	5.0-6.0
Groundcedar	Lycopodium complanatum (flabelliforme)	B	5.0-6.0
Groundpine	Lycopodium obscurum	B	5.0-6.0
Groundsel	Senecio, many species	A	6.0-8.0
Groundsel-bush	Baccharis halimifolia (grows in salt marshes)	A	7.0-8.0
Gypsophila	Gypsophila species	A	6.0-8.0
Hackberry	Celtis species	A	6.0-8.0
Hardhack	Spiraea tomentosa	B	5.0-6.0
Hartstongue	Phyllitis scolopendrium	A	6.0-8.0
Haw, Possum	Ilex Decidua	A	7.0-8.0
Hawthorn	Crataegus, many species	A	6.0-8.0
Hazelnut, Beaked	Corylus rostrata	A	6.0-7.0
Heath	Erica	B	5.0-6.0
Heather	Calluna vulgaris	B	5.0-6.0

* Become chlorotic at 7.5 or 8.0, and soil must then be acidified.

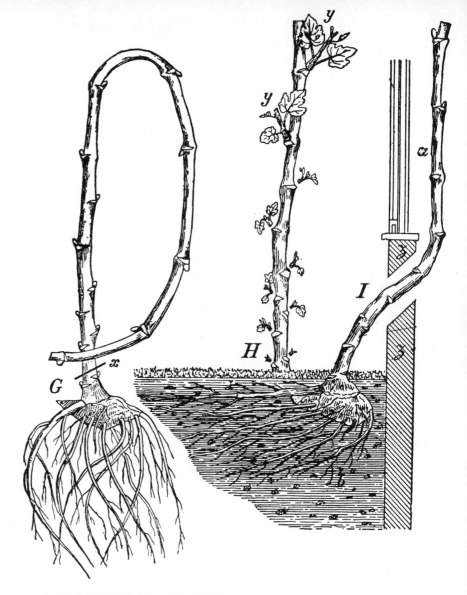

A PLANTING GRAPE VINE

He-huckleberry	Lyonia ligustrinia	B	5.0-6.0
Heliotrope	Heliotropium species	A	6.0-8.0
Hemlock, Carolina	Tsuga caroliniana	B	5.0-6.0
Hemlock, Common	Tsuga canadensis	B	5.0-6.0
Hepatica	Hepatica species	A	6.0-8.0
Hibiscus	Named species and varieties	A	6.0-8.0
Hobblebush	Viburnum alnifolium	B	5.0-6.0
Holly, Inkberry	Ilex glabra	C	4.0-5.0
Holly, American	Ilex, opaca	B	5.0-6.0
Hollyhock	Althaea species	A	6.0-8.0
Honeylocust	Gleditschia, many species	A	6.0-8.0
Honeysuckle	Lonicera, many species	A	6.0-8.0
Hoptree	Ptelea tri foliata	A	6.0-8.0
Hornbeam	Carpinus, many species	A	6.0-8.0
Horseradish	Radicula armoracia	A	6.0-8.0
Houseleek	Sempervivum, many species	A	6.0-8.0
Huckleberry	Gaylussacia	B	5.0-6.0
Hyacinth, Common	Hyacinthus orientalis	A	6.0-8.0
Hydrangea*	Hydrangea species	A	6.0-8.0
Indianpipe	Monotropa uniflora	B	5.0-6.0
Inkberry	Ilex glabra	B	5.0-6.0
Iris	Iris, many species	A	6.0-8.0
Iris, Cubeseed	Iris prismatica	C	4.0-5.0
Iris, Japanese	Iris kaempferi	B	5.0-6.0
Iris, Oregon	Iris tenax	B	5.0-6.0
Iris, Southern Blueflag	Iris carolina	B	5.0-6.0
Iris, Vernal	Iris verna	C	4.0-5.0
Jack-in-the-pulpit, Northern	Arisaema stewardsoni	B	5.0-6.0
Jersey-tea	Ceanothus americanus	B	5.0-6.0
Jetbead	Rhodotypus kerriodes	A	6.0-8.0
Juniper	Juniperus, many species	A	5.5-7.0
Juniper, Common	Juniperus communis and varieties	A	6.0-7.0
Juniper, Creeping	Juniperus horizontalis	B	5.0-6.0
Juniper, Mountain	Juniperus communis montana	B	5.0-6.0
Kale	Brassica oleracea acephala	A	6.0-8.0
Kalmia, Bog	Kalmia Polifolia	C	4.0-5.0
Kentucky Coffee	Gymnocladus dioica	A	6.0-8.0
Kerria	Kerria, many species	A	6.0-8.0
Labrador-tea, True	Ledum groenlandicum	C	4.0-5.0
Laburnum	Laburnum species	A	6.0-8.0
Ladies-tresses, Slender	Spiranthes gracilis	B	5.0-6.0
Ladies-tresses, Sweet	Spiranthes odorata	B	5.0-6.0
Ladyslipper, Pink	Cypripedium acaule	C	4.0-5.0

*Some Hydrangeas yield blue flowers in acid soils, and pink flowers in circumneutral soils.

193

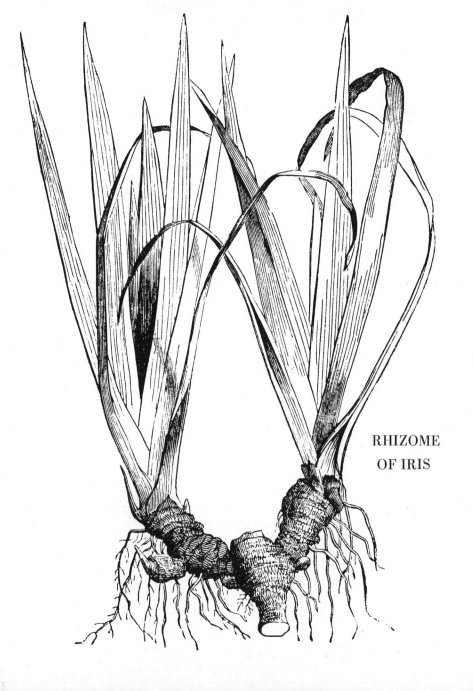

RHIZOME
OF IRIS

Ladyslipper, Ramshead	Cypripedium arietinum	B	5.0-6.0
Lambkill	Kalmia angustifolia	B	5.0-6.0
Larch	Larix, many species	B	5.5-6.5
Larkspur	Delphinium, many species	A	6.0-8.0
Larkspur, Orange	Delphinium, nudicaule	A	6.0-7.0
Leatherleaf	Chamaedaphne calyculata	B	5.0-6.0
Leatherwood	Dirca palustris	A	6.0-8.0
Leek	Allium porrum	A	6.0-8.0
Lemon*	Citrus limonia	A	5.5-7.0
Lettuce, Garden	Lactuca sativa	A	6.0-7.0
Leucothoe	Leucothoe	B	5.0-6.0
Lilac	Syringa species	A	6.0-8.0
Lily, American Turkscap	Lilium superbum	B	5.0-6.0
Lily, Carolina	Lilium carolinianum	B	5.0-6.0
Lily, Grays	Lilium grayi	B	5.0-6.0
Lily-of-the-Valley	Convallaria majalis	B	5.0-6.0
Lily, Orangecup	Lilium philadelphicum	B	5.0-6.0
Lily, Pinebarren	Lilium catesbaei	C	4.0-5.0
Linden	Tilia species	A	6.0-8.0
Lipfern, Hairy	Cheilanthes lanosa	B	5.0-6.0
Lipfern, Woolly	Cheilanthes tomentosa	A	6.0-7.0
Lobelia	Lobelia, many species	A	6.0-8.0
Loblolly-bay	Gordonia lasianthus	B	5.0-6.0
Locust	Robinia, named species and varieties	A	6.0-8.0
Loosestrife	Lysimachia, many species	A	6.0-8.0
Lupine, European Blue	Lupinus hirsutus	B	5.5-6.5
Lupine, Sun-dial	Lupinus perennis	B	5.0-6.0
Lychee	Litchi chinensis	A	6.0-7.0
Loosestrife, Purple	Lythrum salicaria	A	6.0-8.0
Lungwort	Pulmonaria species	A	6.0-8.0
Magnolia	Magnolia (excepting M. glauca)	B	5.0-6.0
Maidenhair-tree	Ginkgo biloba	A	6.0-7.0
Mangosteen	Garcinia mangostana	A	6.0-7.0
Maple	Acer, many species	A	6.0-8.0
Maple, Mountain	Acer spicatum	B	5.0-6.0
Maple, striped	Acer pennsylvanicum	B	5.0-6.0
Mariposa	Calochortus species	A	6.0-8.0
Marjoram	Origanum species	A	6.0-8.0
Marshmarigold	Caltha palustris	A	6.0-8.0
Matrimony-vine	Lycium, many species	A	6.0-8.0
Meadowbeauty	Rhexia	C	4.0-5.0
Menziesia, Allegheny	Menziesia pilosa	B	5.0-6.0
Mignonette, Common	Reseda odorata	A	6.0-8.0
Milkweed, Red	Asclepias rubra	C	4.0-5.0
Mint	Mentha, many species	A	6.0-8.0
Mockorange	Philadelphus, many species	A	6.0-8.0
Molinia	Molinia coerulea	C	4.0-5.0

*Become chlorotic at 7.5 or 8.0, and soil must then be acidified.

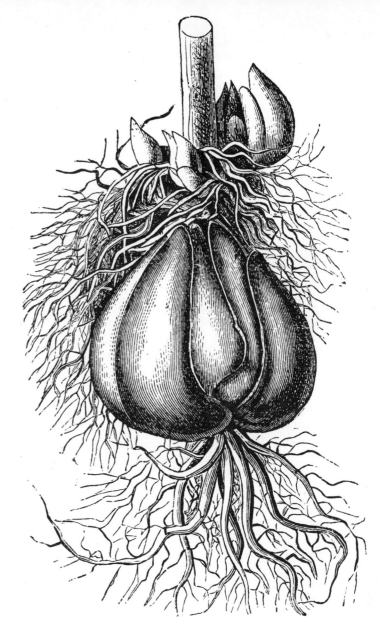

LILY BULBS WITH BULBLETS

Monkshood	Aconitum species	A	6.0-8.0
Morning-glory	Ipomoea species	A	6.0-8.0
Mountain-ash, American	Sorbus americana	C	4.0-5.0
Mountain-dandelion	Krigia montana	B	5.0-6.0
Mountainholly	Nemopanthus mucronatus	B	5.0-6.0
Mountain-laurel	Kalmia latifolia	B	5.0-6.0
Mulberry	Morus, named species and varieties	A	6.0-8.0
Muskmelon		A	6.0-7.0
Nailwort, Allegheny	Paronychia argyrocoma	C	4.0-5.0
Nailwort, Spreading	Paronychia dichotoma	B	5.0-6.0
Narcissus	Narcissus species	A	6.0-8.0
Nasturtium	Tropaeolum species	A	6.0-8.0
Neillia, Tube	Neillia sinensis	B	5.0-6.0
Nightshade	Solanum, many species	A	6.0-8.0
Ninebark	Physocarpus species	A	6.0-8.0
Oak, Black	Quercus velutina	A	6.0-7.0
Oak, Blackjack	Quercus marilandica	B	5.0-6.0
Oak, Pin	Quercus palustris	A	6.0-7.0
Oak, Post	Quercus stellata	B	5.0-6.0
Oak, San Blackjack	Quercus catesbaei	B	5.0-6.0
Oak, Red	Quercus rubra	A	6.0-7.0
Oak, Scarlet	Quercus coccinea	A	6.0-7.0
Oak, Scrub	Quercus ilicifolia	C	4.0-5.0
Oak, Southern Red	Quercus falcata	B	5.0-6.0
Oak, Swamp White	Quercus bicolor	A	6.0-8.0
Oak, Willow	Quercus Phellos	B	5.0-6.0
Oakfern	Dryopteris linnaeana	A	6.0-7.0
Oats	Avena sativa	A	6.0-7.0
Oconne-bells	Shortia galacifolia	B	5.0-6.0
Okra	Hibiscus esculentus	A	6.0-8.0
Onion	Allium, many species	A	6.0-7.0
Onion, Acid-soil	Allium oxyphilum	B	5.0-6.0
Orange*	Citrus sinensis	B	5.0-7.0
Orchid, Grass-pink	Calopogon pulchellus	C	4.0-5.0
Orchid, Green Roundleaf	Habenaria orbiculata	C	4.0-5.0
Orchid, Heartleaf	Listera cordata	B	5.0-6.0
Orchid, Hooker	Habenaria hookeri	B	5.0-6.0
Orchid, Rose-spire	Habenaria peramoena	B	5.0-6.0
Orchid, Satyr	Habenaria bracteata	B	5.0-6.0
Orchid, Small Roundleaf	Orchis rotundifolia	A	6.0-7.0
Oregon Hollygrape	Mahonia aquifolium	A	6.0-8.0
Oxalis	Oxalis, many species	A	6.0-8.0
Pachysandra, Japanese	Pachysandra terminalis (indifferent)	A & B	5.0-8.0
Pansy	Viola tricolor	A	6.0-8.0

FANCY PANSY

PINKS

Parnassia, Brook	Parnassia asarifolia	B	5.0-6.0
Parnassia, Carolina	Parnassia caroliniana	A	6.0-8.0
Parsley	Petroselinum hortense	A-B	5.0-7.0
Parsnip	Pastinaca sativa	A	6.0-8.0
Partridgeberry	Mitchella repens	B	5.0-6.0
Passionflower	Passiflora species	A	6.0-8.0
Paulownia	Paulownia tomentosa	A	6.0-8.0
Pea, Common	Pisum sativum	A	6.0-8.0
Pea, Sweet	Lathyrus odoratus	A	6.0-8.0
Peach	Amygdalus species	A	6.0-8.0
Peanut	Arachis hypogaea	B	5.0-6.0
Pear	Pyrus species	A	6.0-8.0
Peatpink	Silene pennsylvanica	A	6.0-7.0
Pecan		A	6.0-7.0
Pentstemon	Pentstemon, many species	A	6.0-8.0
Peony	Paeonia species	A	6.0-8.0
Pepper	Piper species	A	6.0-6.5
Perwinkle	Vinca, named species and varieties	A	6.0-8.0
Petunia	Petunia hybrida	A	6.0-8.0
Phlox, Annual	Phlox drummondi	A	6.0-8.0
Phlox, Creeping	Phlox stolonifera	B	5.0-6.0
Phlox, Garden	Phlox paniculata	A	6.0-8.0
Phlox, Mountain	Phlox ovata	B	5.0-6.0
Phlox, Sandhill	Phlox amoena	B	5.0-6.0
Pine	Pinus, many though not all species	B	5.0-6.0
Pineapple	Ananas sativus	B	5.0-6.0
Pink	Dianthus, many species	A	6.0-8.0
Pipsissewa	Chimaphila	B	5.0-6.0
Pitcherplant	Sarracenia	C	4.0-5.0
Pitcherplant, California	Darlingtonia californica	C	4.0-5.0
Planetree	Platanus, named species and varieties	A	6.0-8.0
Plum, Common	Prunus domestica	A	6.0-8.0
Pogonia, Rose	Pogonia ophioglossoides	C	4.0-5.0
Poinsettia	Euphorbia pulcherrima	A	6.0-8.0
Poisonlily	Zygadenus	B	5.0-6.0
Polygala, Fringed	Polygala paucifolia	B	5.0-6.0
Polypody, Golden	Polypodium aureum	C	4.0-5.0
Poplar	Populus, named species and varieties	A	6.0-8.0
Poppy	Papaver species	A	6.0-8.0
Potato	Solanum tuberosum	B	4.8-6.5
Potato, Sweet (according to variety)		A or B	5.0-6.0 or 6.0-7.0
Prairiegentian	Eustoma russellianum	A	6.0-8.0
Prickly-ash	Zanthoxylum americanum	A	6.0-8.0
Pricklypear, Common	Opuntia compressa	B	5.0-6.0
Primrose	Primula, many species	A	6.0-8.0
Privet	Ligustrum species	A	6.0-8.0

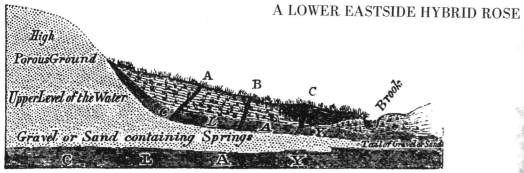

Purpleleaf Plum	Prunus cerasifera pissardi	A	6.0-8.0
Pussytoes, Common	Antennaria dioica	B	5.0-6.0
Pyrola	Pyrola	B	5.0-6.0
Radish	Raphanus sativus	A	6.0-8.0
Raspberry, European	Rubus idaeus	B	5.0-6.0
Rattlesnake-plantain, Checkered	Epipactis (Goodyera) tesselata	B	5.0-6.0
Rattlesnake-plaintain, Downy	Epipactis (Goodyera) pubescens	B	5.0-6.0
Rattlesnake-plaintain, Lesser	Epipactis (Goodyera) repens ophioides	B	5.0-6.0
Redbud	Cercis species	A	6.0-8.0
Redcedar	Juniperus virginiana and varieties	A	6.0-7.0
Redtop	Agrostis palustris (alba)	A	6.0-7.0
Rein-orchid, One-leaf	Habenaria obtusata	B	5.0-6.0
Retinospora	Retinospora, named species and varieties	A	6.0-7.0
Rhododendron	Rhododendron	B	5.0-6.0
Rhodora	Rhodora canadensis	B	5.0-6.0
Rice		A	6.0-7.0
Rose	Rosa, many species	A	6.0-8.0
Rosemallow	Hibiscus, many species	A	6.0-8.0
Rose-orchid	Pogonia divaricata	C	4.0-5.0
Runningpine	Lycopodium clavatum	B	5.0-6.0
Rye	Secale cereale	A	6.0-7.0
Sage	Salvia, many species	A	6.0-8.0
Sally, Blooming	Epilobium angustifolium	A	6.0-7.0
Sandmyrtle	Leiophyllum	C	4.0-5.0
Sandwort, Greenland	Arenaria groenlandica	C	4.5-5.5
Sassafras	Sassafras variifolium	A	6.0-7.0
Savin	Juniperus sabina & varieties	A	6.0-7.0
Saxifrage	Saxifraga, many species	A	6.0-8.0
Sedge, Fraser	Carex fraseri	B	5.0-6.0
Selaginella, Rock	Selaginella rupestris	A	6.0-7.0

Shadblow	Amelanchier	A	6.0-7.0
Shagbark Hickory	Hicoria ovata	A	6.0-7.0
Shootingstar	Dodecatheon species	A	6.0-8.0
Silverbell, Great	Halesia tetraptera	B	5.0-6.0
Silver Buffaloberry	Shepherdia argentea	A	6.0-8.0
Snapdragon	Antirrhinum	A	6.0-7.0
Snapweed	Impatiens species	A	6.0-8.0
Snowbell, American	Styrax americana	B	5.0-6.0
Snowberry	Symphoricarpos species	A	6.0-8.0
Snowdrop, Common	Galanthus nivalis	A	6.0-8.0
Solomonplume	Smilacina racemosa	A	6.0-8.0
Solomonplume, European	Maianthemum bifolium	B	5.0-6.0
Solomonplume, Heartleaf	Maianthemum canadense	B	5.0-6.0
Solomonseal	Polygonatum species	A	6.0-8.0
Sorrel, French	Rumex scutatus	A	6.0-7.0

Sourwood	Oxydendron arboreum C, B, A, (sterile soil)		4.0-8.0
Soybean		A	6.0-7.0
Speedwell	Veronica, many species	A	6.0-8.0
Speedwell, Spike	Veronica spicata	B	5.0-6.0
Spicebush	Benzoin aestivale	B	5.5-6.5
Spiderwort	Tradescanti a, many species	A	6.0-8.0
Spiderwort, Dwarf	Tradescantia rosea	B	5.0-6.0
Spinach, Common	Spinacia oleracea	A	6.5-7.0
Spirea	Spirea, many species	A	6.0-8.0
Spleenwort, Appalachian	Asplenium montanum	C	4.0-5.0
Spleenwort, Lobed	Asplenium pinnatifidum	C	4.0-5.0
Spleenwort, Maidenhair	Asplenium trichomanes	A	6.0-8.0
Spleenwort, Narrow-leaved	Asplenium angustifolium	A	6.0-8.0
Spleenwort, Silvery	Asplenium acrostichrides	A	6.0-8.0
Springbeauty, Carolina	Claytonia caroliniana	B	5.0-6.0
Spruce	Picea	B	5.0-6.0
Squash	Cucurbita maxima	A	6.0-8.0
Squill	Scilla species	A	6.0-8.0
Staggerbush	Pieris	C	4.0-5.0
Starflower, American	Trientalis americana	C	4.0-5.0
Stargrass	Aletris farinosa	B	5.0-6.0
Star-of-Bethlehem	Ornithogalum species	A	6.0-8.0
Stewartia, Mountain	Stewartia pentagyna	B	5.0-6.0
Stock	Mathiola incana var. annv	A	6.0-7.0
Stock	Mathiola incana	A	6.0-7.0
Stonecrop	Sedum, many species	A	6.0-8.0
Stonemint	Cunila mariana	B	5.0-6.0
St. Johnswort	Hypericum, many species	A	6.0-8.0
Strawberries,* most varieties	Fragaria species	B	5.0-6.0
Sugar Cane	Saccharum officinarum	A	6.0-8.0
Sumac	Rhus, many species	A	6.0-8.0
Sundew	Drosera	C	4.0-5.0
Sundrops, Blueleaf	Oenothera glauca	B	5.0-6.0
Sunflower	Helianthus, many species	A	6.0-8.0
Sunrose, Common	Helianthemum chamaecistus	A	6.0-7.0
Swamp-pink	Helonias bullata	C	4.0-5.0
Sweetbay	Magnolia glauca	C	4.0-5.0
Sweet Birch	Betula lenta	B	5.0-6.0
Sweetclover	Melilotus species	A	6.0-8.0
Sweetfern	Comptonia asplenifolia	B	5.0-6.0
Sweetgum	Liquidambar styraciflua	A	6.0-7.0
Sweetleaf, Common	Symplocos tinctoria	A	6.0-7.0
Sweetshrub	Calycanthus species	A	6.0-8.0
Sweetspire	Itea virginica	A	6.0-7.0
Tamarix	Tamarixk, named species and varieties	A	6.0-8.0

*Some 6.0-7.0; some Florida-Texas varieties 7.0-8.0

198

BLUE SPRUCE

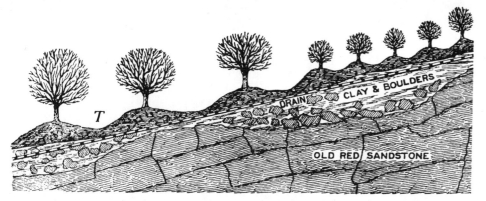

Tea			B	5.0-5.5
Timothy	Phleum pratense		A	6.0-7.0
Tobacco	Nicotiana species	A or B	5.0-6.0 or 6.0-8.0	
Tomato	Lycopersicum esculentum		A	6.0-7.0
Trailing-arbutus	Epigaea repens		C	4.0-5.0
Trefoil, Birdsfoot	Lotus corniculatus		A	6.0-7.0
Trillium, Painted	Trillium undulation		C	4.0-5.0
Trillium, Rose	Trillium stylosum		A	6.0-7.0
Trillium, Snow	Trillium grandiflorum		A	6.0-8.0
Troutlily	Erythronium species		A	6.0-8.0
Trumpetcreeper	Bignonia species		A	6.0-8.0
Tulip	Tulipa species		A	6.0-7.0
Tuliptree	Liriodendron tulipifera		A	6.0-7.0
Tung-oil Tree	Aleurites fordi		B	5.0-6.0
Turkeysbeard	Xerophyllum asphodeloides		C	4.0-5.0
Tupelo	Nyssa sylvatica		A	6.0-7.0
Turnip	Brassica rapa		A	6.0-8.0
Turtlehead, Pink	Chelone lyoni		B	5.0-6.0
Turtlehead, Rose	CHelone obliqua		B	5.0-6.0
Twinflower, American	Linnaea borealis americana		C	4.0-5.0
Twinleaf	Jeffersonia diphylla		A	6.0-8.0
Twistedstalk, Rosy	Streptopus roseus		C	4.0-5.0
Umbrellaleaf	Diphylleia cymosa		B	5.0-6.0
Velvetbean, Deering	Stizolobium deeringianum		A	6.0-7.0
Verbena	Verbena species		A	6.0-8.0
Vetch	Vicia, many species		A	6.0-7.0
Viburnum	Viburnum, many species		A	6.0-8.0
Violet	Viola, many species		A	6.0-8.0
Violet, Birdsfoot	Viola pedata		B	5.0-6.0
Violet, Lilac Birdsfoot	Viola pedata lineariloba		B	5.0-6.0

Walnut	Juglans, many species	A	6.0-8.0
Watercress	Radicula nasturtium aquaticum	A	6.0-8.0
Watermelon	Citrillus vulgaris	A	6.0-7.0
Weigela	Weigela species	A	6.0-8.0
Wheat	Triticum aestivum	A	6.0-7.0
Whitecedar	Chamaecyparis thyoides	C	4.0-5.0
White Oak	Quercus alba	A	5.5-7.0
Wild-indigo, Yellow	Baptisia tinctoria	B	5.0-6.0
Wildginger, Heartleaf	Asarum virginicum	B	5.0-6.0
Wildginger, Mottled	Asarum shuttleworthi	C	4.0-5.0
Willow	Salix, many species	A	6.0-8.0
Willow, Creeping	Salix repens	B	5.0-6.0
Wintergreen	Gaultheria procumbens	B	5.0-6.0
Winter Jasmine	Jasminum nudiflorum	A	6.0-8.0
Wisteria	Wisteria species	A	6.0-8.0
Witch-hazel	Ilamamelis, named species and varieties	A	6.0-7.0
Withe-rod, Smooth	Viburnum Nudum	B	5.0-6.0
Woodbine	Lonicera periclymenum	A	6.0-7.0
Woodfern, Boott	Dryopteris boottii	B	5.0-6.0
Woodfern, Clinton	Dryopteris clintoniana	B	5.0-6.0
Woodfern, Common	Dryopteris intermedia	A	6.0-7.0
Woodfern, Mountain	Dryopteris dilatata (americana)	B	5.0-6.0
Woodfern, Toothed	Dryopteris spinulosa	A	6.0-7.0
Woodsia, Rusty	Woodsia ilvensis	B	5.0-6.0
Woodsorrel, Common	Oxalis acetosella (montana)	B	5.0-6.0
Woodwaxen	Genista tinctoria	B	5.5-6.5
Wormwood	Artemisia species	A	6.0-8.0
Yellowroot	Zanthorhiza apiifolia	B	5.0-6.0
Yellow-wood	Cladrastis tinctoria	A	6.0-8.0
Yew	Taxus, many species	A	5.5-7.0
Yucca	Yucca, many species	A	6.0-8.0
Zenobia, Dusty	Zenobia pulverulenta	B	5.0-6.0
Zinnia	Zinnia elegans	A	6.0-8.0

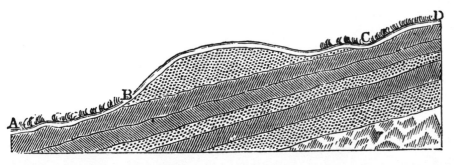

YUCCA GLORIOSA

CHEMICAL ELEMENTS REQUIRED BY HIGHER PLANTS

Some twenty or more chemical elements have been found to be essential to the successful growth of higher plants. Since a plant will require some of these elements in macroquantities (large amounts) and in microquantities ((trace amounts) we may classify them as major, and minor or trace plant foods on the basis of the amounts required. But this distinction does not alter the essential nature of any single one of the elements, nor does it eliminate the possibility that other elements may be required in smaller amounts than their presence as incidental impurities in raw material encountered in present day scientific studies.

Elements required by plants in Macroquantities

Carbon
Nitrogen
Calcium
Hydrogen
Phosphorus
Magnesium
Oxygen
Potassium
Sulfur

Elements required by plants in Microquantities

Iron
Copper
Chlorine
Vanadium
Manganese
Zinc
Cobalt
Boron
Molybdenum
Sodium

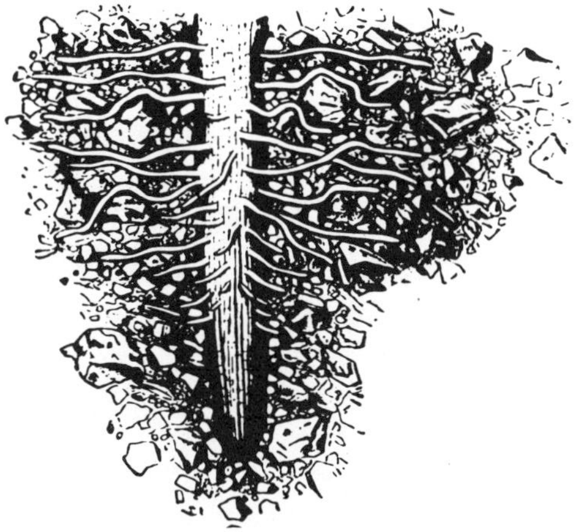

Terminal portion of a root of Pentstemon with Root-hairs penetrating between the particles of soil.

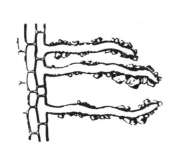

Longitudinal section of surface tissues of young root of Pentstemon showing root-hairs arising as outgrowth of the surface cells.

201

YARD GRASS—CROW FOOT—DOG'S TAIL

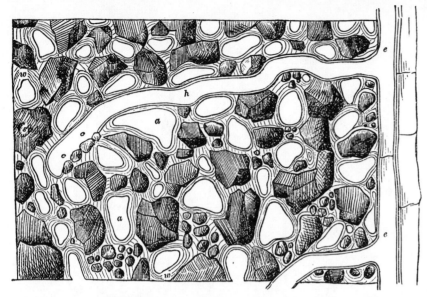

ROOT HAIR IN THE SOIL, SHOWING ABSORPTION OF MOISTURE.

MAJOR PLANT FOODS

Elements required by plants in Macroquantities

The minerals needed by the growing plant must be supplied by the silt fraction of soils, that portion, as mentioned previously, resulting from the slow decomposition of the native rocks. There are perhaps as many as one hundred separate mineral compounds in good soils. The so-called major plant foods, however, consist of the compounds of nitrogen, phosphorus, potassium, calcium and magnesium, sulfur, plus carbon, hydrogen, and oxygen. These will be discussed separately in the order just mentioned.

A. Nitrogen

Nitrogen is the element which stimulates above-ground growth and produces the rich, green color characteristic of a healthy plant. It furthermore encourages the plumpness and succulence of fruit and grains, and increases the protein percentage. The utilization of potash, phosphorus, and other nutrients is stimulated by the presence of nitrogen, but an excess will produce harmful effects, such as delaying maturity or ripening of the crop, lowering its quality, weakening the plant, with consequent "lodging", and decreasing its resistance to disease. Nitrogen then is an important element but must be used in a balanced ratio with the other plant foods.

It might be well to point out in this discussion of nitrogen that recent experimenters have disclosed information which would indicate that the presence of excess nitrates in foods might be detrimental to the health of man and beast. This is based upon the fact that nitrates may be reduced by bacteria to nitrites and in this form, in large quantities, will be poisonous in the blood stream. The investigation has covered many leafy vegetables and plants, including corn. This suggests a new aspect of the importance of controlling nitrates in soils. Some of the diseases mentioned are abortion in cattle, hay poisoning, grass tetany, and reduction of hemoglobin content in the blood.

Soils are often low in nitrogen

Soils ordinarily contain in the neighborhood of 0.1% of nitrogen and a proportionately smaller percentage of available nitrates, consequently it is apparent that the supply would be quickly exhausted by continual cropping. Unavoidable loss due to the leaching action of water would hasten the exhaustion considerably. It is thus apparent that the supply of nitrogen in soils is ordinarily not large at all when considered in relation to the need of crops. Sandy soils, particularly, are low in nitrogen, due to the rapid rate at which decomposition of organic matter and the leaching of resulting soluble products takes place.

Available nitrogen in soils

The nitrogen of the soil usually exists almost entirely in the organic matter. In this form the nitrogen is not available for use by the plants directly, but must first be transformed by soil bacteria (oxidation) to an avaiable form, such as nitrates which are soluble in water and which may then be absorbed by the plant roots. The bacteria bring about this transformation of the un-available nitrogen into the assimilable form, not because of any interest or obligation in the welfare of the crops, but simply because the assimilable forms, ammonia and nitrates, happen to be the by-products of their own feeding activity on the organic matter in the soils. Some forms of organic matter are readily attacked by bacteria and the nitrogen transformed to these soluble nitrates, etc. Animal manure, crop residues, and many fertilizing materials belong to these forms. Under certain conditions, a portion of the organic matter passes over to forms in which the nitrogen is of low availability and not readily assimilable by the plant. In other words, the resulting organic matter is so resistant that the bacteria have difficulty in feeding upon it. Heavy black soils that have been farmed for many years, mucks, and peats may have a large portion of their nitrogen in these resistant forms.

July 15

Effect of fertilizing vegetable soil with phosphates and other substances.

B. Phosphorus

Phosphorus is necessary for the hardy growth of the plant and activity of the cells. It encourages root development, and by hastening the maturity of the plant, it increases the ratio of grain to straw, as well as the total yield. It plays an important part in increasing the palatability of plants and stimulates the formation of fats, convertible starches and healthy seed. By stimulating rapid cell development in the plant, phosphorus naturally increases the resistance to disease. An excess of phosphorus does not cause the harmful effects of excessive nitrogen and has an important balancing effect upon the plant.

Phosphorus in soils

Life, either plant or animal, cannot exist without phosphorus, and, of course, the soil is the chief source of this constituent. A lack of phosphorus, therefore, not only retards growth but also lowers the one and vigor of both plant and animal. Animals secure their phosphorus indirectly by utilizing plants for food, while the plants, themselves, secure the phosphorus directly from the soil.

Soil, as a rule, contains less than 0.1% of total phosphorus (available and unavailable) and a large portion of the cultivated areas of the eastern half of the United States contain less than one-half of this amount. The plowed layer of soil on an acre of ordinary loam soil weighs approximately 2,000,000 pounds, and if it contains 0.05% of the phosphorus it would have 1000 pounds of phosphorus per acre. Since a 100 bushel crop of corn requires about 25 pounds of available phosphorus, the above plowed layer has sufficient phosphorus for over 40 crops of corn of 100 bushels each.

Cropping depletes soil phosphorus

From what has just been said, it is apparent that the supply of phosphorus in the soil can be quickly exhausted by continuous cropping if provision is not made for the return of phosphorus in the form of farm manure and commercial fertilizers. It is further to be noted that as soon as the content of phosphorus in a soil goes below a certain level, maximum crop yields drop below a profitable level.

The seeds of plants are relatively high in phosphorus. The bones of animals consist chiefly of calcium phosphate. Milk, likewise, is rich in phosphorus. Consequently, when it is considered that grain and livestock are raised and sold, such enterprise gradually depletes the soil of phosphorus unless it is replaced from time to time.

Soil phosphates not always in available form

The phosphorus of soils is not only low in amount, but is very often found in forms which are difficult for the plant to assimilate. In acid soils, particularly, the phosphorus may be converted into basic iron phosphate which has a low availability. The calcium phosphate, on the other hand, is more available; therefore, it is desirable to apply phosphates to soils which are properly limed and show slightly acid reaction. Phosphates applied to properly limed soils are kept in available form. It is not meant to infer, however, that basic iron phosphate is entirely unavailable, for plants do feed on it slowly and if the growing season is long they may make a fairly satisfactory growth. For many crops and for maximum yields of practically all crops, however, basic iron phosphate has not been found to supply phosphorus readily enough.

How much available phosphorus should soils contain?

It is extremely important to test soils in order to find out whether or not they contain sufficient readily available phosphorus for good plant growth. Experience has shown that for general farming in the Northern states, silt loam, sandy loam, and clay soils should contain at least 75 pounds of readily

available phosphorus per acre, and sands 50 pounds per acre. More available phosphorus than these amounts is, of course, desirable and beneficial. The desirable bacteria in soils, such as the nitrogen fixing bacteria, are greatly stimulated by an abundance of readily available phosphorus. It is significant, furthermore, that the best agricultural soils are all high in readily available phosphorus, since the abundance of readily available phosphorus favors all the conditions which go to make a real fertile soil. A difference of 25 pounds of available phosphorus per acre in the lower range is sufficient to exert a marked influence on the crop producing power of a soil.

Effect of fertilizing muck soil with different phosphates.

For garden crops and many special truck crops, at least 150 pounds per acre are needed, and higher amounts such as 200 to 300 pounds or more are desirable. In the Southern states, due to the longer growing season, fairly good crops can be secured with about one-half of the amounts just indicated for the Northern states.

If the amount of readily available phosphorus found by testing is less than the amounts just indicated, the application of phosphate fertilizer is recommended.

C. Potassium (commonly called Potash)

Potash has much to do with the one and vigor of plants, encouraging development of healthy root system, and, like phosphorus, it counteracts the harmful effect of excessive nitrogen. Where phosphorus hastens the maturity of the plant, potash tends to counteract undue ripening and thereby exerts a balancing effect on both nitrogen and phosphorus. It is essential for starch formation in the plant and the development of chlorophyll by encouraging the reaction or process known as photosynthesis, which is the action of sunlight in bringing about the formation of important products in the plant juices. Unlike phosphorus and nitrogen, it is believed that potash is not built into the structural part of the plant but serves as a catalyst, encouraging beneficial reactions in the plant juices.

Potassium in Soils

In the case of potassium, soils contain very large amounts of this element, but, unfortunately, most of it is in an insoluble form and therefore unavailable or else very slowly available to the plant. The answer to this in most cases is potassium fertilization. Here again the soil acidity or pH value of the soil plays an important part for the presence of calcium seems to be necessary for the growing plant to take up potassium and if the soil is very acid, naturally, there will be a lack of calcium. In such cases, the plant cannot utilize potassium even though it may be present in large amounts in a soluble form.

On the other hand, in alkaline soils where there is a large excess of calcium, the plant is likely to take up calcium in preference to potassium and again we have the same symptoms of a lack of potassium. We may therefore set the limits for potassium utilization between pH 5.0 and 7.0.

While much experimenting remains to be done to establish definitely the proper potassium levels in the soil it is probable that the amount of water soluble and replaceable potassium in the soil should not be in excess of 200 pounds per acre.

D. Calcium

This is an inexpensive plant food but a highly important one. Calcium forms a structural part of the walls of plant cells. It also neutralizes any harmful acids that are formed, thereby controlling the acid-base balance in plant juices. The addition of calcium to acid soils reduces any toxic acidity and, at the same time, benefits the activity of micro-organisms, indirectly increasing the availability of nitrogen and other elements. Calcium is usually applied to the soil along with green manures, since by stimulating the activity of the soil organisms it hastens the decomposition of organic matter, improves the physical condition of heavy soil, thereby increasing the efficiency of manure and fertilizer applications.

E. Magnesium

Magnesium might be considered a companion to calcium, for it is similar in many of its characteristics and usually occurs in nature along with calcium salts. However, in plant nutrition, magnesium is a working companion of phosphorus and stimulates the assimilation of phosphorus by the plant. It is essential in the formation of chlorophyll, contributing largely thereby to the green quality of vegetation. A deficiency of magnesium causes chlorosis, a disease similar to anemia in animals.

F. Sulphur

Sulphur is a most important element to the plant and will gain considerable prominense as we learn more about its functioning. It is utilized by the plant in the development of essential organic compounds, proteins, vitamins, etc. Very little sulphur is applied to agricultural soils, even though in many cases some is needed. Some sulphur is returned to the earth through current rainfall (rain water absorbs sulphur gases from the atmosphere). Sulphur is usually found also in superphosphate and other fertilizers which carry sulfates. Alfalfa grown on soils deficient in sulphur will not contain as much protein as that grown on sulphur-containing soils. Plants grown on sulphur deficient soils lack the healthy green color of normal plants since sulphur has some bearing on chlorophyll production. Hence, it is readily seen that since plants are one of the chief sources of sulphur for man and animal, it is important that it be properly supplied from the soil.

G. Carbon, Hydrogen, and Oxygen

Carbon, Hydrogen, and Oxygen, in the form of water and carbon dioxide are required by all plants in macroquantities, but since we are concerned principally with chemicals absorbed from the soil, they will not be discussed further in these pages.

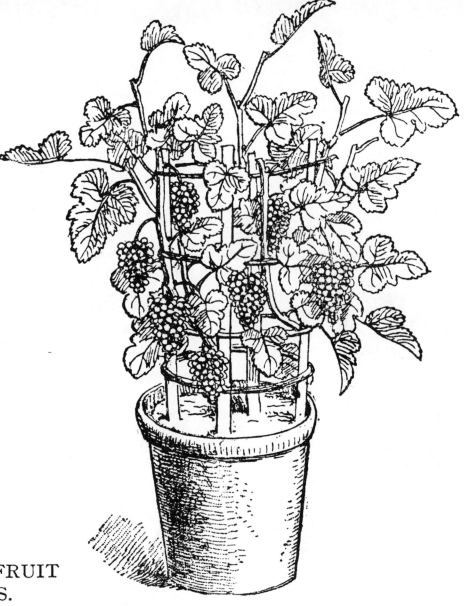

POT GRAPE VINE IN FRUIT COILED ROUND STAKES.

MINOR PLANT FOODS AND SO-CALLED TRACE ELEMENTS

Elements required in Microquantities

It should be the accepted duty on the part of everyone engaged in the growing of food crops to take an increased interest in the new work being done on the minor or so-called trace elements. This research includes studies of their presence or absence in soils, their detection in the plant, but what is more important, the study of the effect of the consumption of these improved plants by the animal world in promoting better health and a higher resistance to disease. There is evidence at hand to encourage the hope that it will soon be shown that such trace elements as zinc, copper, boron and others, are absolutely essential to human well-being. The effect of the absence of some of these is shown clearly in actual cases studied. Medical research is showing some astounding results in studies involving the function of blood cells which have been deprived of some of these trace elements. Manifestations of certain diseases in poultry, livestock and humans can be traced to deficiencies in trace element groups, and some cases are almost entirely relieved by their addition to the diet. Iron, copper, and manganese are important performers in the building of vogorus flesh and blood. Cobalt, while needed in infinitesimally small quantities, fits into this picture. Boron and zinc with manganese are extremely important in the diet of warm-blooded animals. It has been proven that some fluorine in the diet is beneficial in the building of strong animal teeth. Iodine, of course, is essential in body finish and will prevent conditions of hypothyroidism, goiter, and lowered metabolsim. As stated above, there is much yet to be learned but sufficient evidence is before the world to give prominence to the need for trace elements in modern agriculture. Some of these can be added to the feed of livestock but a well-balanced ration could much better come from the soil originally, if these factors were taken care of as needed in the fertilization program. The plant will use them if they are available, and the animal will subsequently get them from plants raised on properly fertilized soils. Much of the popular writing of today deals with the increasing city population over the entire world and the problem of feeding these millions has alarmed quite a few citizens. The fear seems to be with the quantity of food required rather than the quality needed for proper maintenance of health.

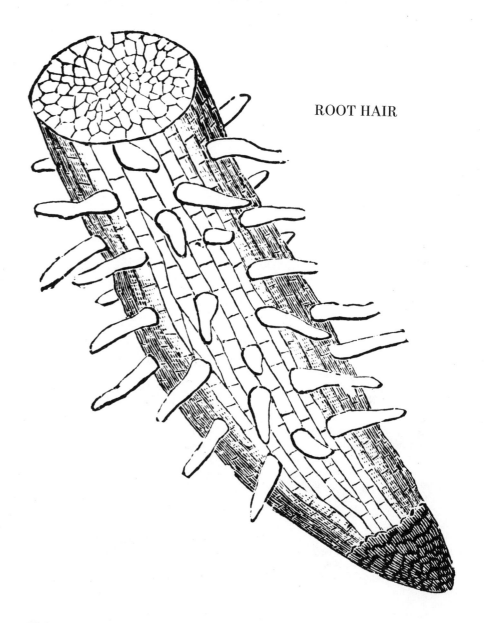

ROOT HAIR

There can be no question about the ability of modern American agriculture to raise a sufficient volume of foodstuffs, but if the proper emphasis is not given to the minor or trace elements in the soil from which this food is to be taken the tragedy will appear in the lack of good health and well-being of future peoples. Hidden hunger will be encountered under such circumstances even though there seems to be an adequate quantity of food for everyone.

In discussing the subject of trace elements here, no effort will be made to differentiate between the various groups and the complete functions which they effect through their presence or absence. It is known that some of these are particularly important in the production of energy and plant health; some as balancing agents to maintain normal vigorous growth; while still others serve as catalysts or intermediate agents essential to the formation of certain chemical compounds readily converted into vitamins, proteins, hormones, etc.

Manganese

Manganese is a minor element which is essential to normal plant development and works along with magnesium in eliminating chlorosis. This element is needed in very small amounts by the plant and must be applied accordingly. A deficiency of manganese usually occurs in soils which are over-limed. It is now believed that manganese is a very important minor element in the soil because of its relation to the production of amino acids and proteins in the plant.

Iron

Iron is needed only in limited amounts as an essential element and is directly connected with the functioning of chlorophyll. A lack of iron contributes to chlorosis and gives rise to malnutritional anemia among humans and cattle. Like manganese, iron may be rendered unavailable to the plant in over-limed and poorly drained soils. While the quantity of iron needed by the plant during its various stages of growth is extremely small. it is essential that it be available. Most soils contain lots of iron but, unfortunately, it is in a form that is not soluble. This is particularly true of soils in the neutral and alkaline zones where the pH will be above 7.0. The oxidation-reduction activity in the organic fraction of good soils has much to do with changing insoluble iron into a soluble form available to the plants. Here is another illustration, not only of the importance of the chemical and biological balance of good soils

Ruby orange graft on old sweet-orange stock, put in March

208

but, also, of the necessity for maintaining normal quantities of organic matter and the proper pH, as discussed previously.

Boron

This element has received a lot of publicity and rightly so. While it is required in very small quantities by the plant, its presence is essential to the health of the plant and its resistance to disease. Alfalfa has probably profited more than any other crop from the recent knowledge of the benefits of boron applications but it serves other plants with equal effectiveness. Studies have shown that alfalfa produced on soils containing an adequate boron and manganese supply develop a higher content of amino acids and protein. Much interest centers in boron because it has been found that a deficiency of this element has caused many types of diseases in plants, particularly of the types known as "root-rot" and "heart-rot" found in beets, turnips, celery, tobacco, apples, cauliflower, and others. Very small quantities of boron are needed to correct existing deficiencies.

Copper, Cobalt and Zinc

Much has yet to be learned about the three elements cooper, cobalt, and zinc in plant nutrition. They are believed to be an important group in the field of substances involved in the regulation of oxidation and reduction processes, both in the soil and also in the plant itself. Traces of these minerals are essential to the well-being of plants, animals, and man and therefore cannot be overlooked in viewing the complete picture of plant nutrition. Plants grown without copper do not show normal growth and are characterized by stunted formation of the young branches.

Lack of cobalt, likewise, shows this effect upon the plant and more particularly upon animals consuming cobalt deficient vegetation. Pastures grown on soils deficient in copper and cobalt produce characteristic diseases in livestock. These diseases, in practically all cases, being eliminated when the proper amounts of these materials were applied to the diet.

Ainc appears to be more closely associated with the formation of chlorophyll than copper or cobalt but bears a similar relation to the latter in passing on symptoms of anemia to livestock fed on zinc deficient plants. It is interesting to note that when investigators suspected the deficiency of copper, cobalt, and zonc as being the cause of certain nutritional diseases, they were able to produce these symptoms in animals at will by eliminating these elements from the diet.

Oak in its deciduous state, in the Exeter Nursery. Height 75 ft.; diameter of trunk 6 ft.; diameter of the head 65 ft.

209

Oak in full foliage, in the Exeter Nursery.

Iodine, Chlorine, Fluorine, Sodium and Lithium

This group of elements represents two chemical families which are of extreme importance in the plant and animal world. Iodine, chlorine, and fluorine are members of the so-called halogen family and are widely distributed in nature.

Iodine, of course, is essential to good human health and is one of the important regulators of metabolism. Most of the iodine supplied in the human body is of course related to the throid gland, and a deficiency of iodine will cause weakness and faulty growth. The supply of iodine to animals through the plant is a distinct advantage in the raising of livestock. Plants absorb iodine without difficulty, particularly the larger leafed vegetables. Pastures treated with potassium iodide increase the iodine content of the herbage sufficiently to show an improved reproduction rate in the animals consuming it. Since it is not known to be absolutely essential for the normal growth of plants its absorption will vary with the iodine content of the soil upon which they are grown.

While it has only recently been reported that there is a chlorine requirement for higher plants, the need of chlorides by the animal kingdom is well known as a stimulant for various body functions and its presence in plants is therefore of significance from the point of view of animal nutrition, although this substance can be added to the diet as a common salt with safety and convenience.

Fluorine is not considered essential to plant life but, undoubtedly, has some minor function in the development of certain useful compounds in the plant juices. The amounts appearing in the plant are small and do not increase appreciably even when the soil may contain large amounts of the element. It has been recently found that fluorine is important in the development of sound teeth and could therefore fill an important place in livestock development. It may be said of the three elements iodine, chlorine, and fluorine, while they are not particularly essential to plant life their absorption by edible vegetation furnishes important body building material for both animal and man.

Sodium and lithium are two members of the family of alkali metals and their salts are among the most soluble known.

Sodium is closely related to potassium and in instances where a limited potash supply in the soil is experienced much sodium is absorbed as a plant food. Being a very soluble substance it is extremely active in the soil water and liberates potassium and perhaps other elements which are then taken up by the plant.

Lithium has not been very thoroughly studied but is probably a companion substance in these reactions. The use of lithium to increase the growth of leaf tissue has been reported by some investigators, particularly in connection with the cultivation of tobacco, where it is said to greatly improve the quality of the leaf for use as a wrapper in cigar manufacturing. Both sodium and lithium are prevalent in nature in adequate quantities and there is no evidence at this time to indicate that any great deficiency of these elements exists.

Aluminum and Molybdenum

Aluminum is widely distributed in nature but its essential nature has not been established. In some plants it appears to be toxic. The presence of soluble aluminum in the soil is of no great significance except in cases where it may be present in excess quantities. Its solubility is greatly reduced by liming such soils.

Molybdenum, on the other hand, may be considered as an essential trace element for many plants. It serves both as a catalyst and a promotor even though it is required in very small amounts. It is thought by some investigators to be required in the process of nitrogen fixation by leguminous plants, but some studies seem to show that the essential nature of molybdenum is not limited to leguminous plants.

It will be well to repeat here that a great deal more knowledge is required before these trace elements can be classified properly in their degree of importance to plant life. They have been mentioned in this discussion in order to acquaint the reader with the significance of their presence or absence in the soil and to emphasize the complexity of nature's processes in the production of the delicate parts of our common plants.

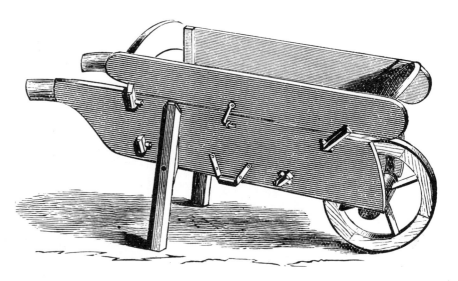

WOOD BARROW WITH MOVABLE TOP

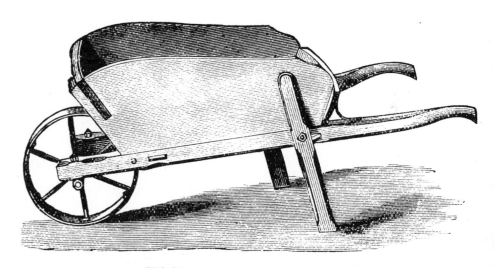

WOODEN WHEELBARROW

211

RELATIVE NITROGEN, PHOSPHORUS AND POTASSIUM REQUIRE-
MENTS FOR COMMON CROPS AND PLANTS
VH = very high; H = high; M = medium; L = low
(L* = nitrogen supplied by legume organisms)

	Nitrogen	Phosphorus	Potassium
Alfalfa	L*	H	H
Apples	M	L	L
Asparagus	VH	H	VH
Barley	M	H	M
Beans, Lima or String	L	M	M
Beets, Early	VH	VH	VH
Beets, Late	H	VH	H
Bent Grass	M	L	L
Blackberries	L	L	L
Blueberries	L	L	L
Blue Grass, Kentucky	M	M	L
Broccoli	H	H	H
Brussels Sprouts	H	H	H
Buckwheat	M	L	L
Cabbage, Early	VH	VH	VH
Cabbage, Late	H	H	H
Carrots, Early	H	H	H
Carrots, Late	M	M	M
Cauliflower, Early	VH	VH	VH
Cauliflower, Late	H	H	VH
Celery, Early	VH	VH	VH
Celery, Late	H	H	VH
Clover, Alsike	L*	M	M
Clover, Ladino	L*	M	M
Clover, Red	L*	H	H
Clover, Wild White	L*	M	M
Corn, Field	M	M	M
Corn, Sweet, Early	H	H	H
Corn, Sweet, Late	M	M	M
Cucumbers	H	H	H
Deciduous Plants	M	L	L
Deciduous Shrubs	M	M	L
Deciduous Trees	M	L	L

CELERY

212

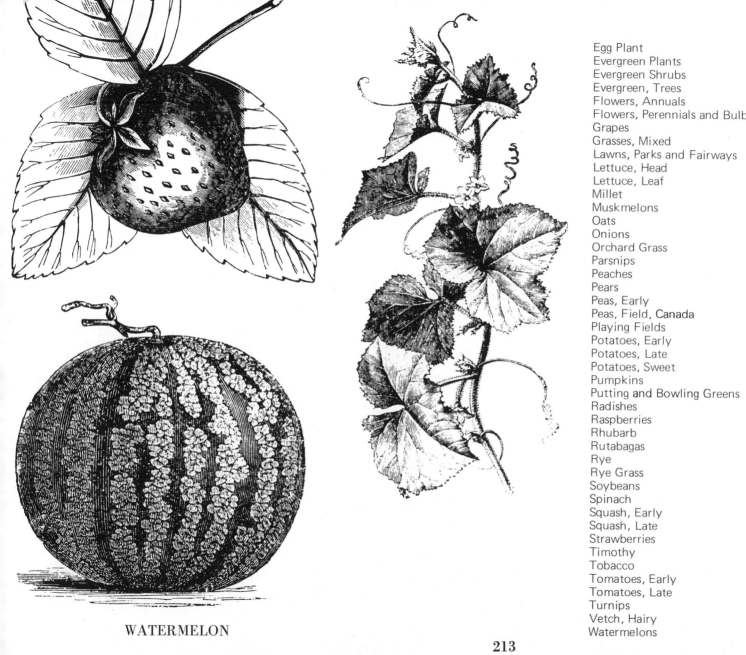

WATERMELON

	Nitrogen	Phosphorus	Potassium
Egg Plant	H	H	H
Evergreen Plants	L	L	L
Evergreen Shrubs	L	L	L
Evergreen, Trees	L	L	L
Flowers, Annuals	H	H	H
Flowers, Perennials and Bulbs	M	M	M
Grapes	M	M	M
Grasses, Mixed	M	L	L
Lawns, Parks and Fairways	M	M	L
Lettuce, Head	VH	VH	VH
Lettuce, Leaf	H	VH	VH
Millet	M	L	M
Muskmelons	H	H	H
Oats	H	M	M
Onions	H	H	H
Orchard Grass	M	M	M
Parsnips	M	M	M
Peaches	M	L	M
Pears	M	L	L
Peas, Early	M	H	H
Peas, Field, Canada	L*	M	M
Playing Fields	M	M	L
Potatoes, Early	VH	VH	VH
Potatoes, Late	H	VH	VH
Potatoes, Sweet	L	M	H
Pumpkins	M	M	M
Putting and Bowling Greens	H	L	L
Radishes	H	VH	VH
Raspberries	L	L	L
Rhubarb	H	H	H
Rutabagas	M	H	M
Rye	M	L	L
Rye Grass	M	L	L
Soybeans	L*	M	M
Spinach	VH	VH	VH
Squash, Early	H	H	H
Squash, Late	M	M	M
Strawberries	M	M	L
Timothy	M	L	M
Tobacco	VH	M	VH
Tomatoes, Early	M	H	H
Tomatoes, Late	H	H	H
Turnips	L	H	M
Vetch, Hairy	L*	M	M
Watermelons	M	M	M

ORGANIC MATTER

Organic matter is that fraction of soils which results from the decomposition of vegetable and animal matter through the action of bacteria. It is one of the important constituents of soils because it provides the natural home for the millions of bacteriological creatures which are so necessary to plant life. In addition, it serves as a spongy mass to retain water, carbon dioxide, and other chemical products produced in the bacterial world.

In looking at the function of organic matter in soils, a definite and helpful picture can be obtained if one will try to visualize this colloidal material as a coating around each soil particle in the top soil. Its color is usually black, although it does contain some inorganic colloids derived from the silt fraction which are colorless. This coating on the soil particle is moist and forms one of the most active agents for exchange of mineral elements from soil to plant. Its preservation in the soil is of the utmost importance, for without it the rate at which minerals will be made available to the plant will be serious reduced.

A good soil should have between three to five per cent organic matter as a safe margin for continuous rotational cropping use. The examination of soils in good farming areas will show that the organic matter content will vary from one per cent in the lower group to five per cent in the upper levels (peat soils of course run very much higher than this). Organic matter is probably the most expensive of the constituents to build into a depleted soil. It is destroyed by overcropping, burning, and washing. It can be restored through the application of animal manures, the return of stubble and roughage to the land, and by the use of green manures in combination with lime or other products which hasten decomposition. Since it is being used up continuously, every rotational system should be designed to return some organic matter intermittently to the soil.

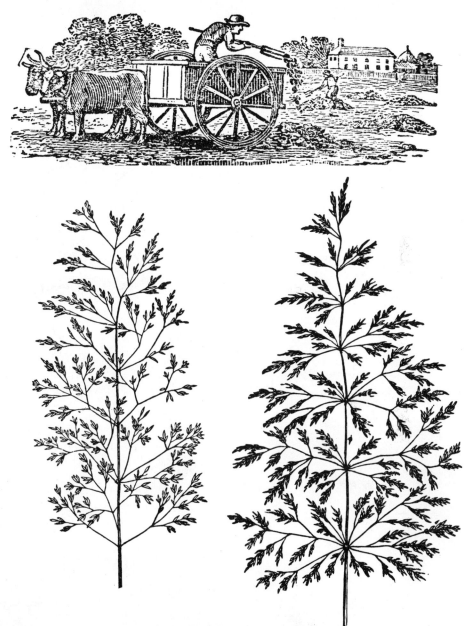

BUYING NURSERY STOCK

NURSERY STOCK—WHAT TO BUY AND WHAT TO EXPECT

Sales of trees, shrubs, vines and other plants purchased at nurseries and other retail establishments offering nursery stock in 1973 are estimated at $2.3 billion. In recent years, with the heavy emphasis on ecology and environmental improvement, the number of plant purchasers has increased markedly, particularly among the younger age groups in their late teens and twenties.

It is not at all unusual today to find "plant boutiques" and other retail plant specialty shops in the major metropolitan areas where young people live and shop. This market is in addition to the garden centers, retail nurseries, hardware stores, department stores, produce departments, roadside markets, and other nursery plant outlets well known to the older age groups.

In addition, local retail outlets, mail order nursery catalogs, magazine advertisements, and newspaper ads continue to furnish information on sources of nursery-produced plants.

As is the case in just about any other field, the nursery industry has its own jargon. Purpose of this article is to review some of these terms, as well as give some information on where and how to buy nursery-produced plants.

Within the nursery industry, nurseries specializing in the production of plants—or growing nurseries—are referred to as wholesale nurseries. Many of the wholesale nurseries choose not to sell to individuals, but only to retail nurseries and other retail outlets selling to the general public, to government agencies such as parks departments, departments of streets and highways, and other commercial users of plants.

On a year-round basis garden centers and retail nurseries offer plants as well as garden tools, mulches, soil conditioners, fertilizers, and other supplies and equipment used in gardening. It is not at all unusual to find that these establishments have a landscape department which will prepare a design plan as well as make actual plantings for the customer.

Some landscape firms do not have a retail sales department and only provide design, planting and landscape maintenance services.

Many other types of retail establishments offer plants and garden supplies only during the peak of the spring and fall planting seasons. These include many department stores, multi-outlet retail stores, hardware stores, grocery stores, roadside markets, and others.

Generally speaking, those retail nurseries, garden centers, and other retail establishments with year-round garden or nursery departments are most apt to have sales personnel with professional or "on the job" horticulture training. Thus they are better prepared to offer sound horticultural suggestions to the purchaser.

Many mail order nurseries offer a wide selection of shade trees, flowering trees, conifers, flowering shrubs, broad leaf evergreens, vines, fruit trees, small fruits, and other plants of interest to both the homeowner and the apartment dweller.

Citizens associations, garden clubs, and other local groups often arrange with a local garden center or retail nursery for special plant sales such as spring bulbs, azaleas, roses, bedding plants, or other landscape plants.

At one time practically all nursery plants, especially those which lose their leaves (deciduous plants), were offered for sale "bare root."

This means that plants were grown in the nursery row or field and after they had shed their leaves in the fall were dug and held dormant in special nursery storages over winter. During the winter months these were sorted, labeled, and inspected for freedom from insects and disease damage.

With the advent of polyethlene and other plastics following World War II, the roots of these plants frequently are wrapped in plastic or placed in a plastic bag with a moisture holding material such as sphagnum moss, or "shingle toe," to keep the roots moist and healthy during transportation and display at the retail outlet.

Mail order nurseries usually ship dormant, deciduous nursery stock in cartons or packages lined with plastic or waterproof paper.

Needle evergreens (conifers) and broadleaf evergreens are plants which do not lose all their leaves at the same time. Such plants are never completely dormant, that is, their leaves are continuing to function although at a reduced rate even at temperatures below 40 degrees F.

Customarily these evergreens are sold as "balled and burlapped." This means the plants are dug from the nursery row with the ball of earth about the roots intact. Burlap wrapped around the ball of earth and roots is fastened with pinning nails or twine to keep the ball intact, avoiding injury to the fine feeding roots and rootlets.

Care should always be taken when handling B & B nursery plants by picking the plant up by the ball. Rough handling or picking them up by the stem or trunk is very apt to result in root injury. One of the advantages of B & B stock is that large size, even mature shrubs and trees, can be moved in this fashion.

Container grown plants are plants grown in the container in which they are sold. To be considered container grown, the plants should have been transplanted into the container and grown there sufficiently long for new fibrous roots to have developed so the root mass will retain its shape and hold together when removed from the container. On removal from the container only the fine or fibrous roots should be evident.

It is currently estimated that over 30 percent of the annual U. S. production of nursery plants sold at retail is container grown.

As the nursery industry continued to develop and specialize in production of different plants in various regions of the country, a standardized system of sizing and describing plants became necessary. Since 1921 the American Association of Nurserymen (AAN) has maintained an active committee on standards.

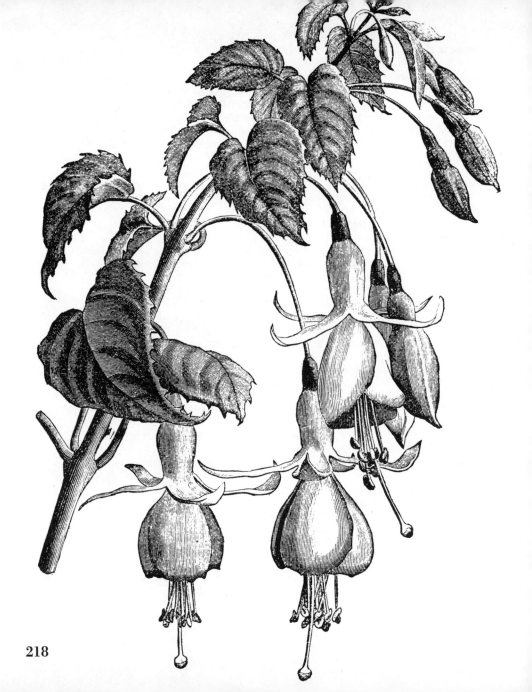

Standards have been periodically revised, and the current edition of American Standard for Nursery Stock ANSI Z60.1—1973 was authorized on Feb. 1, 1973, by the American National Standards Institute, Inc.

In addition to the AAN's Standards Committee, 15 national and regional societies, associations, and governmental agencies reviewed and endorsed the latest revisions.

These technical standards describe the system for sizing various kinds of nursery plants as well as indicating numbers of branches, height of branching, numbers of canes, minimum root ball sizes and grades for roses and small fruits.

Where to Buy

Depending on the type of nursery stock one wants to purchase, there are alternatives. For example: if one is seeking small plants at a minimum cost realizing that they will have to be cared for over several years before they mature, one should look for special advertisements in horticultural magazines and special sections in the mail order catalogs devoted to lists of liner or seedling stock.

For a consumer who wishes a little larger stock which has already begun to branch and develop into its natural shape, mail order catalogs as well as local garden centers and other retail establishments are good sources. Fruit trees, small fruit plants, bare-root shrubs, and small shade trees as well as perennials may be purchased by mail order or at local retail nurseries.

Catalogs and advertisements in magazines and newspapers should indicate the regions of the country where the plants are adapted, or restrict their advertising to only those regions.

Consumers wishing landscape size plants will usually find it to their advantage to purchase such plants locally at garden centers and retail nursery outlets. In this case one has the advantage of examining the plants to select those characteristics most desired, before purchasing.

Some customers prefer to purchase from garden centers or nurseries with a landscape department which provides planting services. When the planting is done by the firm a more favorable customer guarantee will usually be offered.

Because digging, transporting, displaying, and transplanting result in a shock to the plant, it should be carefully transplanted and tended during the recuperative—or establishment—period. Good mail order nurseries furnish specific planting and care instructions. Local garden center and lanscape firms are able to supplement the written planting instructions with added verbal explanation.

Each firm is responsible for its own guarantee, which should be clearly stated in the advertising copy and the sales slip.

These and other points are covered in the Amended Trade Practice Rules

for the Nursery Industry, promulgated by the Federal Trade Commission after extensive public hearings held at the request of the nursery industry.

To assist the consumer in analyzing advertising and sales claims on nursery stock, the American Association of Nurserymen in cooperation with the Council for Better Business Bureaus has recommended standards which include:

When a plant has a well recognized common name it should be used. If an advertiser coins a new name, the common name or the complete botanical name should be included.

A guarantee should be limited to obligations the seller can and will fulfill. It should clearly and conspicuously disclose the nature and extent of the guarantee, the manner in which the guarantor will perform, and the identity of the guarantor.

No reference to "nursery" or "nurseries" should be made for trees or shrubs collected from the wild state and sold without cultivation in a nursery. "Nursery stock" is that which is grown under cultivation, or transplanted from the wild and grown under cultivation for at least one full growing season.

There are many sources of information on the characteristics and description of plants as well as information on the planting and care of various kinds of plants. Horticultural and gardening magazines are valuable for this purpose, as are the public libraries.

Most metropolitan newspapers carry good gardening columns with the writers adapting the recommendations to local climate and soil conditions.

Many plant societies maintain libraries, have membership publications, and hold educational meetings. Among these are the American Boxwood Society, American Rose Society, the Holly Society of America, Inc., the American Camellia Society, American Horticultural Society, Men's Garden Clubs of America, Garden Club of America, National Council of State Garden Clubs, Inc., and the Women's National Farm and Garden Association, Inc.

For information on addresses of these as well as other organizations consult your local library. Or you may wish to purchase the Directory of American Horticulture, available from the American Horticultural Society, Inc., Mount Vernon, Va. 22121.

Another valuable source of information adapted to a local area is the Cooperative Agricultural Extension Service Office in each county of the United States. For the phone number look under your county government listing in the phone directory.

In the United States there are over 100 major arboretums and botanic gardens maintaining outstanding plant collections and display gardens, and providing horticultural information.

Retail garden centers and landscape firms often answer questions and work with garden clubs, service clubs, chambers of commerce, or municipal agencies in community environmental improvement projects.

DEUTZIA

INTERNATIONAL
BUYERS GUIDE

Suggestions to Applicants for Permits to Import Plant Propagating Material

IMPORTANT. Permits are issued only to persons or firms resident in the United States, its territories, and its possessions; and only upon receipt of applications from them. THE APPLICANT'S HOME ADDRESS MUST BE SHOWN on the application. Members of the armed forces must show their home address as well as their APO or comparable address.

ATTENTION. Many plant propagating materials are prohibited entry; many others are enterable subject to special restrictions. Most plant propagating materials require a formal permit for entry. The purpose of the permit requirement is to minimize the necessity of having to intercept prohibited material, the mere arrival of which may constitute a pest risk to the United States.

1. Material to be Imported: Applicants should not ask for permits for "plants for my garden," "flowering plants," "shrubs," "trees," "perennials," "rock plants," "alpines," etc. Permits can be issued, however, for such definite categories as "orchids," "ferns," "cacti," "succulents," and "seeds." If acceptable categories cannot be given, applicants should list the plants, preferably by scientific names; otherwise, by well-known English names. The provincial name by which a plant is known in a foreign country is seldom adequate; the scientific name should be ascertained from a competent horticultural authority in that country. Applicants should state whether plants, cuttings, seeds, or other parts of the plants are desired. In the case of woody plants, applicants should state how the plants were propagated; that is, by budding, grafting, layering, or cuttings. Only seeds may be imported in the case of certain woody plants which can be grown from seed.

2. Origin of Material: Since prohibitions vary according to country of origin, applicants should list the country or countries from which each item is desired. For material from Canada, the City and Province should be shown. For material from Mexico, the State should be indicated.

3. Medium of Importation: Applicants should state whether importation is to be made by surface parcel post, air parcel post, air mail, express, air express, freight, air freight, or as personal baggage. The word "air" alone is not sufficient.

4. Mail Importations necessitate the procuring of a mailing label for each parcel for transmission to the foreign shipper. The label bears the name of the proper Inspection Station and routes the parcel directly to that station, where, after plant quarantine clearance, it is returned to the mails for forwarding to the permittee under the original postage.

5. Importations to be made other than through the mails necessitate pre-arrival arrangements for employment of a customs broker to attend to customs formalities and to arrange for shipment to and from an Inspection Station, if required.

6. Port of Arrival should be indicated, if shipment is to be made other than by mail.

7. Number of Importations Involved: Applicant should indicate whether he wishes to make (a) a single importation; or (b) a number of importations over a period of time.

8. Permits should be procured in advance, if loss of material, delay in clearance, and unnecessary expenses are to be avoided. ORDERS SHOULD NOT BE PLACED UNTIL THE PERMIT AND INSTRUCTIONS HAVE BEEN RECEIVED. There is no charge for a permit or mailing labels.

NOTE: Time will be saved if complete information is given when applying for a permit.

PLANT IMPORTING PROCEDURES AND RESPONSIBILITIES OF PLANT IMPORTERS

1. To avoid delay in the clearance of importations of plant propgating material importers have four important responsibilities to assume. Failure to assume all of these may result in loss or deterioration of material.

These responsibilities are:

a. To obtain, before placing order, an import permit or to make certain that an existing permit provides for the entry of the desired material. If in doubt, obtain written assurance from the Permit Unit, APHIS, PPQ, USDA, Federal Center Building, Room 638, Hyattsville, Maryland 20782.

b. To transmit appropriate instructions to the foreign shipper. Please read carefully No. 2 below and the paragraphs cited therein.

c. To make advance arrangements for meeting all Customs requirements. See No. 14.

d. To supply labor, materials, etc., through broker or agent, when necessary. See No. 17.

WHAT THE FOREIGN SHIPPER MUST BE TOLD

2. The permittee should instruct the foreign shipper concerning the freedom from soil requirement; the use of approved packing materials; the prohibition on certain woody plants which have been or can be grown from seed; the size-age limitations; the defoliation requirement, when necessary; the need for labeling, invoicing, and certification; and the means by which shipment is to be made. Information on these requirements appears in Nos. 3 to 13 which follow.

3. FREEDOM FROM SOIL. All plant material must be free from sand, soil, and earth. Leafmold and other decayed vegetable molds are considered as soil. Plants arriving in or contaminated with sand, soil, or earth will be refused entry.

4. PACKING MATERIAL. (a) Only approved packing material should be used. Leaves, forest litter, woods moss, and any similar material taken from or out of the ground and dried grasses, weeds, hays, and straws are not approved. Among the commonly used packing materials which are approved are peat moss, sphagnum, pulp-free coconut or other vegetable fibers (excluding sugarcane and cotton), osmunda fiber, excelsior (woodwool), shavings, sawdust, ground cork, buckwheat hulls, polymer stabilized cellulose, and vermiculite. Willow withes should not be used to tie bundles.

AGREEMENT TO CONDITIONS GOVERNING THE RECEIPT, HOLDING, GROWING, HANDLING, TREATING, AND RELEASE OF PLANT MATERIAL SUBJECT TO POSTENTRY QUARANTINE PROVISIONS OF NURSERY STOCK, PLANT, AND SEED QUARANTINE 37

As a condition of importation of plant material required to be grown under postentry quarantine provisions of Regulation 19 of Nursery Stock, Plant, and Seed Quarantine 37, I/we the undersigned, agree with the Agricultural Quarantine Inspection Program as follows:

1. That, for the purpose of this agreement the term "plant material" means any plant material subject to the provisions of Regulation 19 of Quarantine 37 which I am/we are authorized by a permit to import and any increase or other parts of plants derived from such material, including cuttings and flowers.

2. That I/we will grow such plant material for the period required on premises controlled by me/us located at (give *actual location-do not use Rural Route numbers or Post Office Box numbers*):

_____

_____

3. That I/we will permit authorized inspectors to have access to the said premises at all reasonable daylight hours. An authorized inspector may be the Chief Nursery Inspector or chief plant quarantine official of the State in which the said premises are located, a member of the staff of such official, or an inspector of the Agricultural Quarantine Inspection Program.

4. That the plant material will be labeled by specific plant name, port accession number, and date of importation.

5. That the plant material will not be intermixed with other importations, and will be reasonably separated from domestic plants.

6. That I/we will make no distribution from the specified premises of the plant material or increase therefrom until I am/we are so authorized in writing by the Agricultural Quarantine Inspection Program, or cut and distribute blooms therefrom until authorized in writing by the inspector.

7. That I/we will apply any remedial measure prescribed by the inspector to the imported plant material, increase therefrom, or other plants growing on the premises, including destruction of any or all of same, if necessary in the judgment of the inspector, to prevent the dissemination of a plant pest.

8. That I/we will promptly notify the authorized inspector with whom I/we have been in contact regarding the plant material in the event I/we notice the development thereon of any unusual insect infestation or disease.

9. That I/we will promptly notify the Agricultural Quarantine Inspection Program of any change of address.

10. That I/we agree to the cancellation of my/our import permit if the terms of this agreement are violated.

This agreement has been read and the responsibilities thereof are hereby accepted.

NAME OF APPLICANT OR FIRM (Please TYPE or PRINT)

ADDRESS OF APPLICANT OR FIRM (Include Zip Code)

SIGNATURE OF APPLICANT OR AUTHORIZED REPRESENTATIVE | DATE

SAMPLE FORM

AQI FORM 546   PREVIOUS EDITIONS ARE OBSOLETE
DEC 1971

(b) Nursery stock which has been wrapped, coated, dipped, sprayed, or otherwise packaged in plastic, wax, or other impermeable material that renders acequate inspection and treatment unreasonably difficult or impracticable may be refused entry if the objectionable condition is not corrected by the importer.

5. WOODY PLANTS. Only seed may be imported in the case of forest trees, woody plants used as understocks, and fruit and nut plants to be grown-on for what they are, if such plants can be grown from seed. For example: hemlock trees, rose stocks, fig plants, and walnut plants which have been or can be grown from seed are not allowed entry. Exceptions can be made only if the applicant presents evidence in writing in advance that it is impossible or impracticable to obtain viable seed.

6. SIZE-AGE LIMITATIONS. (a) All restricted trees and shrubs to be imported shall be limited to the youngest and smallest, normal, clean, healthy plants which can be successfully freed from soil, transported to the United States, and established. Only plants no more than two years of age when they have been grown from cuttings or seeds (see No. 5) or having no more than one year's growth after severance from the parent plant when produced by layers, or having no more than two seasons' growth from the bud or graft when they have been produced by budding or grafting are admissible except that for rhododendron (including azalea) or other genera or species of similar slow growth habit, an additional year is allowed. The size-age limitations do not apply to naturally dwarf or miniature forms of woody plants not exceeding 12 inches in height from the soil line nor to artificially dwarfed forms of the character popular in parts of the Orient.
(b) Cacti, cycads, yuccas, dracaenas, and other plants whose growth habits simulate the woody character of trees and shrubs may not be more than 12 inches in height from the soil line, exclusive of foliage.
(c) Herbaceous perennials which are usually imported in the form of root crowns or clumps shall be limited to one year old plants produced from single propagating units.

7. DEFOLIATION. Certain material from several subtropical and tropical sources must be defoliated prior to shipment if the material is to clear through ports other than New York or Seattle. Full details on this requirement will be found in No. 19 of this circular.

8. LABELING. All material must be plainly and legibly labeled as to genus, species, and variety. Lack of labeling delays handling. Therefore, it is important that plants or bundles of plants be labeled, preferably with scientific names. If the latter are not available a good English common name may suffice. When only a provincial common name is known, its scientific name should be determined from a competent horticultural authority near the source.

9. INVOICES. The copies of invoices required for agricultural quarantine clearance are in addition to those required by Customs, the broker, and the importer. For cargo importations: A copy must accompany the USDA Notice of Arrival filed at the time Customs entry is made. In addition, a packing list must accompany each container of material or a copy of the invoice must be enclosed within container No. 1. For importations by mail: One copy of the invoice must be enclosed within the parcel or within one of the parcels in the event of a lot shipment.

10. CERTIFICATION. Quarantine No. 37 requires that material be appropriately certified by the proper phytopathological official of the country of origin. For cargo importations: A copy of the certificate must be attached to the outside of each container and the original certificate must be submitted with the USDA Notice of Arrival when Customs entry is made. For importations by mail: A copy of the certificate must be attached to the outside of each parcel, and the original certificate must be enclosed within the parcel or within one of the parcels in the event of a lot shipment.

11. MEDIUM OF IMPORTATION. The importer may import material by any medium he wishes and should instruct the foreign shipper as to the means by which shipment is to be made. Mail shipments, whether by letter mail, parcel post, air parcel post, or other classes of mail do not require a bonded carrier to get the material to an inspection station. This does not apply to importations made by other mediums. AIR EXPRESS AND AIR FREIGHT SHOULD NOT BE CONFUSED WITH AIR MAIL AND AIR PARCEL POST.

12. MAIL SHIPMENTS. (a) There are several kinds of mail service as mentioned in the preceding paragraph. Not all countries offer air parcel post; moreover, the character of air parcel post service may vary with the country. From some countries air parcel post moves by air only to the United States port of first arrival and thence by surface transportation to destination; other countries provide air movement to final destination; still other countries provide both types of air parcel post service leaving the shipper to select the type desired. Information on air parcel post can best be obtained from the foreign shipper or at your local post office. Letter-rate airmail, sometimes used for seeds, valuable cuttings, etc., when air parcel post is not available, carries material through to destination by air. Shipments sent letter-rate airmail or first class mail should be marked "This parcel may be opened for inspection." Importers who plan importing by air will find that when air parcel post is not available, there will be times when even letter-rate airmail is as economical as air express.

(b) After agricultural quarantine clearance at an inspection station, mail shipments are returned to the mails and go forward to destination under the original postage. If the value of the shipment is less than $250, Customs duty, if any, is collected at the post office of destination. If valued at $250 or more, the shipment goes to the Customs port nearest the destination post office where the importer must either employ a Customs broker to make formal entry or attend to this himself. The importer is notified by Customs of the arrival of the shipment and the port at which entry must be made.

(c) Addressing mail shipments. When shipments are to be imported by mail, the permittee should request a green-and-yellow mailing label for each parcel involved. Instructions on their use appear on the reverse side of the labels. The same instructions in French, German, and Spanish will be supplied upon request for transmittal to the foreign shipper along with the labels. For mail shipments, it is especially important that the permittee's name, address, and permit number be enclosed within each parcel. GREEN-AND-YELLOW LABELS ARE TO BE USED ONLY FOR MAIL IMPORTATIONS.

13. SHIPMENTS OTHER THAN BY MAIL. (a) Importations arriving by means other than mail require a Customs Entry regardless of value. The importer or his agent must make arrangements for this and for delivery to an inspection station, if necessary, and to final destination.

(b) Addressing other than mail shipments. Each case, box, or other container of a shipment shall be clearly and plainly marked to show the general nature and quantity of the contents and the country where grown, bear distinguishing marks, be individually numbered, and be addressed in the following way:

United States Customs Service
(Name of port where material is authorized to clear quarantine)

For delivery to Plant Protection and Quarantine Inspection Station.

For account of   Permit No.
          (Name & address of permittee)

From
          (Name & address of foreign shipper)

14. MEETING CUSTOMS REQUIREMENTS. For Non-Parcel Post Importations.

(a) Numerous delays resulting in loss or deterioration of material occur because importers fail to make arrangements in advance for a Customs broker or other agent to attend to Customs formalities in connection with freight, air freight, express, or air express consignments. Such shipments are in Customs custody and, unless under an IT entry [see subparagraph (c) (3)], cannot go forward until all Customs requirements have been completed. AGRICULTURAL QUARANTINE INSPECTORS ARE WITHOUT AUTHORITY TO ACT AS OR RENDER THE SERVICES OF A CUSTOMS BROKER. Government employees cannot employ a Customs broker on behalf of an importer nor should they be requested to recommend one.

(b) All arrangements with the Customs broker or other agent should be made well in advance of importation. He will need to know the expected time of arrival and the vessel, train, or plane on which the material is expected to arrive, and should be supplied with invoices, other necessary documents, the importer's permit number, instructions on forwarding the importation, and the type of Customs entry to be made. The broker is in a position to arrange, on the importer's behalf, for transportation, labor, and materials, if needed. The inexperienced importer will do well to consult his Customs broker or agent ahead of time and ascertain what is expected of him (the importer).

(c) There are three kinds of Customs entries normally used for plant material imported other than through the mails. They are as follows:

(1) Informal Entry. This type of entry may sometimes be employed to advantage when the port of arrival is the same as the authorized port of agricultural quarantine clearance and the shipment is valued at less than $250. The duty must be paid in cash or check to a Customs Inspector at the port of entry (pier, airport, etc.).
At times an informal entry, if allowable, may not be practical or convenient for the broker or agent.

(2) Duty Paid Entry. Here duty is paid in cash or by check and any increased or additional duties are generally covered by a bond. When the port of arrival is not the same as the authorized port of agricultural quarantine clearance, the shipment must move under a Customs Special Manifest to the port of agricultural quarantine clearance.

(3) IT (Immediate Transportation) Entry. Under this type, the broker or agent (or carrier acting as such) merely makes the entry and arranges for handling and for movement onward towards destination. At the Customs port nearest to destination, the services of a Customs broker are again necessary to make a consumption type entry (an Informal or Duty Paid) and to pay the duty before the shipment can be delivered. The "double" service makes this a more costly type of entry.

PARAGRAPH 12 EXPLAINS CUSTOMS PROCEDURES GOVERNING MAIL IMPORTATIONS

15. BAGGAGE ENTRIES. The importation of most plant material (except certain bulbs and flower seeds) by baggage may prove more costly than entry by mail because it may be necessary to arrange for a bonded carrier (if available at the port of arrival) to transport the material to the nearest inspection station. Upon completion of agricultural quarantine handling, someone will also have to care for the forwarding of the material to final destination and the costs attending such forwarding. For those reasons, travelers in foreign countries may wish to consider mailing plants to the United States whenever possible, thereby avoiding the inconvenience of having to make arrangements for bonded cartage and forwarding to final destination and eliminating the charges for such transportation. Inspection stations are generally open from 8:30 a.m. to 5:00 p.m., Monday through Friday, except on Federal holidays.

16. PORTS OF QUARANTINE CLEARANCE. Material may be offered for agricultural quarantine clearance at New York, New York (including John F. Kennedy International Airport and Hoboken, N. J.); Miami, Florida; New Orleans, Louisiana; Brownsville, El Paso, and Laredo, Texas; Nogales, Arizona; Los Angeles (San Pedro), San Diego, and San Francisco, California; and Seattle, Washington, for mainland destinations; at Honolulu and San Juan, respectively, for destinations in Hawaii, Puerto Rico, and the American Virgin Islands. If your permit does not provide for handling of the importation at the logical point of agricultural quarantine clearance, application should be made to have it revised. When doing so, bear in mind that uninspected and untreated material may not move long distances overland for inspection and treatment but must be inspected and treated at the authorized point at or nearest the port of arrival. For example: South American material arriving by air usually clears at Miami. The same material coming by water would enter at New York and clear at Hoboken. Asiatic material coming via the Suez Canal and African material by water usually clear at Hoboken. Most Mexican material clears at Laredo and Brownsville. Trans-Pacific material clears at Los Angeles (San Pedro), San Francisco, or Seattle, depending upon the time and method of dispatch from origin. See No. 15 for hours during which inspection stations are open.

17. LABOR, SUPPLIES, ETC. Labor is usually required for the handling of shipments imported other than by mail. It is needed to unpack and repack material and to move the containers into and out of the inspection station. Labor costs vary with the size of the shipment and the amount of work which may be involved. Customs brokers can readily arrange for labor. Supplies such as lumber, material for reconditioning, etc., may or may not be necessary depending upon the condition of the shipment.

18. TREATMENTS. It is the purpose of the Plant Quarantine Act to protect the United States against introductions of plant pests and that purpose must receive first consideration. To protect his country and himself against pest introductions, the importer should emphasize to the shipper the necessity for sending clean, healthy material. Treatments which are given as a condition of entry are those which, in the light of present knowledge, are deemed most effective for the pest concerned and least likely to cause injury to the plants involved. In those exceptional cases where injury might result from treatments given, the importer must regard this as the price of protecting himself and other plant growers against pest introductions. All treatments are given entirely at the risk of the importer. In most cases of alleged fumigation injury which have been investigated, the plant material reached the inspection station in a deteriorating condition because of too much or too little moisture, inadequate ventilation, or other adverse factors encountered in transporation. When the plants reach the inspection stations, the injury done to plants as a result of such adverse factors has not always run its course and the injury which subsequently develops is often erroneously attributed to fumigation. It is important to all concerned, therefore, that vigorous, healthy plants be shipped and that they be so packed as not to lose their vitality in transit. Suggestions on packing plants will be sent upon request.

19. MATERIAL REQUIRING DEFOLIATION. Because of the risk of introducing citrus blackfly (Aleurocanthus woglumi), plants and cuttings of the following genera from all foreign sources except Canada, Europe, Asia Minor, and those countries in Africa bordering the Mediterranean Sea must be defoliated before shipment from the country of origin if they are to be imported through any port other than New York or Seattle. Defoliation is not required when plants and cuttings of these genera enter directly through New York or Seattle for agricultural quarantine clearance.

*Achras	†Cydonia	Parmentiera
*Anacardium	*Diospyros	*Persea
*Annona	Duranta	Plumeria
Ardisia	*Eugenia	††Populus
Bouvardia	††Fraxinus	*Psidium
Bumelia	††Hibiscus	*Punica
Bursera	Hura	††Pyrus
Buxus	Ixora	Sapindus
*Calocarpum	Jatropha	Solandra
Capsicum	Lagerstroemia	*Spondias
Cardiospermum	*Lucuma	Strelitzia
Cedrela	Magnolia	Tabebuia
Cestrum	*Mammea	††Vitis
Cnidoscolus	*Mangifera	Zingiber
Coffea	Melia	
**Crataegus	Myroxylon	
	Myrtus	

*Varieties cultivated for fruits or nuts are subject to growing in postentry quarantine.

**Varieties of C. Monogyna are subject to growing in postentry quarantine.

†Subject to growing in postentry quarantine.

††Prohibited from some sources; subject to growing in postentry quarantine from all approved sources except possibly Canada.

ABOVE MATERIAL ARRIVING IN FOLIAGE contrary to the regulations will be refused entry and immediately become subject to the application of such safeguards as may be deemed necessary and prescribed by the inspector to prevent possibility of pest escape, including immediate destruction if in the opinion of the inspector the circumstances warrant.

BULB NOTICE

The underground parts (bulbs, corms, rhizomes, tubers, pips, and fleshy roots) of the genera listed in the enclosed Administrative Instructions 319.37-1a do not require a formal permit for entry. However, such materials are subject to 1) inspection and 2) treatment if plant pests of quarantine significance are found.

To quality for entry the materials must be free from soil and accompanied by a phytosanitary certificate issued by the agricultural officials of the country of origin.

Anemone grown in Germany and Gladiolus grown on the continent of Africa are prohibited entry.

Mail shipments of bulbs may be addressed directly to the recipient. Green-and-yellow mailing labels are not required. Such parcels must be plainly labeled to identify the contents.

If the post office in the country of origin hesitates to accept parcels without green-and-yellow labels, a copy of this notice should be presented to them. An extra copy is enclosed for that purpose and should be sent along with your order to the foreign shipper.

(a) Most or all of the species of the genera listed in this paragraph, and all of the species listed in this paragraph, have underground parts that conform to the definition of bulbs contained in 319.37-1(h):

Achimenes (Gesner.).
Acidanthera (Irid.).
Agapanthus (Lil.).
Albuca (Lil.).
Allium (Lil.).
Alstroemeria (Amar.).
Amarcrinum= Crinodonna.
Amaryllis (Amar.).
Amianthium (Lil.).
Ammocharis (Amar.).
Anapalina (Irid.).
Androcymbium (Lil.).
Androstephium (Lil.).
Anemone (Ranun.) (Anemone is prohibited entry from Germany.).

Anomatheca=Lapeirousia.
Anthericum (Lil.).
Antholyza (Irid.).
Arum (Ar.).
Babinia (Irid.).
Begonia (Begon.).
Bellevalia=Hyacinthus.
Bessera (Lil.).
Bletia (Orch.).
Bletilla (Orch.).
Bloomeria (Lil.).
Bongardia chrysogonum (Berber.).
Boophane (Amar.).
Bottionea (Lil.).
Bowiea (Lil.).
Bravoa (Amar.).
Brevoortia (Lil.).
Brodiaea (Lil.).
Brunsdonna (Amar.).
Brunsvigia (Amar.).

Bulbocodium (Lil.).
Buphane=Boophane.
Caladium (Ar.).
Calla=Zantedeschia.
Caliphruria (Amar.).
Calochortus (Lil.).
Calostemma (Amar.).
Camassia (Lil.).
Canna (Cann.).
Chasmanthe (Irid.).
Chionodoxa (Lil.).
Chionoscilla (Lil.).
Chlidanthus (Amar.).
Choragalum (Lil.).
Cipura (Irid.).
Clivia (Lil.).
Colchicum (Lil.).
Convallaria (Lil.).
Cooperanthes (Amar.).
Cooperia (Amar.).
Corydalis (Fumar.).
Crinodonna (Amar.).
Crinum (Amar.).
Crocosmia (Irid.).
Crocus (Irid.).
Curcuma (Zingiber.).
Curtonus (Irid.).
Cyclamen (Prim.).
Cyclobothra=Calochortus.
Cypella (Irid.).
Cyranthus (Amar.).
Dahlia (Compos.).
Dicentra (Fumar.).
Dielytra=Dicentra.
Dierama (Irid.).
Dipcadi (Lil.).
Dipidax (Lil.).
Drimia (Lil.).
Drymophila (Lil.).
Elisena (Amar.).
Eranthis (Ranun.).
Eremurus (Lil.).
Erythronium (Lil.).

Eucharis (Amar.).
Eucomis (Lil.).
Eurycles (Amar.).
Eustephia (Amar.).
Eustylis (Irid.).
Ferraria (Irid.).
Freesia (Irid.).
Fritallaria (Lil.).
Funkia=Hosta.
Gagea (Lil.).
Galanthus (Amar.).
Galtonia (Lil.).
Geissorhiza (Irid.).
Geranium tuberosum (Geran.).
Gesnera (Gesner.).
Gladiolus (Irid.) Gladiolus is prohibited entry from African sources.
Globba (Zingiber.).
Gloriosa (Lil.).
Gloxinia=Sinningia.
Griffinia (Amar.).
Habenaria radiata (Orch.).
Habranthus (Amar.).
Haemanthus (Amar.).

Hastingsia (Lil.).
Hedychium (Zingiber.).
Helonias (Lil.).
Heloniopsis (Lil.).
Hemerocallis (Lil.).
Herbertia (Irid.).
Hermodactylus (Irid.).
Hesperantha (Irid.).
Hesperocallis (Lil.).
Hessea (Amar.).
Hexaglottis (Irid.).
Hippeastrum (Amar.).
Homera (Irid.).
Homoglossum (Irid.).
Hosta (Lil.).
Hyacinthus (Lil.).
Hydrotaenia (Irid.).
Hyline (Amar.).
Hymenocallis (Amar.).
Hypoxis (Amar.).
Incarvillea (Bignon.).
Ipheion (Lil.).
Iris (Irid.).
Ismene (Amar.).
Isoloma (Gesner.).
Ixia (Irid.).
Ixiolirion (Amar.).
Kaempferia (Zingiber.).
Kohleria (Gesner.).
Lachenalia (Lil.).
Lapeirousia (Irid.).
Lapeyrousia=Lapeirousia
Leucocoryne (Lil.).
Leucojum (Amar.).
Lilium (Lil.).
Littonia (Lil.).
Lloydia (Lil.).
Lycoris (Amar.).
Manfreda (Amar.).
Massonia (Lil.).
Melasphaerula (Irid.).
Merendera (Lil.).
Mertensia (Borag.).
Milla (Lil.).

Montbretia=Tritonia.
Moraea (Irid.).
Muilla (Lil.).
Muscari (Lil.).
Naegelia (Gesner.).
Narcissus (Amar.).
Nemastylis (Irid.).
Nerine (Amar.).
Nomocharis (Lil.).
Notholirion (Lil.).
Nothoscordum (Lil.).
Ornithogalum (Lil.).
Ostrowskia magnifica (Campan.).
Oxalis (Oxal.).
Paeonia herbaceous (Ranun.).
Pamianthe (Amar.).
Pancratium (Amar.).
Papaver (Papaver.).
Pasithea (Lil.).
Phaedranassa (Amar.).
Placea (Amar.).
Polianthes (Amar.).
Polyanthes=Polianthes.
Polyanthus=Polianthes.
Prochnyanthes (Amar.).
Pulsatilla=Anemone (Anemone is prohibited
    entry from Germany.)
Puschkinia (Lil.).
Pyrolirion (Amar.).
Quamasia=Camassia.
Ranunculus (Ranun.).
Rechsteineria (Gesner.).
Rhodohypoxis (Amar.).
Rhodophiala (Amar.).
Rigidella (Irid.).
Romulea (Irid.).
Salpingostylis (Irid.).
Sandersonia (Lil.).
Sauromatum (Ar.).
Saxifraga granulata (Sax.).
Schizobasopsis=Bowiea.
Schizostylis (Irid.).
Scilla (Lil.).
Sinningia: the "Gloxinia" of florists (Gesner.).

Smithiantha (Gesner.).
Sparaxis (Irid.).
Spiloxene (Amar.).
Sprekelia (Amar.).
Stenanthium (Lil.).
Stenomesson (Amar.).
Sternbergia (Amar.).
Streptanthera (Irid.).
Synnotia (Irid.).
Tecophilaea thomosonia (Ar.).
Tigridia (Irid.).
Trimeza (Irid.).
Tristagma (Lil.).
Triteleia=Brodiaea.
Tritonia (Irid.).
Tropaeolum tuberosum (Trop.).
Tulbaghia (Lil.).
Tulipa (Lil.).
Tydaea (Gesner.).
Urceocharis (Amar.).
Urceolina (Amar.).

In the list in this paragraph the correct botanical name follows the equal sign after each synonym. Botanical family abbreviations are in parentheses and have the following meanings: (Amar.) Amaryllidaceae; (Ar.) Araceae; (Begon.) Begoniaceae; (Berber.) Berberideae; (Bignon.) Bignoniaceae; (Borag.) Boraginaceae; (Campan.) Campanulaceae; (Cann.) Cannaceae; (Compos.) Compositae; (Fumar.) Fumariaceae; (Geran.) Geraniaceae; (Gesner.) Gesneriaceae; (Irid.) Iridaceae; (Lil.) Lilliaceae; (Orch.) Orchidaceae; (Oxal.) Oxalidaceae; (Papaver.) Papaveraceae; (Prim.) Primulaceae; (Ranun.) Ranunculaceae; (Sac.) Saxifragaceae; (Trop.) Tropaeolaceae; (Zingiber.) Zingiberaceae.

(b) A determination as to whether a particular shipment of plant material qualifies as bulbs will be made at the time of offer for entry.

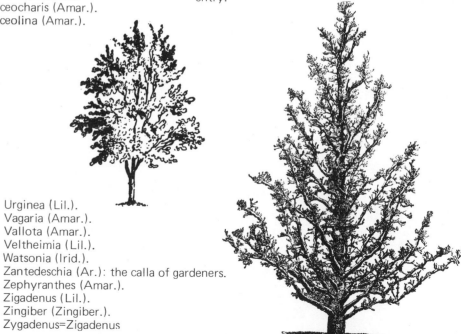

Urginea (Lil.).
Vagaria (Amar.).
Vallota (Amar.).
Veltheimia (Lil.).
Watsonia (Irid.).
Zantedeschia (Ar.): the calla of gardeners.
Zephyranthes (Amar.).
Zigadenus (Lil.).
Zingiber (Zingiber.).
Zygadenus=Zigadenus

ENTRY STATUS OF SEEDS UNDER FEDERAL PLANT QUARANTINES

I. Field crop, flower, vegetable, and other herbaceous plant seeds — as distinguished from seeds of trees and shrubs. Except as indicated immediately below, seeds in this category are allowed entry under the general authorization of paragraph (a) of Regulation 4 of Quarantine No. 37 and no formal permit is needed from this Agency for their entry. All seeds in this category are nevertheless subject to inspection and, if findings warrant, to such treatment as may be deemed necessary to prevent the risk of pest introduction. The exceptions are as follows:

    Alfalfa — enterable under Quarantine 37 seed permit.

    Bamboo and related plants— prohibited from all sources.

    Broad bean (Vicia faba) — see Vetch.

    Corn and related plants — enterable from some sources under separate permit; prohibited from other sources. Write for details naming seeds, country of origin, and purpose of importation.

    Cotton — entry limited to small samples under separate permit for experimental or scientific purposes.

    Kenaf — fumigation required if destined to certain areas.

    Lentils (Lens spp.) — prohibited from South America. Enterable from other sources under Quarantine 37 seed permit.

    Okra — enterable under Quarantine 37 seed permit.

    Rice — enterable under separate permit from Mexico; prohibited from other sources.

    Sweet pea (Lathyrus spp.) — enterable under Quarantine 37 seed permit.

Vetch (Vicia spp.) — enterable under Quarantine 37 seed permit.

    Wheat — Prohibited entry from many sources. Write for details giving country of origin.

II. Tree and shrub seeds including palms and other plants of woody nature. Except as indicated immediately below seeds in this category are enterable under Quarantine 37 seed permits. The exceptions are as follows:

    Avocado — prohibited from Mexico, Central and South America.

    Barberry, Mahonia, and Mahoberberis — prohibited from all sources.

    Coffee (Unroasted) — entry into Hawaii and Puerto Rico prohibited; enterable to other destinations under Quarantine 37 seed permit.

    Currant and Gooseberry — prohibited to many destinations. Write for details, naming variety of seed.

    Mango — enterable from Mexico, Central and South America, and West Indies, and Bermuda under Quarantine 37 seed permit; prohibited from other sources.

ENTRY STATUS OF CUT FLOWERS

The entry of cut flowers from all foreign countries except Canada is regulated by Quarantine No. 74. No restrictions are imposed on cut flowers of Canadian origin.

Cut flowers of Azalea, Camellia, Gardenia, Rhododendron, Rosa (rose), and Syringa (lilac) are admissible under permit issued by this Agency. Permits are granted only to persons or firms resident in the United States and only upon receipt of written application from them.

Applications for permits should name the cut flowers to be imported, the country of origin, the means of shipment, and the port at which shipments will first arrive in the United States. The applicant's name, address (both street and P. O. Box, if any), and telephone number should be given.

No formal permit is required for importations of cut flowers of admissible genera other than those named above.

All admissible cut flowers whether entering under permit or not, are subject to inspection at the United States port of arrival and to treatment should pests of quarantine significance be found. Treatments, when required, are at the risk and expense of the importer and must be performed under the supervision of an inspector of this Department. Phytosanitary certification from the country of origin is not necessary.

Cut camellias and gardenias are prohibited entry when consigned to destinations in Florida. Shipments of cut camellias and gardenias may enter at Florida ports for movement to points outside of that state provided they are securely wrapped in polyethylene or an equivalent material.

Cut gardenia are required to be given a precuationary fumigation when entering at California ports regardless of destination.

233

COMMON PLANT GENERA NOT PROHIBITED OR SUBJECT TO POSTENTRY QUARANTINE UNDER QUARANTINE 37

1. The following is a list of the more common plant genera, or groups of genera, which are enterable under Regulation 6 of Quarantine 37 and, except as noted, are not subject to prohibition or postentry quarantine.

2. If a genus is not listed, it may be prohibited or subject to special restrictions. To avoid rejections or delays, an inquiry should be addressed to the Permit Unit before ordering unlisted genera.

3. Most aroids, bromeliads, cacti, ferns, orchids, succulents, and tree ferns are listed only as group names. Horticultural references should be consulted for the genera included in these broad categories.

4. Volume importations of all genera included in this list are subject to clearance at an especially equipped Agricultural Inspection Station at the approved port of entry listed in the permit.

5. Genera marked with an asterisk (*) from all sources except Canada, Asia Minor, and Mediterranean Africa, must be defoliated at time of shipment if entering at ports other than New York (including Hoboken, New Jersey) and Seattle.

6. Orchids - Plants from south of 30 degrees north latitude are subject to postentry quarantine when destined to Hawaii.

Abelia
Abeliophyllum
Abrus
Abutilon
Acalypha
Acanthus
Achillea
Achimenes
Archyranthes
Aconitum
Adenostylis
Adlumia
Aeschynanthus
Aethionema
Agapanthus
Agave
Aglaonema
Aira
Arjuga
Albizzia
Alchemilla
Allamanda
Allium
Allosorus
Alnus
Aloe
Alpinia
Alyssum
Amelanchier
Amomum
Ampelopsis
Andromeda
Androscace
Angelonia
Anthemis
Anthericum
Antigonon
Aponogeton
Aposeris
Aquilegia
Arabis
Aralia
Araucaria
Archtostaphylos
*Ardisia
Arenaria
Aretia
Argemone
Aristolochia
Armeria (Statice)
Aroids (except Anthurium)
Aronicum
Artemisia
Aspidistra
Asplenium
Aster
Astilbe
Astragalus (Phaca)
Astrantia
Aubrieta
Aucuba
Azalea
Azaleondendron
Barleria
Bassia
Bauhinia
Beaumontia
Begonia
Beloperone
Bergenia
Bertolonia
Betula
Bignonia
Biota (Thuja)
Bougainvillea
*Bouvardia
Braya
Breynia
Bromeliads (except to Hawaii)
Brunfelsia (Franciscea)
Buddleia
Bupleurum
*Bursera
*Buxus
Cacti
Caladium
Calla (Zantedeschia)
Callicarpa
Calliopsis (Coreopsis)
Callistemon
Calluna
Calophyllum
Camellia (except from Ceylon)
Campanula
Campsis
Canna
Caragana
Cardamine
Carex
Carpinus
Cassia
Catalpa
Ceanothus
*Cedrela
Centaurea
Cerastium
Cercidiphyllum
Cerinthe
Ceropegia

*Cestrum
Chaenomeles
Chamaecyparis
Chionanthus
Chorizema
Cimicifuga
Cineraria (Senecio)
Cirsium
Cissus
Clematis (Atragene)
Cleome
Clerodendron
Clethra
Clitoria
Clivia
Clusia
Cocculus
Codiaeum
*Coffea (free of berries)
Coleus
Colocasia
Coprosma
Cordyline
Coreopsis (Calliopsis)
Cornus
Corylopsis
Costus
Cotinus
Cotoneaster
Crassula
Crepis
CRossandra
Croton
Cryptomeria
Cryptostegia
Cupressus
Cycas
Cytisus
Dephne
Davidia
Delphinium
Deutzia
Dieffenbachia

Diervilla
Diplandenia
Dizygotheca (Aralia)
Dodonaea
Dombeya
Doronicum
Draba
Dracaena
Dryas
*Duranta
Durio
Elaeagnus
Enkianthus
Epilobium
Epimedium
Episcia
Eranthemum
Erica
Erigeron
Eriophorum
Eryngium
Erythrina
Euphorbia
Euphrasia
Eurya
Exochorda
Fagus
Fatshedera
Fatsia (Aralia)
Ferns
Festuca
Firmiana
Fittonia
Forsythia
Franciscea (Brunfelsia)
Franklinia (Gordonia)
Fuchsia
Gaillardia
Galium
Galphimia (Thryallis)
Gardenia
Gaya

Genista
Gentiana
Geranium
Gerbera (Gerberia)
Geum
Ginkgo
Gleditsia
Globularia
Gnaphalium
Gordonia (Franklinia)
Graptophyllum
Grevillea
Gymnocladus
Gypsophila
Halesia
Hamamelis
Haworthia
Hedera
Hedychium
Hedysarum
Helenium
Helianthemum
Helianthus
Heliconia
Heliopsis
Helleborus
Heracleum
Heuchera
Hieracium
Higginsia (Hoffmannia)
Hoffmannia
Horminum
Hoya
Hunnemannia
Hutchinsia
Hypericum
Iberis
Idesia
Idria
Elex
Indigofera
Inga

Iresine
Isoloma
*Ixora
Jacaranda
Jacobinia
*Jatropha
Juncus
Justicia
Kalanchoe
Kelmia
Kerria
Kniphofia (Tritoma)
Kobresia
Koelreuteria
Kolkwitzia
Laburnum
*Lagerstroemia
Lantana
Lapageria
Laserpitium
Lasiagrostis

Laurus
Leontodon
Leucothoe
Ligularia
Lilium
Linnaea
Listera
Lobelia
Lomatogonium
Lonicera
Lupinus
Luzula
Lychnis
Lythrum
*Magnolia
Malaxis
Malvastrum
Malvaviscum (Achania)

Manettia
Maranta
Marcgravia
Marica
Maurandia
Medinilla
*Melia
Mentha
Mesembryanthemum
Mimosa
Moehringia
Montia
Muehlenbeckia
Musa
Myosotis
Myricaria
*Myrtus
Nandina
Nardus
Nepenthes
Nerium
Nicotiana
Nolina
Oenothera
Orchids (except to Hawaii—see par. 6)
Osmanthus
Ostrya
Oxydendrum
Oxyria
Oxtropis
Pachysandra
Paederota
Pandanus
Pandorea
Papaver (except P. somniferum)
Parkinsonia
Parthenocissus
Paulownia
Pedicularis
Pedilanthus
Pelargonium
Penstemon (Pentstemon)
Peperomia

Pernettya
Petasites
Petrea
Petrocallis
Peucedanum (Imperatoria)
Philadelphus
Phillyrea
Philodendron
Phleum
Phlox
Phormium
Photinia
Physalis
Phyteuma
Pieris
Pilea
Pimpinella
Piper
Pittosporum
Plantago
Platanus
Platycodon
Plumbago
*Plumeria
Poa
Podocarpus
Poinciana
Poinsettia (Euphorbia)
Polygala
Polygonum
Polyscias (Aralia)
Porana
Potentilla
Primula
Pyracantha
Quisqualis
Ranunculus
Rauwolfia
Rhamnus
Rheum
Rhinanthus
Rhododendron
Rhodotypos

Rhoeo
Rhus
Rhynchosperum (Trachelospermum)
Robinia
Rudbeckia
Rumex
Russelia
Sagina
Saintpaulia
Sambucus
Sanchezia
Sansevieria
*Sapindus
Saponaria
Satureia (Calamintha)
Saussurea
Saxifraga
Scabiosa
Schefflera
Schinus
Schizophragma
Scirpus
Sedum
Selaginella
Sempervivum
Senecio
Sesleria
Sibbaldia
Silene
*Solandra
Soldanella
Solidago
Sophora
Soyeria
Sparmannia
Spathodea
Sphaeralcea
Spiraea
Stachys (Betonica)
Stapelia
Statice (Armeria)
Stellaria (Alsine)
Stephanotis
*Strelitzia

Strobilanthes
Succulents
Symphoricarpos
Symphytum
Syringa
*Tabebuia
Tabernaemontana
Tamarix
Taxus
Tecoma
Thalictrum
Thespesia
Thevetia
Thryallis (Galphimia)
Thuja
Thujopsis
Thunbergia
Tibouchina
Tilia
Trachelospermum (Rhynchospermum)
Tradescantia
Tree fern

Trichostigma
Trifolium
Tritoma (Kniphofia)
Trollius
Tsuga
Valeriana
Veronica
Viburnum
Vinca
Viola
Weigela
Wisteria
Wulfenia
Yucca
Zantedeschia
Zebrina (Tradescantia)
*Zingiber

PLANT PROPAGATING MATERIAL PROHIBITED INTO THE UNITED STATES[1]

PLANT MATERIAL[2]	Foreign Country or Countries from Which Prohibited
ABIES spp. (Fir)	All foreign countries except Canada
ACACIA spp. (Acacia, wattle—erroneously called mimosa)	Australia and Oceania
ACER spp. (Maple)	Bulgaria, England, France, Germany, and Japan
AESCULUS spp. (Horsechestnut, buckeye)	Czechoslovakia, England, and Germany
ALTHAEA spp. (Hollyhock)	Africa and India
ANEMONE spp. (Anemone)	Germany
BAMBUSEAE (Bamboo) including seed	All foreign countries except Canada
BERBERIS spp. (Barberry) Plants of all species and horticultural varieties not designated as resistant to black stem rust	All foreign countries
BERBERIS spp. Plants of all species and horticultural varieties designated as resistant to black stem rust	All foreign countries when destined to Colorado, Illinois, Indiana, Iowa, Kansas, Michigan, Minnesota, Missouri, Montana, Nebraska, North Dakota, Ohio, Pennsylvania, South Dakota, Virginia, Washington, West Virginia, Wisconsin, and Wyoming
BERBERIS spp. seed	All foreign countries
CASTANEA spp. (Chestnut)	All foreign countries when destined to California, Idaho, Oregon, or Washington
CASTANOPSIS spp. (Chinquapin)	All foreign countries when destined to California, Idaho, Oregon, or Washington
CEDRUS spp. (Cedar)	Europe
CHIONACHNE spp. including seed	Countries listed in footnote 3

CITRUS spp. and other genera, species, and varieties of the Rutaceous subfamilies Aurantioideae, Rutoideae, and Toddalioideae	All foreign countries
COCOS NUCIFERA (Coconut) Plants, including sprouted seed, and nuts capable of propagation	All countries except Canada when desgined to Hawaii, and all countries when destined to Florida (nuts capable of propagation are enterable from Jamaica into Florida under permit)
COFFEA spp. (Coffee)	All foreign countries when destined to Hawaii or Puerto Rico
COIX spp. (Job's tears) including seed	Countries listed in footnote 3
CORYLUS spp. (Hazelnut, filbert)	Canadian provinces east of Manitoba, when destined to California, Oregon or Washington
DATURA spp. (Jimson weed)	England and India
DIANTHUS spp. (Pink, carnation)	England
EUCALYPTUS spp. (Eucalyptus)	Argentina, Ceylon, Europe, and Uruguay
EUCHLAENA spp. (Teosinte) including seed	Countries listed in footnote 3
EUONYMUS spp. (Euonymous)	Germany
FRAGARIA spp. (Strawberry)	Austria, Czechoslovakia, England, France, North Ireland, Republic of Ireland, Scotland, and U.S.S.R.
FRAXINUS spp. (Ash)	Europe
Fruit and nut seedling understocks	All foreign countries except Canada
GLADIOLUS spp. (Gladiolus)	Africa
GOSSYPIUM spp. (Cotton) plants	All foreign countries
GOSSYPIUM spp. (Cotton) seed	All foreign countries except Mexico

HIBISCUS spp. (Hibiscus	India, Nigeria, Sudan, and Trinidad
HYDRANGEA spp. (Hydrangea)	Germany
IPOMOEA BATATAS (Sweetpotato)	All foreign countries when destined to the continental United States, including Alaska and Hawaii
JASMINUM spp. (Jasmine)	Belgium, England, and Germany
JUNIPERUS spp. (Juniper)	Finland, Romania, and Canada when from certain areas in British Columbia
LARIX spp. (Larch)	Europe
LENS spp. seeds (Lentil)	All South American countries
LIGUSTRUM spp. (Privet)	Germany
MAHOBERBERIS spp. (Barberry x Mahonia) Plants of all species and horticultural varieties not designated as resistant to black stem rust	All foreign countries
MAHOBERBERIS spp. Plants of all species and horticultural varieties designated as resistant to black stem rust	All foreign countries when destined to Colorado, Illinois, Indiana, Iowa, Kansas, Michigan, Minnesota, Missouri, Montana, Nebraska, North Dakota, Ohio, Pennsylvania, South Dakota, Virginia, Washington, West Virginia, Wisconsin, and Wyoming
MAHOBERBERIS spp. seed	All foreign countries
MAHONIA spp. (Mahonia) Plants of all species and horticultural varieties not designated as resistant to black stem rust	All foreign countries
MAHONIA spp. seed	All foreign countries
MAHONIA spp. Plants of all species and horticultural varieties designated as resistant to black stem rust	All foreign countries when destined to Colorado, Illinois, Indiana, Iowa, Kansas, Michigan, Minnesota, Missouri, Montana, North Dakota, Ohio, Pennsylvania, South Dakota, Virginia, Washington, West Virginia, Wisconsin, and Wyoming

239

MALUS spp. (Apple)	All foreign countries unless from certified nursery[4]
MANGIFERA spp. (Mango) seeds	All foreign countries except those in the Western Hemisphere
MORUS spp. (Mulberry)	China and Japan
Nut and fruit seedling understocks	(See Fruit and Nut seedling understocks)
ORYZA SATIVA (Rice) seed	All foreign countries except Mexico
PERSEA spp. (Avocado) seed	Mexico, Central and South America
PICEA spp. (Spruce)	Europe, Japan, and Siberia
PINUS spp. (2- or 3-leaved) (Pine)	Europe and Japan. Also see PINUS spp. below.
PINUS spp. (2-, 3-, or 5-leaved) (Pine)	Canada when destined to the State of Montana
PLANERA spp.	Same as ULMUS spp.
POLYTOCA spp. including seed	Countries listed in footnote 3 at end of table
POPULUS spp. (Poplar)	Europe
PRIMULA spp. (Primrose)	Australia and Great Britain
PRUNUS spp. (Almond, apricot, cherry, peach, plum, nectarine, etc.	All foreign countries unless from certified nursery[4]
PSEUDOTSUGA spp. (Douglas fir)	Europe
PYRUS spp. (Pear)	All foreign countries except Canada unless from certified nursery[4]; and from Canada originating in certain areas on Vancouver Island, B. C.
QUERCUS spp. (Oak)	Japan
RIBES NIGRUM (Black currant)	British Isles, New Zealand, and Sweden, and all countries to certain destinations[1]

ROSA spp. (Rose)	Australia, Italy, New Zealand, and Republic of South Africa
SALIX spp. (Willow)	England and the Netherlands
Seeds of all kinds when in pulp	All foreign countries except Canada
SACCHARUM spp. (Sugarcane)	All foreign countries
SCLERACHNE spp. including seed	Countries listed in footnote 3 at the end of table
SOLANUM tuber-producing species (Potato)	All foreign countries except Bermuda, Canada, other than Newfoundland and Vancouver Island, and the Dominican Republic
SORBUS spp. (Mountain ash)	China, Germany, Japan, Southeastern Asia, Philippine Islands, Oceania (including Australia and New Zealand)
TRILOBACHNE spp. including seed	Countries listed in footnote 3 at end of table
TRITICUM spp. (Wheat) including seed	Countries listed in footnote 5 at end of table
ULMUS spp.	Canada and Europe when destined to California, Nevada, and Oregon
VITIS spp. (Grape)	Europe
WISTERIA spp. (Wisteria)	Australia
Zea mays (Indian corn or maize)	Countries listed in footnote 3 at end of table
ZELKOVA spp.	Same as ULMUS spp.

1. For additional information, write to the Plant Importations Office, Plant Protection and Quarantine Programs, Animal and Plant Health Inspection Service, U. S. Department of Agriculture, 209 River Street, Hoboken, New Jersey 07030.

2. The term "spp." as used after a generic name in this subpart includes all species, varieties, and hybrids of the genus. Unless otherwise specifically indicated, all items of plant material appearing in this subpart refer to the plants as well as all vegetative parts thereof, including buds, cuttings, scions, and layers, but seeds are not included unless specifically mentioned.

3. Australia, Burma, Cambodia, China, Formosa, India, Indonesia, Japan, and adjacent islands, Laos, Malaya, Manchuria, New Guinea, New Zealand, North Viet-Nam, Oceania, Pakistan, Philippines, Ryukyu Islands, South Viet-Nam, and Thailand.

4. Admissible from nurseries designated as producing material grown from parent plants that have been tested by the plant protection service of the countries of origin and found apparently free of all diseases of plant quarantine significance. Such nurseries must be designated by the Deputy Administrator, Plant Protection and Quarantine Programs, Animal and Plant Health Inspection Service, of the U. S. Department of Agriculture as eligible to ship disease-free material to the United States. A list of authorized nurseries may be obtained by writing to the address shown in footnote 1 above.

5. Aden, Afghanistan, Australia, Bulgaria, Caucasus, Chile, China, Cyprus, Egypt, Greece, India, Iran, Iraq, Israel, Italy, Japan, Jordan, Oman, Pakistan, Palestine, Portugal, South Africa, Saudi Arabia, Sinai Peninsula, Spain, Syria, Tunisia, Turkestan, Turkey, and Yemen.

UNITED STATES DEPARTMENT OF AGRICULTURE
ANIMAL AND PLANT HEALTH INSPECTION SERVICE
Plant Protection and Quarantine Programs
209 River Street
Hoboken, New Jersey 07030

ARTIFICIALLY DWARFED TREES FROM JAPAN

GENERAL INFORMATION. This circular applies to dwarfed trees from Japan only. Consult this office to ascertain the entry status of trees from other areas. Importation are likely to prove disappointing unless the importer obtains detailed information on the reestablishment and care of the trees from competent Japanese sources. While agricultural inspectors handle plant material with all the care and understanding that is required, it should be realized that such services are limited to those necessary while the plants are in the Department's custody awaiting agricultural clearance.

PERMITS should be obtained in advance of importation. The entry status of most trees can be determined by consulting the reverse side of this sheet. A permit to import trees subject to postentry quarantine growing will be issued only to the person who will be responsible for the care of the trees for the required detention period, approximately the first 2 years after entry. Such persons must execute and file with his application (Form 587) an agreement (Form 546) which obligates him to grow the trees on premises under his control. When importations are to be made by mail, the applicant should request mailing labels, one for each parcel. Detailed instructions for their use appear on the reverse side of the labels. IF THE APPLICANT WRITES FROM AN APO OR FPO ADDRESS, HE SHOULD ALSO GIVE HIS HOME ADDRESS.

APPROVED INSPECTION STATIONS. Material must clear agricultural quarantine at the inspection station nearest to the first port of arrival. The most likely stations for the clearance of dwarfed trees from Japan are Honolulu, Los Angeles, San Francisco, and Seattle.

BAGGAGE ENTRIES. When material is brought in by a passenger, it will be his responsibility to get it to the inspection station. This may require the employment of a bonded carrier.

TREES MUST BE FREE OF SOIL before shipment. Moistened peat moss, sphagnum, coconut fiber, or damp newspaper may be packed around the roots.

PLANTS MUST BE LABELED, preferably with their scientific names. Names can usually be obtained from the grower or from horticultural authorities in the areas where the plants are purchased.

PLANTS MAY BE SUBJECT TO FUMIGATION or other treatment necessary to eliminate danger of pest introduction. This will be done at the importer's risk.

CUSTOMS CLEARANCE is the responsibility of the importer or his broker and is required for all entries except mail entries valued at less than $250.

FOR ADDITIONAL INFORMATION AND PERMITS write to the Permit Section, Plant Importation Office, PPQ, APHIS, USDA, 209 River Street, Hoboken, N. J. 07030.

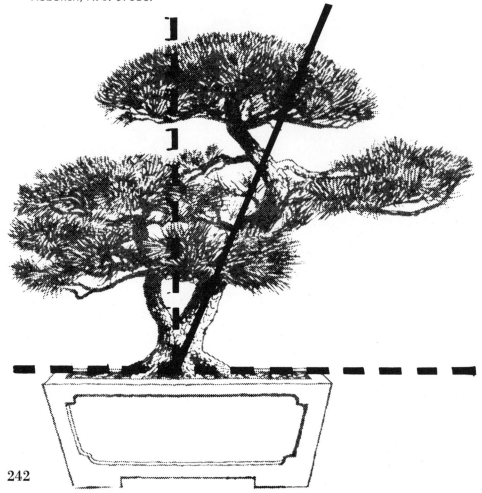

242

ARTIFICIALLY DWARFED TREES FROM
JAPAN

Section I ENTERABLE UNDER REGULA-
TION 6

Abelia
Agave
Akebia
Albizzia
Aleurites
Alnus
Aloe
Amelanchier
Ampelopsis
Araucaria
†Ardisia
Azalea
Betula
†Buxus
Camellia
Caragana
Carpinus
Celastrus
Celtis
Cephalotaxus
Cercidiphyllum
Cercis
Chaenomeles (flowring quince)
Chamaecyparis (Jap. cedar)
Chionanthus
Cornus
Corylopsis
Corylus
Cotoneaster
†Crataegus (hawthorn)
Cryptomeria
Cupressus
†Cydonia
Cytisus
Daphne
†diospyros
Elaeagnus
Enkianthus

Fagus (beech)
Ficus
Firmiana
Forsythia
Gardenia
Ginkgo
Hamamelis
Hedera
Ilex (holly)
Juglans
Laburnum
†Lagerstroemia
Lonicera
†Magnolia
Nandina

243

Osmanthus
Parthenocissus
Paulownia
Philadelphus
Pinus, 5-leaved
Pittosporum
Podocarpus
†Punica (pomegranate)
Pyracantha
Rhododendron
Robinia
Salix
Sciadopitys
Serissa
Styrax
Syringa
Tamarix
Taxodium
Taxus
Thea (tea)
Thuja (arbor vitae)
Thujopsis
Torreya
Trachelospermum
Trachycarpus
Tsuga (hemlock)
Viburnum
Wisteria
Zelkova

Section II ENTERABLE UNDER REGULA-
TION 19 SUBJECT TO POSTENTRY QUAR-
ANTINE GROWING

Aesculus (horse chestnut)
Cedrus (true cedar)
Eucalyptus
Euonymus
†Fraxinus (ash)
†Hibiscus
Hydrangea
Jasminum
Juniperus
Larix (larch)
Ligustrum (privet)
†Populus
Pseudotsuga (Douglas fir)
Rosa
Ulmus

Section III PROHIBITED ENTRY

Abies (fir)
Acer (maple)
Bambuseae (bamboo)
*Berberis (barberry)
**Citrus plants and relatives
*Mahoberberis
*Mahonia
Malus (apple)
Morus (Mulberry)
Picea (spruce)
Pinus, 2- and 3- leaved species
Prunus (apricot, cherry, plum, peach)
Pyrus (pear)
Quercus (oak)
Sorbus (mtn. ash)

* All species prohibited to some States; many
species prohibited to other States.

** A list of citrus plants and their relatives
may be obtained upon request.

† Must be defoliated if entered at ports other
than New York or Seattle.

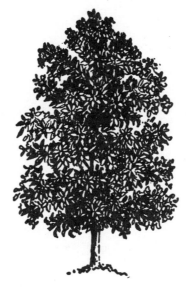

BULBS

Aylett Nurseries Ltd.
North Orbital Road
London Colney, St. Albans
Herts, England
    Dahlias

Ballydorn Bulb Farm
Killinchy, County Down
N. Ireland
    Daffodils

Bloem Erf Nurseries
P. O. Box 2010
Stellenbosch, South Africa
    Wildflowers, hardy perennials, trees,
    shrubs and bulbs

Bloemhove Nurseries
Rynsburgerweg 131-33
Luden, Holland

Walter Blom & Son, Ltd.
Coombelands Nurseries
Leavesden, Watford
Herts, England
    Hardy Border Plants & Spring Bulbs

Broadleigh Gardens
Barr House
Bishop's Hull
Taunton, Somerset
England
    Small bulbs & daffodils

Thomas Butcher Ltd.
Garden Centre, Wickam Rd.
Shirley, Croydon, Surrey
England
    Unusual & exotic plants, bulbs & seeds

Carncairn Daffodils Ltd.
Broughshane Ballymena
County Antrim
N. Ireland

Dix & Zijerveld
Kerklaan 97, Postbus 94
Heemstede, Holland

W. J. Dunlop
Dunrobin Bulb Farm
Broughshane, Ballymena
Northern Ireland
    Daffodils

Dutch Gardens, Inc.
P. O. Box 30
Lisse, Holland

Export Marketing
P. O. Box 5009 WLT
Auckland, New Zealand

Ken Farmer Nurseries
21 Tarawera Road
Rotorua, New Zealand
    Daffodils

Ferncliff Bulb Gardens
Hatzic, B. C.
Canada

J. Gerritsen & Son
Veurseweg 81
Voorschoten, Holland
    Daffodils

J. N. Hancock & Co.
Jackson's Hill Road
Menzies Creek, Victoria
Australia

R. E. Harrison & Co. Ltd.
P. O. Box 1
Palmerston North
New Zealand
    Liliums & Bulbs, Herbaceous plants and
    ornamental shrubs, trees. Wholesale only,
    no catalogue

W. Jackson
Dover, Tasmania 7116
    Daffodils

Kelways Nurseries
Langport, Somerset TA109SL
England
    Daffodils

P. Kohli & Co.
Park Road
Srinagar, Kashmir
India
    Wholesale list of hardy Himalayan
    flower bulbs, shrubs and herbaceous
    perennials

Koppe & Co.
P. O. Box 661
Palmerston, North
New Zealand
    Lily bulbs in variety

Ludwig Amaryllis
Ludwig & Co. N. V.
P. O. Box 18
Hillegam, Holland
    Amaryllis

J. A. Mars of Haslemere
Surrey Gu27 3DW
England
    Cyclamen & others, uncommon bulbs,
    corms, and plants

Nerine Nurseries
Welland, Worcestershire
England
    Hybrid nerine bulbs

N. Z. Horticultural Exports Society Ltd.
P. O. Box 30-095
Lower Hutt.
New Zealand
    Bulbs, Unrooted & rooted cuttings, ornamental
    trees & shrubs, N. Z. natives, N. Z. tree ferns,
    fruit tree perennials. Indoor plants

Niagara Highland Lily Gardens
T. Ross Martin
Binbrook, Ontario
Canada

Orpington Nurseries Ltd.
Rocky Lane, Catton Park
Reigate, Surrey, England
    Rare bulbs

Riverside Gardens
A. E. Delahoy
1088 East Centre
Saskatoon, Sask. S7J3A3
Canada
    Hybrid Patterson lilies

Rodick Agriculture Ltd.
Donabate, Co. Dublin
Ireland

Rosewood Iris Gardens
P. O. Box 2
Witfield, TVL
South Africa

William Smith
Lispopple House
Swords Co. Dublin
Ireland

The Spalding Bulb Co. Ltd.
Dept. 17 Horseshoe Road
Spalding, Lincs.
England

Universal Bulb & Plant Nurseries
P. O. Kalimpong
Kalimpong, West Bengal
India

W. J. Unwin Ltd.
Histon, Cambridge
England
    Seeds & bulbs

Von Tubergen
Zwanenburg Nurseries
Koninginneweg 86
P. O. Box 116
Haarlem, Holland

Von Tubergens Ltd.
Fulham, London SW6
England
    Small plants & bulbs, early flowering
    iris (dwarf)

Woco Nurseries Ltd.
21 View Street
Balclutha, New Zealand
    Tulips, iris, crocus

ORNAMENTALS

Avenue Nurseries
The Avenue
Levin, New Zealand
    Roses, trees & shrubs. Ornamental flax
    (plants & ornamental foliage for florists—
    not dried flowers)

Bell Roses Ltd.
P. O. Box 211-44
Henderson, Auckland
New Zealand
    Nursery plants: rose plants, shrubs, etc.
    in all varieties

The Clifton Geranium Nurseries
Earnley Gardens Ltd.
Cherry Orchard Road
Chichester, Sussex
England

Devon Nurseries Ltd.
Box 478
Devon, Alberta, Canada
    Trees, shrubs, perennials & ground covers

Duncan & Davies, Ltd.
P. O. Box 340
New Plymouth, New Zealand
   Ornamental trees & shrubs, N. Z. natives, azaleas,
   camelias, rhododendrons, magnolias, roses,
   conifers, Chinese gooseberry

Fibrex Nurseries
Evesham
Worcestershire, England
   Primroses, cultivars & cultivated forms of wild
   primrose, raised from seed collected from a
   natural stand, & greybridge geraniums

Fisk's Clematis Nursery
Westleton
Nr. Saxmundham, Suffolk
England
   Clematis

Hillier & Sons
Winchester, Hampshire
England
   Ornamental & flowering trees & shrubs

Hortag Products (N. Z.) Ltd.
P. O. Box 590
New Plymouth, New Zealand

Model Nurseries Ltd.
P. O. Box 15-029
New Lynn, Auckland
New Zealand
   Ornamental trees & shrubs, kiwi fruit
   (rooted cuttings)

Notcutts, Ltd.
Woodbridge
Suffolk, England
   Flowering trees

Perry's Hardy Plant Farm
Enfield, Middlesex
England

Pickard's Magnolia Gardens
Stodmarsh Road
Centerbury, Kent
England
   Magnolias & azaleas, wholesale only overseas

Prop and Grow, Ltd.
Farnley Gardens, Farnley Lane
Otley, West Yorkshire
England
   Geraniums, begonias, fuchsias

L. R. Russell Ltd.
Richmond Nurseries
London Road (A30)
Windlesham, Surrey
England
   Ornamental and flowering trees & shrubs

Tara Exports Ltd.
P. O. Box 6057
Auckland, New Zealand
   Trees & shrubs

J. Timm & Co.
Papenhohe 22, Postfach 1129
22 Elmshorn
Holstein, Germany
   Trees & shrubs, alphabetized catalog, with
   an illustration of every plant

James Trehane & Sons
Winborne, Dorset
England
   Camellias

Trenoweth Valley Flower Farm
St. Keverne
Cornwall, England

E. J. Wills Fuchsias Nursery
Chapel Lane, West Wittering
Chichester, Sussex, England
   Fuchsias, geraniums & begonias

ALPINES

Broadwell Alpines
Broadwell Nursery
Moreton-in-Marsh
Glos.
England
   Plants & seeds

C. G. Hollett
Greenbank Nursery
Sedbergh, Yorks.
LA10 5AG
England

Home & Garden Pride (AG35)
Freepost, Abergele
North Wales, United Kingdom

W. E. Ingwersen, Ltd.
Gravetye
East Grinstead
Surrey, England
   Bulbs & Rock Garden Plants

Jack Drake
Inshriach Alpine Plant Nursery
Aviemore
Inverness-shire
Scotland, United Kingdom

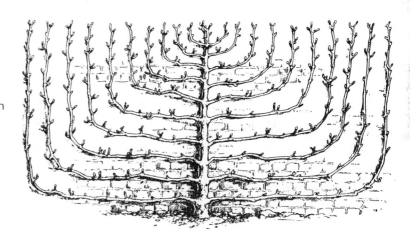

Little Heath Farm Nursery
Potten End
Berkhamstead
Herfordshire, England

AQUATICS

Blagdon Watergarden Centre Ltd.
Blagdon, Bristol
England

Moore Water Gardens
Port Stanley
Ontario, Canada

Stapely Water Gardens, Ltd.
Dept. AG2318 London Road
Stapely, Nantwich, Cheshire
England

Wildwood's Water Gardens Ltd.
AG24 Theobold's Park Rd.
Enfield, Middlesex
England

FRUIT & VEGETABLE

J. C. Allgrove Ltd.
Slough, England
  Apple, pear, quince, medlar

R. Barrett & Co. Ltd.
Barrett Street
Ballina, Co. Mayo
Ireland
  Potatoes & seed potatoes

Blue Mountain Nurseries & Orchards Ltd.
Clarksburg, Ontario
Canada

W. Drummond & Sons Ltd.
Pembroke, Carlow
Ireland
  Fruit trees & shrubs

Irish Potato Marketing Co. Ltd.
4 Merrion Square
Dublin, Ireland
  Seed potatoes & potatoes

Model Nurseries Ltd.
P. O. Box 15-029
New Lynn, Auckland
New Zealand
  Kiwi Fruit (Rooted cuttings) Ornamental
  trees & shrubs

Ken Muir
Dept. AG75
Weeley Heath
Clacton-on-Sea CO169BJ
England
  Strawberries

New Zealand Horticultural Exports Society Ltd.
P. O. Box 30-095
Lower Hutt., New Zealand
  Fruit tree, perennials

Whitaker's Hatcheries Ltd.
Camden Quay, Cork
Ireland
  Fruit trees & seeds

W. Robinson & Sons
Sunny Bank, Forton, PR 3)BN
England
  Onions, Leek, and Celery

HERBS

World-Wide Herbs Ltd.
11 St. Catherine St. East
Montreal, 129
Canada

SEEDS

Alberta Nurseries and Seeds Ltd.
Bowden, Alberta
Canada
  Flower, Fruit & Veg. seeds

The Scottish Seed House
Alexander & Brown
P. O. Box 13
South Methuen St.
Perth Phi, Scotland

The General Swedish Seed Co. Ltd.
S-268 OO Svalov
Sweden

Allwood Bros. Ltd.
Haywards Heath
Sussex, England
  Carnation & others, dianthus

Asmer Seeds Ltd.
Asmer House
Ash Street
Leicester, LES ODD
England

Barnhaven
Brigsteer, Kendal
Westmorland, England
  Plants, too

Barr & Son
11-13 King St.
Covent Garden, London WC2
England
  House plants & seeds

David Bell (Eire) Ltd.
21 City Quay
Dublin 2, Ireland

Blossfeld Seeds
D-2400 Lubeck 1
Postfach 1550
Germany
  House plants, too

Bord Na Mona
28/32 Upper Pembroke
Dublin 2, Ireland
  Fruit trees, grass seed

Carter's Tested Seeds, Ltd.
80 Victoria St. S.W. 1
Raynes Park, London S.W. 20
England

Correvon Fils et Cie
Avenue Petit-Senn 50
1225 Chene-Bourg
Geneve, Switzerland

Dardis & Dunns Seeds Ltd.
15/16 Usher's Island
Dublin 8, Ireland

Samuel Dobie & Son, Ltd.
11 Grosvenor Square
Chester, England

249

Dominion Seed House
Georgetown, Ontario
Canada
    Flower & veg. seeds & others

Peter B. Dow & Co., Ltd.
P. O' Box 696
Gisborne, New Zealand
    Exotics

Finneys Toogoods Brydons
Finneys Seeds Ltd.
P. O. Box 1 PB
Newcastle Upon Tyne
England

Gunson Seeds
P. O. Box 9861
Posbus
Johannesburg, South Africa

Hem Seed Company
Hem, Holland

Honingklip Nurseries
c/o W. J. & Mrs. E. R. Middlemann & Son
13 Lady Anne Ave.
Newlands, Cape
South Africa
    Flower, Fruit, & Veg. seeds

Irish Agricultural Wholesale Society Ltd.
151/156 Thomas St.
Dublin 8, Ireland
    Grass Seed

Pennell & Sons Ltd.
Nurserymen & Seedsmen
Princess St., Lincoln
England

Power Seeds Ltd.
Glenville, Dunmore Road
Waterford, Ireland
    Bulbs, Seeds, Seedling trees, ryegrass seed,
    shrubs, trees

T. Sakata
2 Kiribatake
Kanagawa-Ku
Yoko, Japan

Seed Center, Ltd.
127th St. & 144th Ave.
P. O. Box 3867, Station D
Edmondton, Canada

Paul Sexton & Co.
Cornelscourt, Foxcroft
Co. Dublin, Ireland
    Bulbs, seeds, seed potatoes, shrubs & trees

Suttons Ltd.
1 South Mall
Cork, Ireland
    Grass seed screenings, seed barley, seeds, rye-
    grass seeds

Suttons Seeds
The Royal Seed Establishment
Reading, Berks.
England
    Fruit, flower & veg. seeds

J. Swain
The Seedhouse
Bristol, England

Thompson & Morgan
London Rd.
Ipswich
Suffolk, England
    Flower & veg. seeds & bulbs

Vilmorin-Andrieux
4, Quai de la Megisserie
Paris, France

Watkins & Simpson Ltd.
Pound Hill
Crawley, Sussex
England
    Wholesale only, flower & veg. seeds

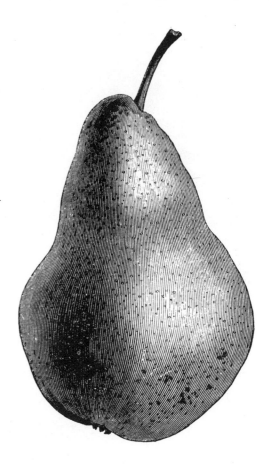

INDOOR PLANTS

La Germinadora, S. A.
Auda. Franklin D. Roosevelt 5459-(31/6)
Buenos Aires, Argentina
   Trees & shrubs

Thomas Rochford & Son Ltd.
Braxbourne, Hertfordshire
England

G. Zimber & Cia
Rua de Consolacao
Sao Paulo, Brazil

Kwekerij Abbing
Antwoordnummer 48
Zeist-2740
Holland

J. N. Anderson & Son Ltd.
P. O. Box 106
Napier, New Zealand
   Rooted & unrooted cuttings, plants

Stuart Boothman
Nightingale Nursery
Maidenhead, England

Bransford Nurseries
Branford, Worcester
England

Chilstone Garden Ornaments
Great Linford Manor
Newport Pagnell
Buckinghamshire, England

J. W. Cole & Son
16 Holdrich St.
Midland Road
Peterborough, England

Comalfi
AA 29688
Bogota, D. E.
Colombia, South America

John Connon Nurseries Ltd.
Box 200
Waterdown, Ontario
Canada

Cramphorn Ltd.
Cuton Mill
CHelmsford
Essex, England

L. Daehnfeldt
P. O. Box 15
DK 5100
Odense, Danmark

F. Delaunay
100, Route des Ponts-de-Ce
Angers, France

R. Delmore Ltd.
Sutton Road
Wisbech, Cambs.
England

F. Despalles
Aux bonnes semences
76 bd. Saint-Germain
75005 Paris, France

Dickson's Hawlmark
Newtownards
Co. Down
Northern Ireland

Gordon Douglas
67 Church Road
Great Bookham
Surrey, Bookham
England

E. F. G. Nurseries Ltd.
Fordham, Cambridgeshire
England

Edrom Nurseries
Coldingham Eyemouth
Berwickshire
Scotland, United Kingdom

Elm-House Nurseries Ltd.
Walpole, St. Peter, Wisbech
Cambs., England

J. E. Ohlsens Enke
Copenhagen-Taastrup
Denmark

Erfurter Samenzucht KG
Weigelt & Co.
6229 Niederwalluf
Postfach 27
Rheingau, West Germany

Fernley Gardens
Fernley Lane
Otley, West Yorkshire
England

Gardenquest for Garden Lovers
London Road
Ipswich, England

I/S Geisler-Nielsens
Planteskole
8723 Løsning, Denmark

H. DeGraff & Sons
Lisse, Holland

251

A. Hansen
2770 Kastrup
Danmark

J. Heemskerk
c/o P. Van Deursen
P. O. Box 60
Sassenheim, Holland

Herm. A. Hesse Garden-Center-Bremen
Osterholzer Heerstrasse, B75
Ruf (0421) 453882
Postfach 240
Germany

The Himalayan Nursery, R. Regd
Bagaicha Kothi East Main Road
P. O. Kalimpong
West Bengal, India

Honeywood Nursery
A. J. Porter
Parkside, Sask.
Canada

Hortus Botanicus
Universitatis Scientiarum
Budapest VIII Illes U. 25
Hungaria

The Imperial Nursery
9 Rai Charan Pal Lane
Calcutta 46
India

Irish Forest Products Ltd.
28 Upper Baggot St.
Dublin 4, Ireland
    Trees & seedling trees

Irish Nurseries Ltd.
Kimmage Road West
Dublin 12, Ireland
    Potted plants

Jackmans of Woking
Jackmans Nurseries Ltd.
Woking, Surrey
England

Kanda La Flor de las Flores
Viaducto Vallcarca 3
Barcelona 6
Spain

Karlheinz Uhlig Kakteen
7053 Rommelshausen
Kreis Waibligen
Lilienstrasse 5
Postfach 1107 Germany

Reginald Kaye Ltd.
Waithman Nurseries
Silverdale, Carnforth, Lancs.
England

V. Kraus Nurseries Ltd.
Carlisle, Ontario
Canada

Lakeshore Nurseries Ltd.
Sub. P. O. 11
Saskatoon, Sask. S7M IXO
Canada

Maxwell & Beale
Corfe Mullen
Wimborne, Dorset
England

Mountain's Nursery
3915 - 47th Ave.
Lloydminster, Sask.
Canada

Mount Congreve Gardens
Waterford, Ireland

Murrells of Shrewsbury
Portland Nurseries
Shrewsbury, England

C. Newberry & Son
Bulls Green Nursery
Knebworth
Herts., England

Nissho-Iwai Co. (N.Z.) Ltd.
P. O. Box 5108
Mt. Maunganui, New Zealand

A/S Norsk Frø
Frysjaveien 40
Oslo 8, Norway

Norton Hall Nurseries
St. Stephens Road
Cold Norton, Chelmsford
England

Nursery International
Dr. B. L. Dikshit Road
Kalimpong, India

Old Court Nurseries Ltd.
Colwall, Near Malvern
Worcs., England

Pajotin-Chedane
La Maitre-Ecole
Angers, France

Patmore Nursery Sales
Box 582
Brandon, Manitoba R7a 5Z7
Canada

Pepinieres
Louis Lens
Mechelbaan N 117
2860 Onze-Lieve-Vrouw-Waver
France

Pepinieres Pinquet
22 Avenue du Mans
Boite Postale 45
37-Tours-02
France

Piante e Sementi Ansaloni
40100 Bologna
Casella Postale 2068 (E.L.)
Italy

J. R. Ponton
The Gardens
Kirknewton
Midlothian, Scotland
United Kingdom

G. B. Rawinsky
Highlands Nursery
Farmham, Surrey
England

M. Reis
Bernhardt St.
Albury 33
N.S.W.
Australia

Mrs. Lionel Richardson
Prospect House
Waterford, Ireland

Riverside Gardens
A. E. Delahey
1088 East Centre
Saskatoon, Saskatchewan
Canada

Rivoire
24, Rue St. Mathieu
69 Lyon
France

Robinsons Gardens Ltd.
Rushmore Hill Nurseries
Knockholt, Sevenoaks
Kent, England

W. H. Rogers
Red Lodge Nursery
Chestnut Ave.
Eastleigh, Hants. England

B. Ruys
Dedemsvoort, Holland

H. Schilpzand
Box 1
Isle Texel
Holland

Simpson & Sons
209 Monument Rd.
Edgbaston, Birmingham
England

Royal Sluis
Postbos 22
Enkhuizen, Holland

Hans Meisert Samenzucht
3 Hannover-Buchholz
Podbielskistr. 409
Germany

E. Sander
2082 Tornesch/Holstein
W. Germany

Albert Schenkel
2000 Hamburg 55 (Blankenese)
Blankeneser Hauptstrasse 53a
Germany

Charles Sharpe & Co., Ltd.
Sleaford, Lincs.
Engla nd

Shelmerdine Garden Centre
3612 Roblin Boulevard
Charleswood, Manitoba
Canada

Sheridan Nurseries
Stobiocke 653
Ontario, Canada

The Slieve Donarfd Nursery Co. Ltd.
Newcastle Co. Down
Northern Ireland

W. Kordes Sohne
2201 Sparrieshoop uber Elmshorn
Holstein, Germany

Spaargaren & Zn.
Ralsmeer, Holland

Springhill Nurseries Ltd.
Lang Stracht, Aberdeen
Scotland, U. K.

W. M. & A. P. Spry
The Basin
Victoria 3154
Australia

Sued-Pflanzen Importe
D 6200 Wiesbaden-Erbenheim
Rennbahnstrasse 8, Germany

Sunningdale Nurseries Ltd.
Windlesham, Surrey
England

Sutton Place Nursery
Sutton Place Farm
Abinger Hammer-Surrey
Dorking 730638 England

smal.

Water Cresses round leavd

Tacolneston Nurseries
Tacolneston, Norwich, Norfolk
NOR 87W
England

Rosen Tantau
2082 Uetersen bei Hamburg
Tornescher Weg 13
Germany

Telston Nurseries
Oxford Road
Sevenoaks, Kent
England

Tezier Freres
26 Valence Sur Rhone
France

F. Toynbee Ltd.
Barnham, Near Bognor Regis
Sussex, England

Treasures of Tenbury Ltd.
Tenbury Wells, Worcestershire
England

Treseder's Nurseries (Truro) Ltd.
The Nurseries
Moresk, Truro
Cornwall, England

Mrs. Desmond Underwood
Colchester, Essex
England

C. J. Van Den Brock
Bousley Farn
Ottershaw
Nr. Chertsey, Surrey
England

Vn Dijk & Co.
P. O. Box 20
Enkhuizen
Holland

Van Gemeren & Co., Ltd.
Hasland, Nurseries
Chesterfield, England

George van der Veld
Lisse, Holland

Nathan Vardi & Son
61000 Tel Aviv
P. O. Box 2231
Israel

Antoine Vermeulen
Labor Nurseries
Postbox 48
Oudenbosch, Holland

Wansdyke Nursery
Hillworth Devizes
Wilts, England

J. Waterer & Sons
The Nurseries
Bagshot, Surrey
England

Weall & Cullen
784 Shepard Ave., East
Willowdale, Ontario M2k Ic3
Westhill Nursery
Winchester, England

G. G. Whitelegg Ltd.
The Nurseries
Knockholt, Sevenoaks, Kent
England

Wilcox Nurseries
Oliver, B. C.
Canada

G. L. Wilson
Broughshane
County Autrin
No. Ireland

Wisbech Plant Co., Ltd.
Lynn Road
Wisbech, Cambs.
England

Young Plants Ltd.
Alveston
Stratford-Upon-Avon
Warwickshire
England

Zena Court
54, Whitehouse Road
Eastwood, Essex
England

Zorzi Sementi
Casella Postale 193
Padova, Italy

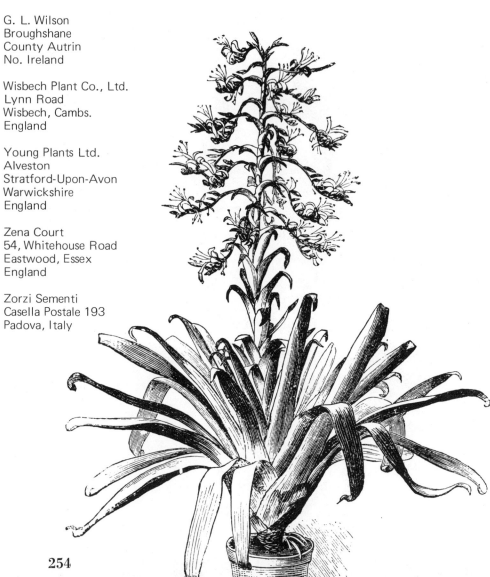

ORCHIDS

Armstrong and Brown
J. L. Humphreys
Tunbridge Wells, Kent
England

The Bangkrabue Nursery
15 Klahom's Lane
Bangkrabue, Bangkok
Thailand

Black & Flory, Ltd.
Slough, Bucks, England

Charlesworth & Co., Ltd.
Haywards Heath, Sussex
England

Chow Cheng Orchids
194 Litoh St.
Taichung, Taiwan

Flandria
Bruges, Belgium

G. Ghose & Co., Orchids
Town-end
Darjeeling, West Bengal
India

J. S. Hannah
RD 2
Papakura, New Zealand

Tom Henry Pty. Ltd.
25 Ruskin Rowe
Avalon Beach
New South Wales 2107
Australia

Juanita Nursery
29 La Boheme Ave.
Caringbah, N. S. W. 2229
Australia

A J. Keeling and Sons
Westgate Hill, Nr. Bratford
Yorks, England

D. J. & G. M. Langdale
22 Wilkins St.
Yagoona, N.S.W.
Australia

Marcel Lecoufle
5 Rue de Paris
94 Boissy St. Leger
France

Stuart Low Co.
Jarvisbrook (Crowborough)
Sussex, England

Mansell and xatcher, Ltd.
Rawdon, Leeds, Yorkshire
England

McBean's Cymbidium Orchids
Cooksbridge, Lewes
Sussex
England

McBean's Proprietory Ltd.
256-262 Jasper Road
McKinnon 3204
Australia

Dr. & Mrs. Yoshio Nagano
261 Eifukucho
Suginami, Tokyo
Japan

Orchidgeen Nursery
25 Ayr St.
Morningside, Queensland 4170
Australia

Orquideario Catarinense
P. O. Box 1
1981 Roberto Seidel St.
Corupu, Santa Catarina
Brazil

Paradise Orchid Nurseries
Box 2107
Tauronga South
New Zealand

Helen Cockburn & Frank Pies
F. L. S. Box 2041
Nairobi, Kenya, E. Africa

L. K. Pradhan Nursery
P. O. Kalimpong District
Darjeeling, West Bengal, India

R & R Ratcliffe (Orchids) Ltd.
Downland Nurseries
Chilton, Didcot, Berkshire
England

Rapee Sagarick
G.P.O. box 953
Bangkok, Thailand

David Sanders Orchids, Ltd.
Selsfield, East Grinstead
Sussex, England

Frank Slattery
12 Eddystone Road
Bexley, N.S.W.
Australia 2207

South Pacific Orchids Ltd.
P. O. Box 2019
Napier, New Zealand

T. Orchids Nursery
30/71 Suthisaanvinichai Road
Soi Thonglor
Bangkok 4, Thailand

Tecson Orchids Center & Nursery
No. E-6 Comp Crame
Quezon City, Philippines

Maurice Vaherot
31 Rue de Valenton
Boissy-St. Leger (V. de M.)
France

Adelaide Orchids
Briardale Road
O'Halloran Hill
South Australia, 5158

Astbury's Orchid Nursery
Bloomfield St.
Cleveland 4163, Queensland
Australia

Bambricks Orchid Nursery
93 Cavan St.
Koongal, North Rockhampton
Queensland, Australia

Blencoe Nursery
48 Jack St.
Atherton, Queensland
Australia 4883

Alvin Bryant
22 Cook St.
Kurnell, N.S.W.
Australia 2231

A. & J. Burrows—Orchids
107 Pohlman St.
Southport, Queensland
Australia 4215

Greenacres Orchid Farm
115 Great Western Highway
Valley Heights, N.S.W.
Australia

Johnston Orchids
1062 Lower North East Road
Highbury
S. Australia 5089

Kirkwoods Orchids
P. O. Box 1281
Cairns, Australia 4870

Limberlost
P. O. Freshwater Nth
Queensland, Australia 4872

Lugarno Orchid Co. Pty. Ltd.
1178 Forest Road
Lugarno, New South Wales 2210
Australia

Nindethona Orchids
16 Rangeview Road
P. O. Box 94
Mitcham, Australia 3132

Olivine May Orchids
12 Old Barrenjoey Road
Avalon Beach
N.S.W. 2107, Australia

Orchid Producers & Supplies
27 Hillview Road
Mount Lawley, Western Australia
6050

Barry Paget's Orchid World
P. O. Box 97
Carina, Queensland
Australia 4152

Sunshine Orchids
Raghan Road
Bald Hills, Brisbane, 4036
Australia

Bamborine Mountain Orchids
Long Road, Eagle Heights
Tamborine Mountain
Queensland 303 Australia

Valley Orchids
70 Somers St.
Brighton, South Australia

Hodgins Orchids
P. O. Box 108
Frankston 3199, Victoria
Australia

Nicky Zurchers
Box 326
Virginia, S. Australia 5120

John Walker's McLead Nursery
325 McLead St.
Carins, North Queensland
Australia 4870

Wandabah Orchids Pty. Ltd.
724 Pennant Hills Road
Carlingford, N.S.W. 2118
Australia

West Coast Orchids Pty. Ltd.
H. J. Lodge
100 Spring Road
Tharlie, Western Australia 6108